Gangland
SYDNEY

James Morton
Susanna Lobez

VICTORY BOOKS
An imprint of Melbourne University Publishing Limited
187 Grattan Street, Carlton, Victoria 3053, Australia
mup-info@unimelb.edu.au
www.mup.com.au

First published 2011
Text © James Morton and Susanna Lobez, 2011
Design and typography © Melbourne University Publishing Ltd 2011

Text designed by Alice Graphics
Cover designed by Nada Backovic
Typeset in 9/14 pt Lino Letter Roman by Pauline Haas
Printed in Australia by Griffin Press, South Australia

Front cover photos, left to right: Tilly Devine, © Newspix/News Ltd; Lennie McPherson, © Newspix/News Ltd; Louis Bayeh, © Newspix/Brendan Esposito; Dulcie Markham, © Newspix/News Ltd; Roger Rogerson, © Newspix/News Ltd; Abe Saffron, © Newspix/News Ltd; Bill Bayeh, © Newspix/Stuart Ramson; Chow Hayes, © Newspix/News Ltd. Background images © iStockphoto.com.

National Library of Australia Cataloguing-in-Publication entry:
Morton, James, 1938–
Gangland Sydney / James Morton and Susanna Lobez.

9780522858709 (pbk.)
9780522860399 (ebook)

Includes bibliographical references and index.

Organized crime—New South Wales—Sydney—History.
Gangs—New South Wales—Sydney—History.
Mafia—New South Wales—Sydney—History.

Lobez, Susanna.

364.106099441

*For Patricia Rose and Alec Masel
and Dock Bateson with love.*

Contents

Preface

In the October 1965 issue of the satirical magazine *Oz*, Richard Neville published a semi-serious top twenty of Sydney-based criminals of the time.

No. 1   There isn't one

No. 2   Lennie

No. 3   Perce

No. 4   Abe

No. 5   Joe T

No. 6   Eric F

No. 7   Norm*

No. 8   Ronnie*

No. 9   Dick*

No. 10   The Yank

No. 11   Smokey

No. 12   Cuffancollar Johnson

No. 13   Sammy

No. 14   Lugs

No. 15   Empty

No. 16   Melbourne John

No. 17   Bondi

No. 18   Hollywood

No. 19   The Scholar

No. 20   Kate & Tilly (retired)

* partners

Nearly fifty years later some of the names are difficult to identify. Delicately, and probably sensibly, *Oz* did not mention George Freeman, who was undoubtedly the prince of the city at the time. Number 2 was Lennie McPherson, certainly a man to be reckoned with. He decapitated a white rabbit and threw its body on the floor of his mother's flat in front of her because he had not been invited to her seventieth birthday party. Such behaviour requires the highest form of recognition. 'You are a flag and should be obeyed,' fawned the Lebanese-born fixer Frank Hakim, who idolised him. Shortly after the *Oz* article appeared, McPherson organised an attempted execution of his rival, Jackie 'Iron Man' Steele, who had offended him by saying first, that McPherson was a fizz (a dobber), which was undoubtedly true, and second, that he, Steele, was the Number 1 in Sydney, which wasn't. Steele bought numerous copies of the magazine and happily distributed them.

Number 3 was the gambler Perce Galea, who in his early days worked for the old-time Razor Wars man Siddy Kelly in his baccarat schools. Galea is generally noted for his gambling as opposed to his criminal activities—outside illegal gaming and bribing the police, that is. He caused a mini-riot by showering the crowd with banknotes after his horse Eskimo Prince won the Golden Slipper Stakes in 1964. There is no doubt, however, that he was an associate of the top men in the city.

Number 4 was the club owner and then 'King of the Cross', Abe 'Mr Sin' Saffron, whose slimy hand stretched over prostitution, drug dealing, sly-grogging, gambling and possibly murder and arson, as well as extortion, for half a century. Number 5 was Joe Taylor, the two-up king who gave the drug dealer Dr Nick Paltos— another seminal figure in Australian organised crime—his start in life. At Number 6 was Eric Farrell, or O'Farrell, who ran nightclubs such as the Forbes and the Ziegfeld, where Chow Hayes killed the boxer Bobby Lee.

At Number 9 is Dick, Richard Gabriel Reilly, standover man and club bouncer from the 1930s, and partner of the crooked detective Ray Kelly in abortion rackets after the war. He was shot dead in his Maserati in June 1967. He could reasonably have expected to be far higher in the credits. Number 8 was Reilly's offsider, Ronald Joseph Sylvester Lee, a baccarat organiser and also a friend of Kelly.

Beyond that, identification becomes more difficult. Norm at Number 7 may well be the New South Wales Police Commissioner Norm Allan, who, at best, turned a blind eye to all sorts of illegal activities. It was he who seized Reilly's diaries and black books after his death, and tried to suppress the confidential telephone numbers and addresses of criminals, police and politicians within them. At Number 10, The Yank may have been the visiting Chicago mafioso Joe Testa, who arrived with an introduction to Ronnie Lee and then linked up with McPherson and Freeman in a series of failed fraudulent companies. Testa was killed in 1981 when a car bomb blew up his Lincoln Continental at the Oakland Park Country Club, Florida. Alternatively, The Yank could have been Bernie Houghton, who ran a series of bars in Kings Cross and was closely linked to the Nugan Hand Bank.

Then comes a long series of blanks—which forty years later even Neville cannot fill—until Number 18: Hollywood is 'Hollywood' George Edser, a flamboyant horse owner and punter whose activities on the track had him warned off in 1961. A close friend of leading identity Richard Reilly, Edser had convictions for consorting and receiving liquor. In March 1958 he survived being shot in the groin in his garage in what was undoubtedly a contract hit, probably over unpaid gambling debts. Number 19, The Scholar, was a shadowy figure involved in the baccarat club wars from the 1940s. There are no prizes for identifying Number 20, Kate Leigh and Tilly Devine, the madams from the 1920s then rapidly coming to the end of their careers.

The *Oz* piece did not go down well. In fact, the police attributed the near fatal shooting of Jacqui 'Iron Man' Steele to McPherson's annoyance with the publication. Neville, who then lived in Paddington, opened his door one evening and found McPherson, admittedly minus another rabbit, on his doorstep wanting to know where he had obtained his information. McPherson, then probably at the peak of his powers, took him for a drive. Neville must have thought it his last, but the great man merely dropped him off at a preview of the Polanski film *Knife in the Water*. On the way, McPherson showed Neville the bullet holes in the roof of his car and explained the facts of gangland life and journalism to him. A suitably penitent piece appeared in the next issue.

Worldwide, the authorities are keen to say there is no 'Mr Big' or Number 1 on their patches. But they will reluctantly accept there are a few 'Big Enoughs'. Quite what you have to do to graduate from Big Enough is difficult to say. Import more than $50 million of cannabis, steal jewellery worth over $20 million, kill more than five people a year?

This book, then, is an account of the careers of both the Mr Bigs and the Mr Big Enoughs, as well as a few Ms Bigs, in what could be called the Golden Age of Sydney's underworld—of those who preceded and predeceased them and those who took over the reins when they were dead or retired.

Our thanks are due first and foremost to Dock Bateson, without whose research skills, help and guidance the book could never have been completed. They are also due in strictly alphabetical order to JP Bean, Anne Brooke, Nicholas Cowdery QC, Michael Drury, Rebecca Edmunds, Tony Gee, Tim Girling-Butcher, Foong Ling Kong, Barbara Levy, the late Paul Lincoln, Richard Neville, Sybil Nolan, Russell Robinson, Adrian Tame and a number of people on both sides of the criminal fence who have asked not to be named. Our thanks also go to Sonya Zadel and Lisa McGregor (NSW SC), Anna Cooper (NSW DPP), the State Library of New South Wales, the National Library of Australia at Canberra, the State Library of Victoria, Public Record Office of Victoria, the National Archives at Kew, England, the British Library and the British Newspaper Library, Colindale, London. The following websites have been invaluable: austlii.edu.au, trove.nla.gov.au/newspaper, paperspast. natlib.govt.nz and news.google.com/archivesearch.

Founding Fathers

1

Although many of those transported to Australia in the eighteenth and nineteenth centuries were politicals and general riff-raff, there were some high-class English criminals among them. It is hardly surprising, therefore, that from the early years Sydney had a ready-made criminal class. Since neither prison nor any other method of punishment, let alone transportation, necessarily prevents recidivism, its members swung into operation almost on landing.

Perhaps the first organised crime worthy of the name in Sydney, still effectively one enormous prison, was the 1828 Bank of Australia robbery. The bank, founded two years earlier, and standing between a private home and a public house on George Street, was regarded as socially superior to the Bank of New South Wales, which had been in existence for a decade.

The plot to rob the bank seems to have been devised by former convict James Dingle, who had obtained his Certificate of Freedom the previous year. He decided there must be a way of tunnelling into the vault through a drain under George Street, and put the plan to George Farrell, who in July 1826 had been charged with robbing a man and had received the relatively lenient sentence of working in irons for three months. Thomas Turner, a cleanskin, was recruited—a great benefit, given he worked on the construction of the bank's premises—and tools were supplied by the former

London safebreaker William Blackstone, known as 'Sudden Solomon', who worked for a blacksmith.

The team decided the digging should be done on Saturday nights; it began on 30 August. Turner, who as a former construction worker on the bank would have been a prime suspect, withdrew after the first night's work, but it was agreed that, as he had provided details of the premises, he should still receive a share in the proceeds. He was replaced by a man named Clayton.

Around 11 a.m. on 15 September they finally removed the cornerstone nearest the street and the smallest of them, Farrell, went in and brought out two boxes. They returned on the Sunday night and the result was probably beyond the team's wildest dreams. By the time they emptied the vault they had taken a total of 14 500 pounds. They also destroyed the bank's ledgers. An immediate reward of 100 pounds was posted, then upped to 120 pounds and, when neither produced a response, the governor, Sir Ralph Darling, offered an absolute pardon and a free passage to England to the man or woman who provided information.

As robbers have found over the centuries, it is the disposal of the proceeds that is sometimes the hardest part of the work. There was no way that passing a fifty pound note, of which 100 had been taken, would not attract attention. Anything over five pounds would cause serious problems. Similarly, bills could not be paid with handfuls of silver. And so, just as many other robbers have done in their time, Blackstone negotiated with a receiver, Thomas Woodward.

Woodward's terms were not onerous. He was given 1133 pounds and told Blackstone that he would pay back 1000 pounds in smaller denominations once he had obtained them. Yet again, as many have found to their cost, receivers are not always reliable. The pair went to the Bank of New South Wales. In a classic example of the rort known as the corner game, Woodward told Blackstone to wait outside, then disappeared through a side door.

Some months later Blackstone tried to rob a gambling den in Macquarie Street and was shot and wounded by a policeman who saw the raid. His colleague on the robbery was killed and Blackstone was sentenced to death, a penalty that was commuted to life imprisonment. He was sent to the feared penal settlement on Norfolk Island where unsurprisingly, he disliked the conditions and so in 1831 he decided to shelve his mates from the Bank of Australia job, something which might mean his freedom and return to England. Meanwhile he was lodged on the prison ship *Phoenix*.

Blackstone did not tell the whole story. Clayton was not arrested; Dingle and Farrell were charged with breaking and entering, and the now retrieved Woodward with receiving. They appeared on 10 June 1831 and, tried under English law, were convicted on Blackstone's evidence. This presented a difficulty. As Blackstone had been convicted of a capital crime, in theory his evidence was inadmissible. The Appeal Court for the first time broke away from the English rules of evidence and, by a two-to-one majority, decided that the law was not applicable in New South Wales. Had it been, no one would ever have been convicted. Dingle and Farrell received a very lenient ten years apiece and the cheating Woodward received fourteen years.

Blackstone did not learn from his experiences. In July 1832 he was acquitted of stealing a gun lock but in February the next year, shortly before he was due to be shipped back to England, he was caught breaking into a warehouse and received another sentence of transportation for life. His co-defendant, Thomas McGrath, was shown a great deal more mercy. He received only seven years' transportation because, said the Chief Justice, 'he was a youth and they [the court] hoped that the lesson of that day would not be forgotten during his future life'. In 1839 Blackstone was sent to Cockatoo Island, and was released in December the following year. Back in Sydney he continued to commit a series of offences and receive relatively short sentences until his death on St Patrick's

Day 1850. The Bank of Australia never recovered its money or its status and folded in 1843.

* * *

By the 1880s clear divisions had been established in the hierarchy of Sydney crime. Amateur, opportunistic thieves, such as domestic servants, used pawnbrokers as the preferred method of disposing of stolen goods. Provided the pawnbroker kept a set of books, and not too many fenced items were recorded in them—and, of course, the stolen goods pawned were never redeemed—there was a measure of a defence if he was charged with receiving. The professional thief went to a professional fence, whose shop had a sign 'Gold and Silver Bought' or 'Wardrobes Purchased'. In the back room there would be a crucible maintained at white heat. One observer noted: 'People go into that room as freely as if it was a public house parlour and empty their pockets of gold and silver, jewellery and plate into their separate crucibles where they are speedily reduced to ingots.' Watches were sent abroad.

Just as the American ethnic street gangs of today broadly divide themselves into supporters of either the Crips or the Bloods, in the early 1870s the Sydney 'pushes', as the gangs were known, divided on religious lines. The Rocks Push (then under the leadership of Sandy Ross), the Gibbs Street Mob and the Glebe Island Boys all broadly supported the Oranges or Protestants. The Greens or Catholics were led by Larry Foley.

The pushes lived on a steady diet of theft, assaults and rolling sailors, using their girls as decoys as well as prostitutes. When the whalers and grain carriers left harbour the pushes amused themselves by attacking anyone foolish enough to stray into the Rocks and by fighting among themselves.

In March 1871 Larry Foley challenged the heavier, older and taller Ross for leadership of the Rocks Push. The fight lasted for some two hours forty minutes before it was broken up in the seventy-first round by the police. One account has it that Ross recognised at the time that he was badly beaten and handed the leadership to Foley. Another is that Ross's backer was dissatisfied and there was a 200-pounds-a-side rematch, which Foley won handily in twenty-eight minutes. There is, however, agreement that Foley became leader of the Rocks Push, with Ross as his first lieutenant. By some accounts he tried to stop the practice of living off immoral earnings but he failed and, now sponsored by local sportsmen, left the Rocks Push. Eight years later he was the undisputed bare-knuckle champion of Australia after defeating Melbourne's Abe Hicken in sixteen rounds on 18 March.

In theory, Foley was never defeated in the ring, but on 28 May 1883, in his last bout, he was badly beaten by strongman and wrestler 'Professor' William Miller. Although Foley was ageing and Miller was heavier, Foley should have had the skill to defeat him. He was saved when the crowd invaded the ring in the thirty-seventh round to give him time to recover, and again when he was knocked out in the fortieth. The contest was declared a draw but Foley later conceded the match and the 500-pound purse.

Over the next twenty years other pushes came and went, including the Straw Hat Push, the Glebe Push and the Forty Thieves from Surry Hills. The Waterloo Push thoroughly disgraced itself over the gang rape of a serving girl, sixteen-year-old Mary Jane Hicks, in what became known as the Mount Rennie case. On 9 September 1886, the unfortunate girl was first molested by a cab driver, Charles Sweetman, who was later sentenced to a flogging and fourteen years' hard labour; then, as she escaped from him, she was chased and attacked by up to a dozen members of the push. Eleven youths were charged and two, George Duffy and Joe Martin, admitted that they had intercourse but claimed it was with the girl's consent. Mary Hicks and a Bill Stanley, who went to her help, identified eight of the eleven and, after a bitter trial before the unpopular Mr Justice Windeyer—in which counsels' speeches finished at 3.30 a.m. and the judge began summing up just five and half hours later—nine (including Duffy and Martin) were found guilty and were sentenced to death.

After a series of appeals and petitions, five were reprieved and four were hanged in a botched execution at Darlinghurst Gaol on 7 January 1887. The hangman had miscalculated the length of rope required and only Duffy died instantly. The seventeen-year-old Joe Martin strangled for ten minutes before he died.

Newspapers such as *The Bulletin* were by no means sympathetic towards the girl, suggesting she was no better than she ought to be, as the phrase went, and that she had brought things on herself. The severity of the sentences was partly due to earlier similar incidents. There had been a gang rape of Elizabeth Phillips in Elizabeth Street in September 1883, and another of Margaret Owen in Mount Carmel on Christmas night 1883, both of which ended with the death of the victim. When a Frances Logan had tried to intervene in the latter rape, she was told to clear out or the same would happen to her. There was an outcry when the men were acquitted. The reprieved boys in the Mount Rennie case served ten years and one, Mick Donellan, later became a city alderman.

Seven years later the Millers Point Push did rather better. In June 1893 Tom Pert, a sailor from the *Royal Tar*, was kicked to death outside the Gladstone Hotel at the corner of Argyle Street as a reprisal for causing the jailing of one of the Millers Point Push. Nine men were put on trial and all were acquitted after, it was alleged, intimidation of the witnesses.

In February 1894 two visiting Victorian burglars, Charles Montgomery and Thomas Williams, were captured after failing to blow a safe at the Union Steamship Company in Bridge Street. When challenged by officers, Montgomery, wielding a 3-foot iron jemmy, fractured the skull of Constable Frederick Bowden and broke the arm of another constable. He then threatened to shoot a third if he chased him. Reinforcements came from the Water Police Station and, after a struggle, Montgomery was captured. Williams surrendered quietly. Both were sentenced to death, with the jury recommending mercy for Williams. For Montgomery, who had already served a six-year sentence in the dreaded Pentridge, there was no hope. Despite a petition signed by 25 000 people, including Bowden, there was none for Williams either. They were both hanged on 31 May. It was this incident that led to the arming of the New South Wales police.

* * *

It was in the years between the two world wars that robber and standover man John 'Chow' Hayes became a dominant figure in the Sydney underworld. He had started his career in the old Sydney gangs of the early twentieth century. In his authorised biography, he sets out the territories occupied by the various pushes of that century. The Surry Hills Mob, also known as the Ann Street Mob, ran the streets from the railway to Darlinghurst and back to Surry Hills; the Loo Mob came from Woolloomooloo; the Glebe Mob from around Bay Street, Glebe; the Newtown Mob from around the railway station there. The last were profitably employed by Joe Taylor—at that time managing The Hub theatre and who later became the king of the two-up schools—who would use them as bouncers for unruly patrons. Their great rivals were the Redfern Mob, who controlled an area off Cleveland Street. Hayes himself belonged to the Railway Gang, who controlled a part of central Sydney from Grace Brothers, the department store on Broadway, up George Street to the Town Hall. The Railway Gang specialised in shoplifting: while one set would distract shop assistants, others would throw toys and sporting equipment from the first floor window to their friends outside.

It is easy to see how youth gang members can progress to crime proper. If the Newtown boys found they could be paid money to protect a theatre, then it was a short step to go to another cinema or theatre and demand money to protect it. In the great days of the two-up rings there had to be people to keep the crowds under control. There would be opportunities to ensure that a successful punter was protected on his way home or to rob him; to point the winning punter in the direction of a prostitute, the sly-grog shop or both, to complete the evening's entertainment; to lend money at exorbitant rates to a loser or at least to collect the debts on behalf of the lender.

Over the years the street gangs of Sydney underwent a steady transformation to become profitable organisations and by the time World War I broke out many of the fighting pushes had died away. Gone were the Woolloomooloo and the Rocks pushes. The last outpost seems to have been in Surry Hills, where the Forty Thieves and the Big Seven still hung on. Lately they had been used by politicians to break up rivals' meetings and to protect their own. Now even their days were numbered. In particular robber and housebreaker Samuel 'Jewey' Freeman, who once ran the Riley Street Gang and who lived in Surry Hills, was regarded as being quite capable of dealing with rival gangs on his own. And if he could not, then there was Ernest 'Shiner' Ryan, described as one of the worst criminals in South Australia, to help him. Ryan's criminal convictions dated from 1902, when he was whipped for larceny in Adelaide, and in 1909 he was suspected of the murder of Constable Hyde, who was shot at Marryatville. Sharing Freeman's bed and, from time to time, that of Ryan, was Kate Leigh, a diminutive woman—barely five foot one—with thick dark hair often worn in a bun and a vitriolic temper, who would go on to carve out a career for herself in the Darlinghurst Razor Wars a decade later.

Born in 1887 in Dubbo, one of thirteen children of a horse trainer, Leigh was badly mistreated and, found wandering on the streets at the age of ten, was sent to the Parramatta Industrial School, where she remained for four years. In 1901 she was released and went to Sydney where she was promptly sentenced to fourteen days for vagrancy. On her release she became a waitress and on 2 May 1902 she married small-time thief and illegal bookmaker James Leigh.

In 1905 she was living with her husband in what might be called reduced circumstances when he allegedly found her in bed with their landlord, Patrick Lynch. Naturally, accounts of what exactly took place vary but it seems to have been a form of the ginger game, in which the apparently deceived and enraged husband beats the seducer of his wife and takes money from him. Leigh claimed they were so poor she had been working off the rent in bed, and the beating Lynch received had been from her husband, incensed at his taking advantage of her. Lynch said that he had never been in bed with Kate but had instead gone upstairs with the pair to look at some work done by a painter when they attacked him, robbing him of his watch and gold chain valued at seventeen pounds. He then called the police. In turn James Leigh said that after he had surprised the pair in bed Lynch had hit him before going to the police. Four trials followed. In the first, the Leighs were acquitted of the robbery. In the second, in which James Leigh sued Lynch for 500 pounds for assault and false imprisonment—giving him over to the police—the jury found for Lynch and the Chief Justice recommended that Kate and James Leigh face perjury charges. Two months later, in separate trials on consecutive days, both were acquitted. Whatever the truth of the incident, one thing is certain: James Leigh did not last long as a husband afterwards. Kate moved on to better things, in the form of Jewey Freeman.

It was in the autumn of 1914 that Freeman, Shiner Ryan and Leigh planned what would become one of New South Wales's most famous crimes to date: the Eveleigh Railway Workshops robbery— an attack on their factory in Wilson Street, Redfern. It was the first time a motor car is known to have been used in an Australian robbery.

It took place on 10 June, four days after Freeman had shot a guard, Michael McHale, in the face during a robbery at the Paddington Post Office in Oxford Street. Now, two Eveleigh employees arrived on a horse and cart at the factory, bringing the payroll, which totalled slightly more than 3300 pounds. They unloaded the first chest of money and, as they were taking the second, Ryan drove up with Freeman in the passenger seat of an old grey car. Freeman put a gun to the head of one employee, Norman Twiss, and threatened to blow his brains out. The second chest was loaded onto the car and away the pair drove. The *Herald* was both enchanted by the robbery and able to use it as a stick with which to beat the administration:

> The Eveleigh hold-up is surely unique of its kind in Australia. For audacity of conception and cool effrontery of execution it could hardly have been surpassed [but had there been a policeman about, the robbers may have been apprehended]. We commend to the Government's notice the increase of the police force.

Unfortunately for Freeman and Ryan, the number of their car had been taken. Even more unfortunately they had not bothered to steal one; they had borrowed one from Arthur Tatham from Castlereagh, who had duly reported it stolen and, when interviewed by the police, seemed to know far too much about things. The man in charge of the payroll also told the police that Twiss had been unusually cool. Indeed it seemed almost as if he had expected the attack. Then Freeman was dobbed in. He was picked up at Strathfield Railway Station on the night of 16 June. Although he claimed that he had been in an oyster bar and then at the races on the day of the McHale robbery, he was charged with both attacks.

All of which left Shiner Ryan very much on his own. For the moment it went well enough. He stayed in Sydney, sending his share of the takings to his friend Sam Falkiner in Melbourne, but then things began to unravel. First, Falkiner decamped to Tasmania with the money. Then Ryan went to Victoria and, finding Falkiner had left, told a girlfriend, a Mrs Edith Kelly, about the robbery. With the sound of reward money ringing in her ears, she went to the police.

Ryan was in bed with Edith in Albert Park, Melbourne, when the police arrived. They found 300 pounds in a glass jar stuffed into the chimney, but that, and a further 280 pounds, was all that was ever recovered. Ryan was returned to Sydney, where he was charged along with Freeman, Twiss and Tatham. The quartet went on trial at the Central Criminal Court, Darlinghurst, in September that year with mixed results. Twiss was acquitted and Tatham received a mere three months as an accessory.

Ryan's defence was hopeless. The reason he had left Sydney was that he had seen a drawing in the paper of one of the robbers which resembled him and, thinking of his criminal record, knew no one would believe him. Totally unable to explain away the money in the chimney, the evidence of an informant and the fact that he had admitted to the crime on his arrest, he was right: the jury did not believe him.

Both he and Freeman took their ten-year sentences well. Saying that he would make a good soldier, Freeman asked to be sent to the front. Mr Justice Sly seems to have had some admiration for the pair: 'I believe you are right. Both of you are bold men apparently afraid of nothing and you would make very good soldiers. Still I cannot send you to be a soldier.'

Freeman asked that an officer in the case, Detective Robson, be given his revolver as a souvenir. Ryan said he wanted his to go to the war effort. He later told a warder he would see the sentence out in twenty-four hours. The next morning he was found in bed soaked in blood. He had tried, and failed, to commit suicide.

Freeman's sentencing was followed immediately by his trial for shooting McHale. Now his alibi changed slightly, principally because the races were not run in the morning when the robbery took place. Instead he had been in bed with Kate Leigh. They had gone ice-skating together at the Exhibition rink and then back to Frog Hollow, Surry Hills, where they stayed in connubial bliss for two days. In the witness box she confirmed it: Freeman had been with her when the robbery took place. Again the *Sydney Morning Herald* was taken in: 'Her admission, made in public and on oath, a woman's confession of her own lack of virtue, would have gone far to swing the scales in favour of Freeman. It seemed unbelievable that a woman would publicly parade her shame unless the facts were correct.'

But, as she would prove time and again, Leigh was not simply a woman. Still, the jury did not believe her and convicted Freeman. He received a death sentence immediately commuted to life imprisonment. He was released in 1939 and seems to have given up his criminal career with one minor exception. In May 1950 he was fined £10 for stealing a blow lamp from a shop. He had been drinking. There is no evidence he ever saw Kate Leigh again.

For the moment Leigh had her own troubles. In March the following year she stood trial for perjury and was convicted in a bare fifteen minutes. She received five years.

With the imprisonment of Jewey Freeman and Shiner Ryan, John 'Snowy' Cutmore, who led the Safe Protection gang—so called because they only stood over other criminals who would not go to the police—temporarily took over the top spot of Sydney's criminal fraternity. Regarded as a clever criminal who always carried a revolver, Cutmore had been driven out of Melbourne in the so-called Fitzroy Vendetta, following a dispute over the proceeds of a robbery in 1918 and the subsequent stripping of one of Squizzy Taylor's girls. Taylor, the king of the Melbourne underworld, was Cutmore's one-time friend and ultimate nemesis.

Like Taylor, Cutmore never served a long sentence. His worst was a twelve-month stretch in 1923 for theft. His acquittals made his reputation more than his convictions. He had been wanted in connection with the death of Edward Cleary, a prizefighter turned newsvendor, found shot dead in a hansom cab at 2 a.m. on 3 June 1917. In August 1920, Cutmore was charged with shooting at Peter Linas with intent to murder, and with having stolen ladies clothing in his possession. When the police went to his house in Barkly Street, Carlton, he tried to escape by climbing the chimney but it was too narrow so he hid under a bed. He was easily retrieved. As was so often the case, nothing came of either incident. And although, along with his offsider Henry Slater, Cutmore was found in Adelaide with an absolute arsenal of weapons in November 1921, again there was a verdict of not guilty.

The Rip Roaring Twenties

2

By the mid-1920s there were four dominant figures in the Sydney underworld. In sharp contrast to the situation in England and the United States, where females usually had subservient roles— providing alibis, arranging for bail, minding stolen goods, finding lawyers—two of these figures were women. One was the feisty Kate Leigh, who was released from Long Bay in 1919 and after her divorce from James Leigh in 1922 had married Edward Barry. The marriage ended when she found him in bed with another woman and gave them both a good beating. The other was Matilda 'Tilly' Devine, a former prostitute. One of the reasons for their rise was the *Public Offences Act 1908*, which made it an offence for a man, but not a woman, to live off the earnings of prostitutes. Later the *Crimes Act 1924* increased sentences for a reconvicted bludger to three years. Legally it was far safer for women to run brothels. Not that Devine and Leigh weren't good at managing the girls.

Even before her Eveleigh Street conviction, Leigh was establishing herself as a madam when girls of her age were usually just working in brothels. She had been convicted for 'being the holder of a house frequented by prostitutes' and, after a spell working the doorsteps of Mark Foys on the corner of Liverpool and Elizabeth streets, she found her true vocation. She opened a series of sly-grog shops in Surry Hills and a string of brothels in East Sydney. She was an enthusiastic recruiter of good-looking, working-class women, promising them that jewellery, furs, clothes and a good time was now almost literally at their fingertips, telling them: 'It's a nasty world, so it's best to enjoy it while you can.' There was also money to be made from receiving, cocaine dealing and, with the help of her male friends, the standover and the ginger game.

In contrast to Leigh, Matilda 'Tilly' Mary Twiss Devine was sometimes described as 'usually good tempered', but others say differently. After all, in May 1925 she did cut the throat of commercial traveller Sidney Cork—apparently to teach him to speak more respectfully of her. She received eighteen months' imprisonment. Born on 6 September 1900 in Camberwell, a poor, working-class district in South London, she had acquired a number of convictions for prostitution before she married James (Jim) Devine, then a small-time racecourse racketeer and thief serving with the AIF, on 12 August 1917. She came to Australia at the end of the war on a 'bride ship', starting work in a factory. Then, like a great many other women, she once again took to the streets. Devine and Leigh were said to be charging six shillings a turn, which would produce a very respectable sum when the average weekly wage was three pounds (sixty shillings).

Devine's first brothel was in Palmer Street, East Sydney, where she rented rooms to girls at two pounds a shift—they had to work off the first seven customers before they really began earning. Within five years she owned eighteen houses and the press had dubbed her 'Queen of the Night'. By 1923 she had racked up sixty-seven assorted minor convictions.

The pair could not stand each other. When they finally left the streets themselves and set up as full-time madams, they had differing lifestyles. Devine lived in some comfort in a red brick house in Torrington Road, Maroubra, with crystal glassware and a dinner service, while Leigh lived on the premises in Riley Street, East Sydney, where she celebrated every Christmas by throwing a great children's street party—with presents stolen for the occasion. There was method in her generosity. The children's fathers thought Kate was 'all right' and so might well visit her girls or work with her.

In October 1931 Leigh was involved in a curious case. While she was working in the laundry at Long Bay, she had befriended Catherine Ikin, who was accused of murdering her husband Albert. Both the Ikins drank methylated spirits and liked to chase each other around the house and garden with sticks. In the middle of July he was badly cut in a knife fight with his wife; the tendons of his right hand were severed. Had he gone to hospital, all would have been well but he did not and died in bed three days later. She was promptly, if a bit ambitiously, charged with his murder. The murder charge was dropped and in October the widow Ikin was duly acquitted of manslaughter. Then followed a little struggle between God—in the form of the Salvation Army, who wanted to take her to a hostel—and Mammon, in the form of Kate Leigh, herself out and about again. This time the flesh triumphed (probably because Leigh was offering a celebratory drink and the Salvos were not) and off she went in Leigh's smart car. It was only a matter of days before Leigh was in the police court again, this time charged with robbing and stabbing Mrs Ikin for her pension money.

It was a short-lived case. Mrs Ikin did not, as lawyers say, come up to proof and the magistrate refused to commit Leigh for trial, but not before she had gone to the expense of hiring King's Counsel to represent her. Clearly there was a great deal of money available to a madam.

The third of the Sydney quartet was Phil 'The Jew' Jeffs, who was born in Riga, Latvia, but, like Devine, grew up on the streets of London. He worked a passage on a tramp steamer and spent time in South Africa before he jumped ship in Sydney in 1912. Then he worked as a boot boy for the gambler and publican Theodore Trautwen at the Coogee Bay Hotel until he was sacked for stealing from the guests. He also worked as a strongarm man for the warned-off racing identity James 'Growler' Kingley.

In 1923, at the age of twenty-nine, Jeffs was arrested following the deaths of Alice O'Grady and Violet Thompson, with whom he had been out on a jaunt. He had managed to overturn their open car. He was acquitted of the manslaughter of O'Grady and the prosecution offered no evidence in the Thompson case. Then, in March 1928, he was charged with rape, which at the time was a capital offence. On the face of it, Ada Maddocks, mother of two, was snatched off Bayswater Road, Darlinghurst, while on her way home to her children after visiting a friend. Taken to a flat, she was repeatedly raped—and subjected to other shameful indecencies which the papers could not name—by at least five men including Jeffs, Fred 'The Crusher' Gordon Payne and Herbert Wilson, a hulking man otherwise known as 'Budgee' Travers. After nearly three hours she was then turned out onto the street. The newspapers were in uproar. The gang rape was the criminal *cause célèbre* of the year. How could any decent woman feel safe in the face of 'perverted satyrs'? 'Compared with this, Mount Rennie is a poor parallel', and so on. The men immediately claimed that what had happened was with her consent and that, in criminal slang, she had agreed to 'pull the train'.

The public and papers were excluded from the committal proceedings but then gradually a very different picture emerged. First, Ada Maddocks had earlier taken out a summons against her husband for threatening her with a razor and accusing her of being a loose woman. On one occasion he had knocked her out and had been bound over to be of good behaviour. Then her uncle gave evidence that whenever he met her he had given her money because she was almost destitute. When she gave evidence of the rape it was clear she was still quarrelling with her unemployed husband and she admitted she had not eaten for twenty-four hours before the attack. Neither had she said anything about her ordeal when two girls, Olive Reynolds and Bessie Crawford, had come to the flat. Rather, while she was powdering her face, she had remarked, 'Mind love or they will do the same to you as they did to me. They will promise you the world and then kick you out.' Jeffs and Herbert Wilson called alibi witnesses, who testified that they were at Rock Lodge flats with two women. The judge summed up against Maddocks, and Jeffs and the others were acquitted in some triumph in less than half an hour. Her allegation seems to have come from her fear of her husband finding out how she had come by some money and particularly because Wilson refused to pay her.

Crusher Payne did not last long on the outside. On 27 November 1929 he was sentenced to ten years for an assault on a garage owner in Manly. The court was told he cultivated shop girls and then persuaded them to steal for him. Payne told the judge his witnesses in the rape case had been congratulated on their evidence, but this time Judge Curlewis, who described him as an 'absolute menace to human life', told Payne, 'I've been considering committing all your witnesses for perjury.' Herbert Wilson continued a career in standover and sly-grogging until he moved into drugs. In February 1938 he was fined the modest sum of fifty pounds over the illegal importation of 110 tins of opium at Port Macquarie.

But for Jeffs himself, it was really a matter of not looking back. By this time he was involved in mugging and in procuring women, often forcibly, for sex. He had a number of girls working for him in the Kings Cross area, was adroit at the ginger game and aligned to the cocaine trade. With great foresight he was also looking at illegal gaming on a grand scale. Regarded as one of the hardest razor men working in Sydney, he was intelligent and self-taught; some thought him to be the most capable criminal of his generation.

The fourth, if rather less permanent, fixture in the Sydney underworld was the standover man Norman Bruhn, who sometimes worked as a labourer on the wharves, and had served, albeit sporadically, in the forty-sixth battalion (he was court-martialled in 1916 and 1919). Ugly, bad-tempered, a beater of women, a thief and pimp, Bruhn was one of Melbourne-based Squizzy Taylor's top men. By the time he left for Sydney in 1926 his record ran the gamut of offences—larceny, vagrancy, cruelty to a horse, shop- and house-breaking and indecent exposure.

Like Snowy Cutmore, it was not the crimes for which Bruhn served time that made him so dangerous—in fact, the sentences were relatively short stints. It was the crimes for which he was never convicted, and often not even arrested, that marked him as one of Melbourne's great criminal figures of the early 1920s. That and the fact that he founded a criminal dynasty, which continues today in the shape of the Faure family. When he arrived in Sydney in 1926, bringing with him his wife Irene and their children, he had only a year to live.

Bruhn's interstate move was highly necessary. He had raided Dot Patrick's Melbourne sly-grog shop and brothel, stripped and assaulted the girls and taken about 1000 pounds. There would almost certainly be reprisals from his rivals, whom he had seriously upset. In the underworld these things could often be sorted out through intermediaries, such as Bruhn's brothers, but a spell interstate never hurt and, for the moment, Sydney seemed a much better option. From November 1926 he worked on the docks, joining the wharf labourers' union under the name Noble and staying until Easter the next year. In an interview after his death, Irene Bruhn, perhaps self-servingly, said that when he left the docks in the autumn of 1927, he had once again begun to mix with undesirables and she had returned with her family to Melbourne.

In fact she was not being wholly accurate. Bruhn had already established a string of prostitutes, including the gorgeous five-foot-three Nellie Cameron, described as a 'redhead with a ripe figure and provocative china blue eyes'. Softly spoken and never raucous but with a flaming temper, she had Bruhn as her lover and pimp, allowing him a percentage of her earnings, said to be the then remarkable one pound a time for sex. One of the many women dubbed a Black Widow, and known in the press as 'The Kiss of Death Girl', Cameron began life as a prostitute in the Surry Hills and Woolloomooloo districts. From time to time she commuted to work in Queensland and she and Bruhn also worked the ginger game. Asked what she saw in the disagreeable man, she replied, 'When I wake up in the morning I like to look down on someone lower than myself.'

Bruhn took offence easily, and his reprisals were always swift and harsh, as standover man and receiver Edward Anthony Waldhoer found out the hard way. Waldhoer, who boxed as the lightweight Billy Chambers and was regarded as the biggest fence in Sydney, would buy anything from a tiepin to a tractor and be able to dispose of it. When Waldhoer rescued prostitute Florrie Masters from Bruhn's clutches, Bruhn was not prepared to stand back and see his stable depleted. On Christmas morning 1926, he attacked Waldhoer as he lay in bed with Florrie at their home in Darlinghurst, cutting the fighter and leaving him with wounds requiring seventy-six stitches.

Poor Florrie had simply exchanged one tyrant for another. On 5 October the next year, Florrie, now euphemistically described as a barmaid, killed Waldhoer. He had been beating her, and the pair had split, then reunited and split again. This time, when she had returned to the flat to collect her furs, Waldhoer chased after her down a lane and she shot him. He died three days later in hospital, but not before he had done the decent thing, telling the police that he had shot himself while cleaning the revolver he had bought to protect himself from Bruhn. No one believed him, particularly since Florrie had told the police she had shot him in self-defence. Charged with his murder, on 15 December she was saved by the prosecutor who, opening the case with the words, 'the girl kept him and in return for his keep he was in the habit of brutally ill-using her', effectively told the jury to bring in a verdict of not guilty, something they did before the end of the defence case.

As Irene Bruhn had said, her husband's companions certainly were undesirables but it wasn't that he was simply mixing with them, as she put it; Bruhn was out leading the pack. Well, one of the packs. During his time in Sydney, he managed to gather a talented supporting cast, with whom he alienated the remainder of the local villains. Aligned with him was the seriously nasty standover man and thief George Wallace, known as 'The Midnight Raper' because of the way he stood over the prostitutes he controlled. Wallace, an ex-wrestler and an adroit pickpocket, would bet his male victims that he could guess their weight within four pounds. When he lifted them up he would steal their wallets, handing them to an offsider. Also acting as Bruhn's enforcers were the gay albino Frank 'Razor Jack' Hayes, John 'Snowy' Cutmore and Lancelot McGregor 'Sailor the Slasher' Saidler—said by his wife to be 'wonderful', keeping cats and tweaking the noses of Chinese children until they squealed with delight.

It was Hayes who slashed the throat of Sydney identity and crooked racehorse trainer Siddy Kelly on Bruhn's behalf. He didn't die, though, and in reprisal, Kelly and his much underrated older brother Tom, a standover man and gym proprietor, followed Bruhn and Hayes into Mack's, a sly-grog shop run by Joe McNamara in Charlotte Lane, Darlinghurst, and gave them a bad beating. Continuing the feud, in early June 1927 Tom Kelly shot and wounded Hayes in Liverpool Street, Darlinghurst. He was acquitted after telling the jury that Hayes had jumped on the running board of his car and demanded money from him.

Overall Bruhn should have been paying closer attention. On 22 June he spent the day drinking in the Courthouse Hotel, Darlinghurst, with racehorse trainer Robert Miller, the gambler Jim Hassett and a Dick O'Brien. They moved on to Mack's, where later that evening, Bruhn was demanding free drinks. When he was refused, he threatened to shoot up the place, but he and Miller eventually left. Outside, in Charlotte Lane, the girls usually sat on their doorsteps or in armchairs in the doorways, soliciting, but on this night there was a sea mist, and they were indoors. Two men pushed Miller aside saying, 'You're not in this' and shot Bruhn five times. 'He was so tough, four would not have killed him,' one admirer told *Truth*. But according to the taxi driver who had taken him to Mack's and had remained nearby, Bruhn's death seems to have been less than heroic. He was wailing, 'Help, I'm shot! Oh, I'm shot.' He was taken to the hospital, and Irene was at his bedside when he died. Although he is said to have told her the names of his killers, she declined to tell the police.

The possible motives for his killing were limitless. There was speculation that there had been a quarrel over cocaine distribution, or that Bruhn had failed to divvy up the proceeds of a robbery. Or that he had robbed Snowy Cutmore's friend, or that it was done on behalf of Tilly Devine, on whose girls Bruhn was leaning. Or that it was standover man Frank Green, trying to separate Bruhn from Nellie Cameron, and that Snowy Cutmore had been with him. Or, as has sometimes been suggested, it was in reprisal for the slashing of Waldhoer. Bruhn was probably also a dobber, something which has never appealed to the underworld. 'Pentridge is half full of men Bruhn betrayed,' said one Victorian detective.

More in hope than expectation, the police did at least arrange an identification parade. On it went Frank Green, along with Tom and Siddy Kelly and another Sydney identity, 'The Little Gunman' George Gaffney. Naturally, neither Miller nor the taxi driver, Noel Infield, was able to make any positive identification. 'I didn't know who these men were and if I did I would not dare to tell you,' Miller told the police. Two of Bruhn's brothers came from Melbourne and took the body and Irene back home. Within a matter of days the less than grieving Nellie could be found on the arms of both standover man Guido Calletti and Green, although not simultaneously.

Snowy Cutmore did not last long. At the end of October, he returned to Melbourne, ostensibly to pick up a horse. He must, however, have expected trouble because he took the hulking standover man Herbert Wilson (then going under the name Roy Travers) with him as bodyguard. Cutmore stayed with his mother and wife but that did not stop him getting about in an evening.

Out on the town, Cutmore, who was known to be violent (it was said he had once branded a girl with a hot iron), was drinking heavily at a brothel in St Kilda which was under the temporary protection of Squizzy Taylor. Cutmore smashed the premises and, pulling a young girl out of bed, stripped her naked before turning her onto the street. It was not something that Taylor could allow to go unpunished. The pair met at Richmond racecourse on 26 October, where there were high words.

The next day Taylor, along with Siddy and Tom Kelly, went looking for Cutmore at his mother's house. Cutmore was in bed, said to be suffering from a sudden attack of bronchitis and influenza. The most popular version of the encounter is that Taylor walked in and shot Cutmore, who, with a pistol under the sheets, returned fire. Between them, they fired fourteen times. Cutmore died on the bed, shot through the right lung. Mrs Cutmore ran into the room and was shot in the shoulder. Taylor then staggered out, to be taken to St Vincent's Hospital, where he died.

Now began the Cocaine War, a series of shootings and knifings, out of which Jeffs ultimately emerged a clear winner. But there was plenty of to-ing and fro-ing before he did. First, immediately after Bruhn's death, the personnel shifted violently. Razor Jack Hayes went to Germany, where he was badly injured in a street fight the next year. George Wallace, 'The Midnight Raper', was in Brisbane when Bruhn was shot and on his return was involved in a losing fight with Tom Kelly in Victoria Street, Darlinghurst. He was hit over the head with a hammer and fled. On 23 July 1928, fuelled with cocaine, Wallace began a fight in the Plaza Café in King Street where—after he had thrown a coffee pot at a waitress and slashed the manager, Harry Murray, with his razor—he was captured and attacked by the customers. Fined a modest two pounds, and a further three pounds towards the Plaza's damages, Wallace left Sydney and twenty years later was stabbed to death in Perth.

The next year the *Crimes (Amendment) Act 1929* made possession of a razor immediately prior to arrest on any charge punishable by six months' imprisonment. There was also a provision for ordering a whipping on a conviction for malicious wounding and grievous bodily harm. The same year the *Vagrancy (Amendment) Act* made consorting with reputed criminals punishable by six months' imprisonment.

The provisions do not seem to have deterred the last of Bruhn's team, the small, pale and thoroughly difficult Lancelot Saidler, who must have suffered from his first name in his youth. He had convictions for assault and riotous behaviour and, for the three years after Bruhn's death, he continued to stand over bars and clubs in Glebe and Elizabeth streets near the Central Railway Station until, on 13 September 1930, he demanded five shillings' protection from Ernie Good, who ran a wine bar. Good refused; Saidler threw a glass of wine in his face and, taking out his razor, threatened to carve him up. According to one witness, Saidler said, 'I'll slice off your smeller with this little beauty.' Good took out a pistol and shot him where he stood. Some stories do have happy endings. Good was charged with manslaughter but the coroner ruled Saidler's death was justifiable homicide.

* * *

There was not only prostitution, sly-grog and the standover from which to make money. From the 1920s the sale of cocaine, opium and morphine was just as important. Top-grade opium from Hong Kong came in through Queensland while lesser quality Dutch opium from Java came via Rottnest and Fremantle. This was an easy route; once the drugs were in Rottnest there was no customs enquiry of the boats that went to and fro. By the middle of the 1920s, however, because of the increasingly jaded palates of the users and the wild swings in quality, Dutch opium was falling out of favour.

The first king of the Sydney drug trade was habitual criminal Charles Passmore who 'has ruined more lives in Sydney than any other person', said Sergeant Tom O'Brien when Passmore was fined fifty pounds for possessing illegal liquor in March 1925. Henry McEwan, who in May 1923 had received six months for selling cocaine at two shillings a packet to prostitutes. A number of women had been found in a stupefied condition and, true to form, the Chinese had at first been blamed.

Passmore was another who went on to greater things. In 1930 he was convicted, along with showman Joseph Williams and sly-grog and cocaine salesman William Poe, of shooting Norman Everitt and Thomas Holdsgrove in a bank raid at Woollahra. They each received ten years. Tom Kelly, now described as a boxing instructor, was acquitted.

The next in Sydney to go down was Harry 'Jewey' Newman, described as the king of Sydney dope traffickers, who bought cocaine from doctors and dentists, cut it with boracic acid and sold it at Paddy's Markets using a gramophone records stall as a front. He would do the rounds of the surgeries, often accompanied by his children, and then break the purchases down into five shilling bags for sale to prostitutes and their clients.

When the prostitute Mary Edwards was raided in Pelican Street, Surry Hills, in 1925, the police found thirty packets of cocaine. She told them she had got them from Newman but, for the next four years, despite constant raids on his runners—including Rose Steele, 'Botany May' Smith (or Lee), who once threw a hot flat iron at Lilian Armstrong, the first policewoman in New South Wales's history, and the fifty-year-old Lilian Sproule, who was engagingly known as the 'Human Vulture'—Newman himself remained untouched.

Indeed he seems to have had a remarkable degree of protection, but his downfall came on 18 February 1929, when he tried to bribe Sergeant Tom Wickham, then half of the Drugs Squad. Wickham declined the offer and from then Newman's days on the outside were numbered in single figures. On 23 February the police raided his shop and found eighteen packets of cocaine hidden in a drainpipe. Even then he was only sentenced to nine months' hard labour and given a small fine. However, the conviction represented a modest breakthrough. Possession of cocaine had only been made an offence in 1927.

By the end of the 1920s the crusading *Truth* claimed, in good old tub-thumping prose, that Darlinghurst was the centre of crime in Sydney: 'Razorhurst, Gunhurst, Bottlehurst, Dopehurst … a plague spot where the spawn of the gutter grow and fatten on official apathy.' The article claimed underworld czars ruled over: 'bottle-men [thieves who bludgeoned their victims, usually from behind with a bottle], dope pedlars, razor slashers, sneak thieves, confidence men, women of ill repute, pickpockets, burglars, spielers, gunmen and every brand of racecourse parasite.' In fact, all the people who make life in the underworld worth living.

So far as Dopehurst was concerned, the courts were beginning to hand out substantial fines and require substantial bail for people charged with possessing cocaine. But the profits were such that it was a worthwhile risk. In July 1929 Ada McQueen and her daughter Helen were charged after drugs had been found when a party at their home was raided. Mère McQueen had been fined 250 pounds earlier in the month. Now she was required to find 300 pounds in addition to the sum she had lodged for an appeal.

Appeals were standard practice. It was sensible from the criminal's point of view to accumulate a number of convictions, lodge appeals and then withdraw them all. The usual effect was that all the sentences were made concurrent.

One noted drug smuggler of the period was Reginald William Lloyd Holmes, a man with seemingly impeccable social and business connections who owned land at McMahon's Point, across the harbour from central Sydney. For no very apparent reason he gave a former boxer, Jim Smith, a contract to erect a block of flats on the land. This was all the more peculiar because, whatever talents Smith may have had as a fighter or billiard marker, he had no experience whatsoever in the building trade.

The likelihood is that Smith was standing over Holmes and his grip tightened because the McMahon's Point scheme was a ramp: Smith went bankrupt and creditors were defrauded. However, Holmes continued to finance Smith and set him up with the grandly named Rozelle Athletic Club—in fact a billiards hall. He also gave Smith a more or less free hand skippering his speedboat.

House building apart, Holmes's great activity was smuggling. This was a time when smugglers usually just took the contraband off the ships at the docks, but Holmes used his boat *Pathfinder* to outrun customs officials as he picked up packages dumped overboard in Sydney Harbour or along the coast. Much of the contraband was cocaine—then, as now, the drug of choice among the bright young things of Sydney and elsewhere. It was a lucrative but highly competitive game, with fights between rival gangs. There were stories that Holmes's gang intended to kidnap the head of a rival organisation and indeed he had once lured a man onto his boat and then fired shots into the water to indicate what would happen if he did not co-operate.

It all began to unravel when, on Anzac Day 1935, Jim Smith's arm, identified by its tattoos, was regurgitated by a captured shark in Coogee Baths. One Patrick Brady was arrested for Smith's murder and police hoped that Holmes would give evidence. But on 11 June, in the midst of police investigations, Holmes was found shot dead in his car in Hickson Road, Dawes Point, a known courting spot.

Without evidence from Holmes, the case against Brady withered and died. On 10 September he was acquitted on the direction of the Chief Justice. Nor was the prosecution any more successful in the cases of two men, John Patrick Strong and Albert Stannard, who were accused of the murder of Holmes. The evidence was again weak—a flimsy identification and fingerprints found on the dashboard of Holmes's car—and the pair were acquitted shortly before Christmas.

In his analysis of the case, author Alex Castles suggests that Smith, not only a blackmailer but also a police informer, was shot and killed by another criminal, Edward Frederick 'Eddie' Weyman, whom Smith had been threatening. Castles also suggests that Holmes, who was heavily insured, hired men to kill him—suicide would have voided his life policies.

* * *

From the time of the First Fleet, coining—making counterfeit coins—was a useful occupation and there was a rash of it in Sydney in the 1920s. One man who went down was the sixty-year-old Arthur Twible, who in October 1920 was sentenced to five years' imprisonment to be followed by detention during the Governor's pleasure, which translated as displeasure. Unsurprisingly, Twible was unhappy, and sawed through the bars of his prison cell, scaled a wall and ran slap-bang into a warder. Twible also worked in Victoria, and over the years was thought to have been sentenced to forty years' imprisonment, including a ten-year stretch for coining in 1905.

Another talented man who seems to have coined for the sheer fun of it was Harold Roy Williams. Along with Louis Somme he received eighteen months at Quarter Sessions in 1932. He had already served a sentence in Western Australia and this time the Attorney General appealed, claiming the sentences were too lenient. They were increased to four and three years respectively.

But the unluckiest of them, and also perhaps the most talented, was Edgar Ronald Stokes (also known as James John Ritchie). One Saturday morning in August 1931, some eight months after his release from prison, neighbours heard a thump in his flat in Darlinghurst. They went to investigate and found Stokes lying dead near the door. He had died of cyanide poisoning. The police found all the windows closed and the door sealed. He had been coining florins (the equivalent of a ten-cent piece) and had inhaled the fumes. Instead of throwing open the window, he had tried to get to the door and failed by a few feet. In the previous weeks he had sold goods from a barrow, where he was thought to change the counterfeit coins. Now the police found a newspaper marked with racing selections and it was clear Stokes had intended to go to Kensington pony races that afternoon to get rid of the florins on bookmakers.

The next year three Chinese businessmen appeared at the Central Criminal Court charged with uttering counterfeit coins. This time shillings totalling 480 pounds were brought in by Kuong Yung Tseng and then passed in their hundreds by Tseng Po Yung and Kwong Khi Tseng. The coins, all dated 1928, contained up to 3 per cent less silver than a genuine Australian shilling. Two things were surprising about the case. The first was that the men used banks to change the coins, though it was some time before the cashiers became suspicious. The second was that in November 1932 they were acquitted. Perhaps it was their openness in going to the banks that created sufficient doubt in the minds of the jurors. Although why someone should carry 9600 coins, all dated 1928, seems odd in itself. The trio immediately left for China.

*   *   *

Shootings continued happily in the underworld, with none of the survivors ever able to say who shot them or why anyone should do such a thing at all. In the autumn of 1928 there were no fewer than twenty, and in most of the cases the victims refused to co-operate with the police. In January 1929, William McKay, accounting for a wound in his chest, said that he had carried a gun and accidentally shot himself when he put his hand in his pocket. No gun could be found and McKay explained he had thrown it away the moment it went off.

The first major trouble in Sydney after the death of Norman Bruhn and the dismantling of his team came two years later—in the form of a half-hour pitched battle in Eaton Avenue, Normanhurst, fought by about twenty men. It occurred because Phil Jeffs had been discovered cutting cocaine with an unacceptable level of boracic acid. Jeffs was at the fore, pulling William Archer, who had been shot in the leg, off the running board of a car and giving him a good kicking. He left the scene of the action and returned home, where at around 4 a.m. he was shot in the shoulder after a break-in. He crawled out of the house and was found by a milkman to whom he called rather piteously, 'Milkie, take me to hospital.'

Fortunately for him, Milkie came up trumps. Jeffs was driven to hospital, In his dying depositions he was at pains to deny that he was the head of an international gang. He survived and Ernest James Taylor was charged with his attempted murder but Jeffs gave evidence he was not the man. In turn he was charged, along with Archer, with causing grievous bodily harm to the fraudsman and fixer Charles Sorlie—who had run out of a block of flats in Normanhurst he was apparently managing to see what the noise was about—and to former all-in wrestler and known thief Frederick Johns, who just happened to be in the neighbourhood. Naturally, by the beginning of September all charges were dismissed, and as far as Jeffs was concerned peace was temporarily restored.

The Game, Gambling and Cocaine

3

The first outbreak of hostilities in the war between Tilly Devine and Kate Leigh for the control of prostitution in East Sydney came at precisely 7.30 p.m. on 17 July 1929. As with all good conflicts, it had been simmering for a couple of days—since Tilly's husband Jim was fined fifty pounds for possessing illegal ammunition when gun cartridges were found in a settee at their Long Bay address. He claimed that, ten weeks earlier at Newtown, he had been robbed of a diamond stickpin and ten pounds, and the gun was for his protection.

In the yard of the courthouse a ring of men formed while Tilly Devine and another woman, Vera Lewis, both later described as fashionably dressed, rolled on the ground fighting. When the police broke it up and hauled the pair into court, Lewis was fined three pounds and Tilly Devine, who was said to have been trying to bite her opponent's finger, was remanded. 'She seemed to think I was responsible for her husband being fined,' complained Lewis. The charge of biting Lewis was dropped and Tilly was fined three pounds for riotous behaviour.

In the early evening of 17 July, the gunman Frank Green, now active in prostitution and illegal betting, met George 'The Little Gunman' Gaffney from the Leigh camp in Nicholson Street, Woolloomooloo. Green, who was accompanied by a Sidney McDonald, received a good kicking from Gaffney and headed for the casualty ward. Three hours later McDonald met the Devines, with whom Green was living, and told them what had happened. They took a taxi and returned to Torrington Road, Maroubra, where Green, who had discharged himself from hospital and modestly taken a tram, arrived a little before midnight. Also on their way to Torrington Road in a taxi were Gaffney and Kate Leigh's long-time bodyguard, Walter Tomlinson.

Shortly after midnight Jim Devine heard someone trying to climb the fence and shouted a warning from the balcony. His revolver had been forfeited by the courts and, because he feared trouble, he had borrowed a .303 from a friend. As Gaffney announced he had plenty of friends with him, yelling, 'I'm out for the blood of you, you bastard', Devine shot him in the chest. He also shot Walter Tomlinson, smashing his arm. The 'plenty of friends' seems to have been something of an exaggeration. A third man escaped in a taxi shortly before the police arrived and Gaffney died on the pavement soon afterwards. Decently, before he died he refused to say who had shot him; in turn Devine refused to prosecute Tomlinson for the home invasion. Devine was, nevertheless, charged with the unlawful killing of Gaffney.

Gaffney's funeral took place in Surry Hills on the Saturday and there was trouble on the streets throughout the day. When Police Constable Strong tried to arrest a group of men for indecent language, he was set upon. A man who went to his rescue was beaten back and the officer was only freed when police reinforcements arrived.

Three months after the party thrown for Devine's acquittal on the grounds of self-defence, Frank Green was out for revenge. On 9 November, admittedly by mistake, he killed a Leigh soldier, the former rugby league player Bernard Dalton, as he and Tomlinson, who had been the real object of Green's attention, stood talking to Tom Kelly outside Sharland's Hotel in William Street, Woolloomooloo. Green and Sidney McDonald went into hiding and Tomlinson, his arm now healed, drove Kate Leigh in her Studebaker to Dalton's spectacular funeral. Green went into smoke and was not found until early December when, following a tip-off, he was traced to a shack in Cronulla.

Tomlinson, forgetting his position in life and possibly thinking he had had enough, picked out Green on an identification parade. It naturally only served to cause more ill feeling. On the tram to Long Bay jail, Green was heard to remark, 'The bastard picked me today. It's a pity I didn't get him as well as Dalton while I was at it.' Amazingly Tomlinson went through with his evidence and for his pains was knocked about by Sidney McDonald during the luncheon adjournment of Green's trial. In March 1930 McDonald received twelve months and Green was acquitted.

Then, in the middle of March, three months after Green's arrest, Leigh's house at 104 Riley Street, East Sydney, was attacked by a gang of men looking for the Judas, Tomlinson. One, Jacky Craig, managed to reach the bedroom and damaged the furniture before the police arrived to evict them. Next day Kate Leigh bought a pea-rifle and fifty cartridges. She was well advised to have done so; on 27 March there was another attack. Giving evidence at the subsequent inquest, Leigh said that she had warned she had a gun and would shoot, but the men, including the Prendergast brothers John (known as 'Snowy' because of his predilection for cocaine) and Joseph, demanded that she give up Tomlinson. She shot John Prendergast in the stomach after he threw a brick at her. When the police were called, Prendergast is said to have told Leigh, 'Shoot me, you ****. I am dying.' The following month at the inquest, Leigh, now described as a shopkeeper, was acquitted by the coroner of Prendergast's killing. Later she would say, 'I have never stopped saying a prayer of repose for the blackguard's soul.'

And if, in a fit of temper, Leigh did go to the police in April 1930, claiming that Joseph Prendergast, Fred Lee and Albert Runnalls had broken into her shop with intent to murder her, by the time the defendants appeared in court, she had thought better of it and would not attend to give evidence.

In April 1930 the lightweight boxer and standover man Arthur Messenger (who boxed as Art Walker) was shot at the corner of Riley and Albion. He had, he said, been eating in a café when a man he did not know called him outside. He was shot four times at close range but amazingly escaped with minor injuries. One shot ricocheted off his waistcoat button. He merely told the police, 'I'll deal with it myself.' On 18 April that year, wharf labourer William Roy Elmer (also known as Walter Williamson) and Charles Bourke (also known as Edward Brown and MacRogers), standover man, greyhound trainer and later husband of the prostitute 'Pretty' Dulcie Markham, were taken to hospital where Elmer died. He had been shot in the back, possibly by a woman with a long-barrelled revolver. Although the coroner was brought in to take a statement, Elmer refused to disclose who had shot him, while Bourke denied even knowing Elmer. The police were convinced that both men had been cornered together and, since both had wounds on their backs, they had been shot as they tried to run away. There was also the suggestion that Elmer's brother Maxwell had been present when the shooting took place.

By now, with the press on their heels, the politicians had acted and the New South Wales *Vagrancy (Amendment) Act 1929* was passed, providing penalties for those consorting with reputed thieves, prostitutes and those with no known means of support— that is, with each other. In 1930 sixty-eight men and women were charged under the 'consorting clause', and nearly double that the next year. Tilly Devine was charged in January 1930 with consorting with prostitutes, which, since she employed them, was hardly surprising. She negotiated a settlement that if she was not tried, she would agree to leave Sydney for two years. She sailed for England the next month, leaving Jim Devine, half the man his wife was, to look after the shop.

The arrangement was not a success. In her absence he hired what might euphemistically be called a housekeeper, an arrangement which did not meet with Tilly's approval on her return well inside her exile time. On 9 January 1931, when he arrived home with the housekeeper, Tilly was enraged. A shot was fired. At me, said Tilly; in the air to pacify her, said Devine. She wanted him kept in custody because she was afraid he would murder her. A week was sufficient for everyone to see sense and she withdrew the charge. For good measure, Devine was also charged with possessing a razor but, after the court was told that it was not in the coat he was wearing at the time he was arrested, he was acquitted of this as well.

Worse, however, was to follow. In March that year Jim Devine was badly slashed and, in the convoluted way in which the underworld conducts its alignments and re-alignments, he now fell out with Frank Green. Devine does not seem to have had a great deal of luck with his diamond stickpins. At about 8.30 on the evening of 16 June, Green, Dulcie Markham and William Hourigan turned up at Torrington Road and robbed Devine of another stickpin at gunpoint.

Devine seized a gun and ran after Green as he was getting into a waiting taxi. He fired at him and missed, killing the driver, Frederick Moffitt. Devine had been using soft-nosed, high-velocity ammunition and the shot tore out the unfortunate man's lungs. Devine, now described as a fruiterer, was charged and, once more, acquitted. Again, Tilly threw a lavish party for her husband but, in truth, her empire was in trouble.

Perhaps mistakenly, Devine decided to give evidence against Green, who was having a bad time of things. First, he was committed for trial on the charge of stealing the stickpin and then, on 26 October 1931, he was found shot in the stomach at the rear of St Vincent's Hospital. He was carried inside by a young man and woman who promptly and sensibly disappeared. Coincidentally, in the hospital at the time was Siddy Devine, Jim's brother, shot in the arm. Siddy had been found staggering in French Street, Maroubra, saying he had been talking to a Guy Neville Kingsbury when he was suddenly (and obviously for no reason) set upon. Kingsbury shot him at close range, severing an artery, and then locked him in a bedroom. Siddy only escaped by smashing a window. He does not appear to have behaved as heroically as might have been wished, repeatedly asking the hospital staff whether he was going to die. Kingsbury was arrested and charged with attempted murder. For once, a conviction resulted and he was sentenced to death. However, the High Court ordered a new trial on the grounds that the police evidence had been fudged and, after a second jury disagreed, he was again convicted in March 1933. This time he received a rather more acceptable two years.

The papers followed the Green shooting case with interest. On 28 October he was said to be sinking slowly and there was no hope for him. Nevertheless his lips remained sealed. The next day he had a 'fighting chance'. On 30 October Charles George Brame, recently arrived from Victoria, was charged over the shooting at what was described as a musical evening in a Darlinghurst flat. But what are a few bullets to a man like Green? By March 1932 he was in court to say Brame was not the man who had shot him and out went the case. Now the judge took the opportunity to issue a few words of unheeded wisdom: gangsters should use their fists, not revolvers. It is possible that Green's shooting was a reprisal by Brame, who had himself been shot in the groin in Belmore Park on 5 August 1929. In the meantime, on 3 January 1932 Brame had been fined 100 pounds for possessing an unlicensed revolver.

Rather unsportingly, Green took a delayed and mean reprisal against Jim Devine over the stickpin charge. In May 1932 a woman telephoned the police to say Devine was planning a robbery and that he had weapons hidden in the bathroom. Indeed he had, along with some cocaine, the police discovered. He was acquitted after telling the court that a friend of Green, Florrie Sharman, had used the bathroom the night before. He received an encomium from Detective Young: 'Devine is a pretty shrewd fellow. In my opinion he is too shrewd to have a revolver and cocaine lying in that spot.'

It was not all Devine/Green, however. In the early hours of 9 May 1931 bookmaker George Cooper was shot when three men raided a sly-grog shop party in Thurlow Street, Redfern, apparently demanding bottles of beer. A fight broke out between sly-grogger Alfred Stanton and one of the robbers, and Cooper was accidentally shot near the heart. He was taken to hospital but of course refused to say anything. At the time he was too weak to have the bullet removed and he died two days later. Although everyone knew everyone else involved, the police claimed it was not part of the then current racecourse wars, in which standover men were demanding money from bookmakers, who in turn were hiring other standover men to protect them. On 14 May, standover man Jack Finnie, who in his younger days could have been a bantamweight contender, appeared in court charged with Cooper's murder. Happily, he was acquitted.

* * *

Meanwhile, Kate Leigh had been in trouble yet again. In 1929 she served a four-month sentence under the consorting law after a raid on one of her brothels, at 25 Kippax Street, Surry Hills. The following year she was raided again and this time cocaine was discovered at her East Sydney home. *Truth* now claimed, 'she had held the dope game in a grip that was as tight as that of any Midas'. Leigh was sentenced to twelve months' imprisonment and fined 250 pounds. Her appeal was dismissed and she was dragged screaming from the dock. She had more fortune shortly before Christmas 1931 when she was acquitted of the attempted murder of Joseph McNamara. He had been shot in the groin but was another who did the manly thing and failed to identify her. There being no other evidence, she was discharged.

Meanwhile, bookmaker Frederick Dangar, described as Leigh's right-hand man, had been in court in February the previous year after attempting to purchase fifteen grams of cocaine from a North Sydney chemist without a prescription. His defence was that he wanted it for a horse. He was given a 250-pound fine or twelve months' imprisonment.

Leigh did not serve the twelve months for her drugs conviction. She used her influence with a Labor alderman to persuade the courts that payment of the fine was sufficient punishment, but her empire was on the wane. In March 1932 her daughter Eileen agreed to exile for three years from New South Wales to avoid a prison sentence and in June 1933 Leigh herself agreed to a five-year rustication at least 200 miles from Sydney after being found in possession of stolen goods. She was given fourteen days in which to prepare for her exile but took no notice of repeated warnings after the time had expired and was back in front of Judge Curlewis on 1 August that year. She had had a touch of pneumonia, but no, she had not been to a doctor. She had nearly packed her bags now, couldn't she have a bit more time? No, she could not. Two years' imprisonment. 'Won't you make it twenty-three months?' she asked. 'No, I won't,' replied the judge and received a volley of abuse for his troubles.

Deprived for the time being of Tilly Devine's guiding hand, Frank Green's career was another to decline. He had achieved his pinnacle in 1930 when he was regarded as Sydney's top gunman. Now he spent the next five years of his life in hiding, in prison, in hospital or locked in battle with another top standover man, Guido Calletti, for the favours of the delectable Nellie Cameron. One street fight with Calletti over Nellie was said to have lasted three-quarters of an hour and ended with honours even and the clothes of both men in tatters.

Nellie Cameron's love life apart, all the Devine/Leigh shootings left the retiring and very smart Phil Jeffs on top of the pile to became one of the great sly-grog dealers in the city. In the 1930s he had a half share in the appropriately named 50-50 Club, a sly-grog shop on the corner of William and Forbes, when, bored with constant raids by the police, his partner upped and left. Jeffs was now the de facto owner and made of sterner stuff. He transformed the large hall—now with a piano and, more importantly, a string of prostitutes—into one of the best-known drinking rooms in the city. It had all the scams of a 'near beer' joint, with the girls drinking water and the customers paying for their 'gin'. The girls themselves were not charged admission but paid five shillings every time they left with a customer. Frank Green was hired to calm the more rowdy element. Above the club there were apartments for the prostitutes to whom the leading and lesser lights were steered. The customers could be drugged and photographed in compromising positions but fortunately the negatives were always available for purchase to avoid family or public embarrassment.

Now Jeffs had his head firmly below the parapet. When in April 1933 the 50-50 Club was raided, Harold 'Snowy' Billington took the rap. Jeffs was there only for his protection, he said. This was rather contradicted by the evidence that it was Jeffs who took control during the raid, telling the staff to say nothing and reminding them that the cash receipts were for food and not liquor. The police generously described him as a 'former' gunman.

Curiously, this robber and pimp acquired a certain measure of social respectability. Perhaps more importantly he acquired a defender in the form of Anthony Alexander Alam, a member of the state parliament. In 1936 *Truth* named Alam as the part owner, with Jeffs, of Graham's on Hunter Street, where he could be found on a regular basis. Alam sued the paper for 10000 pounds but the case was settled for a derisory five pounds.

Jeffs also opened a classier establishment, the 400 Club in Phillip Street, Darlinghurst, which for a time he owned in partnership with the fashionable doctor–abortionist Reginald Stuart-Jones. Their relationship came to an abrupt end in 1937, with the good doctor being slipped a Mickey Finn, thrown out of the club by Jeffs and the doorman, and barred further entry. Jeffs also opened Oyster Bill's Club, complete with a swimming pool and band, at Tom Ugly's Point.

By that year, Jeffs had organised his contacts in the police force so well that it was tacitly accepted that his 400 club was almost immune from prosecution. Almost but not quite. When the club was raided in March 1938 the thirty or so upper-class patrons were reported as saying they had found the whole experience, including their ride in the police van, rather exciting. And there was Alam in the state parliament denouncing these bully-boy tactics. After all, the club was run on the most respectable lines—why, the Governor's wife could go in unattended. As sociologist Alfred McCoy points out: 'It was indicative of Jeffs' influence that the major address-in-reply to the Governor's speech should be a passionate defence of the city's leading criminal and that not a word of objection should be raised.'

* * *

For a time in the 1930s cocaine temporarily disappeared from the streets of Sydney and the standover men had to turn their hands to some other occupation. This time their chosen victims were the SP bookmakers. In 1936 another war broke out. On one side were ranged the standover men and on the other the equally violent men employed as guards by SP bookmakers in Darlinghurst, East Sydney and Surry Hills.

The spring of 1937 saw a partial clearing of the decks. On 17 September, the 250-pound George Jeremiah 'Jerry' Lynch was shot in the Tophatter's Cabaret in Darlinghurst Road, Kings Cross. Naturally he would not tell the police who had shot him, saying, 'I can square the matter myself.' He could not. Like so many of the time, he developed peritonitis and died four days later. Names in the frame included Frank Green and a man, Cunningham, but it was Thomas Ernest de Valle who was charged with his murder. In a dying deposition Lynch said it was not de Valle, whom he had known for some twelve years, and the only evidence against him was from the doorman, who had picked him from a line-up. Lynch may have been right that it was not de Valle. His shooting may have been over gambling debts but in a series of articles in *The Argus*, the Melbourne gunman 'Pretty Boy' Robert Walker claimed he had shot Lynch because he believed he was either going to be beaten up or shot and that Lynch's death was the culmination of a quarrel which had begun in Parramatta jail. On 27 October the Attorney-General filed a no-bill.

Clarence Henry John 'Clarrie' Thomas had been one of the youngest men to serve in World War I but after his discharge he became a standover man and receiver. In May 1924 Thomas was a leader in the Bathurst jail mutiny in which an attempt was made to liberate the top men in the jail, including the aboriginal Roy Governor. On 18 November 1937 he was shot dead in Castlereagh Street by Richard Gabriel Reilly, who would later become a major player in the city's underworld. Thomas and his cousin Jack Finnie went to stand over the Ginger Jar Club, which later became the Ziegfeld. Club bouncer Reilly took a gun, followed them up Castlereagh Street and shot Thomas. Claiming he was protecting his brother Gerald, whom Thomas had been standing over, Reilly was acquitted on a plea of self-defence.

Certainly there had been bad blood between Thomas, Finnie and Reilly. Finnie had been charged with assaulting former boxer Gerald Reilly, giving him a beating that afternoon in the lavatory of the Surrey Hotel, claiming that Richard was a dobber. Everything worked out nicely. With Finnie blaming the dead Thomas for the assault, he was acquitted without the jury leaving the box.

* * *

Even when there was no actual gang war going on, the underworld's casualty rate was still high. At a time when guns were still carried as a matter of course, quarrels over women and perceived insults, not to mention business troubles, ended not with a slap but with a bullet. In his memoirs, Chow Hayes recalled that among his Sydney friends who went to the long early bath were Barney Dalton and Henry 'Sap' Johnson, a shoplifter and thief killed in Surry Hills. In February 1938 thief and standover man Harold Robert Tarlington was shot twice in the stomach after a house in St Peters was wrecked in a fight over women. He refused to help the police, telling the magistrate, brought to his bedside to take his dying deposition, 'I would never squeal.' Another standover man, Harold George Baker, shot in the same blue, survived. Myles Henry McKeon, known as 'Face', was charged with Tarlington's murder and, naturally, was acquitted.

In July 1936 the Scottish-born Cecil Charles 'Hoppy' Gardner was acquitted of shooting another standover man, Alfred 'Nigger' Fox, but his luck soon ran out. On 15 August Gardner was himself shot while trying to stand over Paddy Roach's two-up game at Erskineville. It was another shooting that did not go anywhere. He refused to tell the police the name of his attackers but, before he died three days after the shooting, he did tell his mother, Jean, 'Mum, I've got to tell you who shot me. Ted 'Alan' Pulley shot me. Ted shot me four or five times.' Later she told the coroner, 'I asked him if Big Bill had anything to do with it and he replied that Big Bill had told Pulley to "give him the lot".' 'Big Bill' George Plaisted and Pulley were charged and quite properly acquitted.

In fact Pulley did not last too long himself. A talented housebreaker from New Zealand, whose *modus operandi* was to break a leadlight over the front door and release the lock, Pulley was also a feared standover man. Always expensively dressed except when he was working, he had been drinking in the Town and Country Hotel in St Peters on 6 March 1937 when he went to stand over an SP joint run by sisters Florrie Riley and Elsie O'Halloran. The official story was that Pulley came into the backyard while a race from Randwick was being broadcast and demanded three pounds from the women. Florrie said he was too late and that they had paid out to other standover men. The women then went into the house and shut the back door. If they thought that was the end of the matter they were swiftly disabused when Pulley leapt in through the window. O'Halloran grabbed the chocolate tin where they kept their money and Pulley tried to snatch it from her. Riley ran upstairs to get a gun. As Pulley and her sister were fighting, she shot him twice. Pulley fell down and asked, 'What have you done to me? I can't get up.' At first he thought she had stabbed him with a pencil, but in fact two bullets had lodged in his spine. Six days later he died doing the right thing—not blaming the women. He was right not to blame them, and not just for the sake of not snitching. According to Chow Hayes, Pulley had gone to the house expecting only the women to be there but found instead that Elsie's husband Ned O'Halloran was in attendance. It wasn't the women who shot Pulley, it was Ned.

The gamest of the game must have been William Joseph 'Billy' McCarthy. A list of underworld members who took a pop at him reads like a roll of honour. And, despite what they did to him, McCarthy never gave one of them up. Chow Hayes took a tram hook to him; Charlie Bourke shot him; he had his throat cut in Brisbane. Back in Sydney in February 1944, Charles 'Kicker' Kelly and John O'Connor shot him in Bourke Street after he was caught stealing from a two-up game, and in 1951 he needed more than fifty stitches after an attack in Wilmot Street off Pitt Street. Throughout he remained silent, until in 1957, it all came to an end when he quarrelled over prossie Faye Payton at the Avalon Sports Club, Bondi Junction, and Charles 'Chicka' Reeves killed him. Naturally Reeves was acquitted but not before Ms Payton told the court that Reeves, to whom she gave thirty pounds a week from her earnings, had taken a can opener to her face when she displeased him.

Occasionally there were chinks in the armour. On 9 July 1938 Charlie Madden and his offsider, John Thomas 'Ike' Harvey, went to tax the Green Street, Waterloo, bookmaker James Young, threatening to 'clean him up'. They found him unco-operative. As a result Madden pinned the bookmaker's hand to the windowsill with a knife. Young was fortunate. His cockatoo pulled the knife out and stabbed Madden. Bravely, Young was not prepared to leave things as they were and he went to the police. He also arranged some protection for himself and when Madden and Harvey returned to Young's premises the same day they found Edward Perry there barring the way. Harvey stabbed him in the ribs.

Until then Madden had been fortunate. He had been acquitted three times of shooting with intent to kill when his victims either declined to give evidence or could not be sure that he was their attacker. Nor was Harvey a cleanskin, despite his counsel describing him as being from a family 'of excellent reputation'. He had convictions for assault going back ten years and in 1932 had sued *Smith's Weekly* for 1000 pounds over an article in the paper regarding his association with the murderer William Moxley. But Young was prepared to go through with it and both Madden and Harvey, described by the judge as 'a grave menace to decent citizens', received ten years' imprisonment. Nor did they get any change from the Court of Appeal, where the Chief Justice, calling the pair 'parasites', said that racketeering must be stamped out.

Bookmaker Jack Keane had not been as fortunate as Young. In late August 1933 Jack Finnie and Norman 'Mickey' McDonald, another whose speciality was standing over SP bookmakers, were shot as they visited a former colleague in Mascot. McDonald was hit in the chest and Finnie in the neck but, amazingly, both men survived. Once at the Royal South Sydney Hospital, the pair indicated to the police that the identity of whoever shot them was their business and theirs alone. Labourer Thomas Craig was charged with attempted murder but acquitted. At about 5.20 a.m. on 29 September, Jack Keane's body was found dumped near the house in Coward Street where Finnie and McDonald had been shot. One theory was that Keane had been killed following a blue at a party. Another was that his crime had been to tell the police who the Mascot gunman had been. His penalty was a beating and three bullets in the left side of his head. No charges were ever brought.

Three years later Finnie and McDonald fell out, and in September 1936, in an argument over money, Finnie shot his friend near the greyhound track at St Peters. Amazingly, McDonald identified him and Finnie stood trial. He was acquitted after telling the jury that he had fired in self-defence when McDonald had threatened him with a gun. Finnie later received a six-month sentence for consorting, which was reduced to three after the Rev Albert Morris made an impassioned plea to the magistrate that Finnie had reformed and would never offend again. 'I am pleading for this man's life; for his soul,' he told Judge Markell, adding, 'I am a parson but not a fool.' Parson he may have been, fool he certainly was. Finnie continued his high-profile criminal career for years to come.

If matters could not be squared between the parties prior to a court hearing, then complainants and witnesses could be scared off. There is nothing that concentrates the mind of a girl who lives off her looks like the threat of a razor slash to the face. After Maisie Wilson accused Siddy Kelly, Guido Calletti and Anthony Cummins of criminally assaulting her in late 1929, she became so frightened she headed for Brisbane and remained there until the case against the men was dismissed. On 23 September that year Tom Kelly received five years for holding down a John Alfred Penfold for Joe 'The Pig' Sinclair to slash. Penfold had attacked a Poppy Kindy, who was under Kelly's protection. Sinclair and Kelly were acquitted. Occasionally the girls did go through with their evidence. Dolly Carslake was made of stern stuff when Gordon Henry Barr turned up at her Kings Cross flat to see his wife. When she tried to evict him he slashed her. Curiously, the jury recommended mercy but Judge Curlewis sent them back to reconsider, after which they again returned with the same recommendation. They suggested he had been provoked and even when the judge pointed out that he had gone armed with a razor they still refused to change their minds. He gave Barr five years and, when asked by the Court of Appeal why he had disregarded the jury's recommendation, he wrote a note: 'I sentenced him to five years' penal servitude because I could not give him ten.' The superior court agreed with him.

The case had a series of repercussions. Barr's wife, 'Diamond' Dolly, and her friend Jean Ryan (also known as Joyce Thelma Branch) believed Siddy and Tom Kelly had shelved Barr, and later that year on 4 August Dolly travelled to Melbourne to the Richmond Pony Races to tell the stewards that Siddy, who was running a horse there, had put a battery in the saddle. He was disqualified for life. In turn Siddy Kelly shot at, and missed, Jean Ryan as she left a Melbourne brothel, and was bound over for it.

On 6 August 1939, Guido Calletti, the standover man described in 1930 as 'the worst man in Sydney', was shot twice in the stomach and killed. His practice had been to stand over standover men, in his case the Brougham Street mob, who collected from bookmakers. He would isolate members and deal with them. He also worked as a debt collector for the crooked trainer and bookmaker James Kingsley. Calletti had already survived a number of shootings and soon began to boast of his invulnerability. On the day of his death, he had been to his grandmother's funeral, taking the opportunity to stop and have a drink with his friend Dulcie Markham.

Calletti decided he would gatecrash a birthday party being held that evening in Brougham Street for a nurse. Nellie Cameron was away, working in Queensland, so he went with Markham. At first all was well, albeit on a tentative basis, but then Calletti began to drink and boast of how he would deal with his hosts. In the ensuing fight he was outnumbered and, as he went for his gun, the lights went out, his arm was turned, two shots were heard, and indeed the lights went out for Calletti, who lay dying in Dulcie's arms. When the police arrived, naturally he told them he did not know who shot him—on this occasion he may actually have been right.

The funeral was spectacular even by gangland standards of the period. Five thousand people were said to have either filed past his body as it lay at the Reliance Funeral Chapel in Darlinghurst or to have attended the service, many simply checking for themselves that he was indeed dead. There were 200 wreaths at the funeral, including one from Nellie Cameron, who did not make the journey back, contenting herself with sending a four-foot-high floral cross. Dulcie Markham wept bitterly at the graveside. The maple and silver coffin was paid for by a whip. As it was carried out, Calletti's football blazer was thrown across it.

The police thought the birthday girl, Peggy Patterson, might actually solve the killing for them. Promised immunity from prosecution as an accessory, she gave the names of those who had been at her party and on 10 August two men, Robert Branch (also known as Jackson) and George Allen (also known as Cave), were arrested. Branch was discharged at the committal proceedings, leaving Allen to face the murder charge. Patterson was now tucked away safely in a boarding house in Moss Vale and the proprietor was told to report any suspicious behaviour to the police. However, the best laid plans often go astray. It would not have seemed suspicious when the girl's 'sister' visited her, had the sister not been Nellie Cameron, back from Queensland to help out.

The trial went badly wrong for the prosecution. First, Patterson did not appear and a warrant was issued for her. Then, when she was brought to court, she was convinced she had made a mistake and that Allen was not the man responsible. She was just as convinced that Nellie Cameron had not been to see her. Treated as a hostile witness, she refused to answer questions. Not guilty. It was a good time for both men. On 10 October Branch had been acquitted of the attempted murder of standover man Richard Mealing in a quarrel on Bayswater Road. The same day Allen was charged with bank robbery in King Street and stealing 1267 pounds. He was acquitted on the direction of the judge on 12 March the following year.

Occasionally the standover man did come off second best. Cornelius Wilson, proprietor of the Pirates Cave Cabaret in Dowling Street, Woolloomooloo, was accused of the murder of taxi driver and boxer Stanley James 'Mickey' Leonard on 15 March 1939. Leonard, together with Kicker Kelly, had tried to gain entry to the club, breaking down the door after being turned away. Wilson shot Leonard through a peephole in the door of his office, claiming he had fired only to frighten, and that Kelly had been standing over his club. On 2 June he was found not guilty.

Despite all this mayhem, in 1939 it was Melbourne which had a higher crime rate per capita than both Sydney and London. It had the worst record in Australia for violent robberies, noted the *Sydney Morning Herald* complaisantly. And that, more or less, was the picture of major crime before war broke out and the screen changed completely.

Some Grey and Other Fleeting Shadows

4

There is a maxim in the underworld that one's best partner in crime is oneself—and it is one largely followed by Australian identities. In the late 1920s Sydney was plagued by the Grey Shadow, the name given by newspapers to a lone robber who wore a long grey coat as he carried out a series of armed hold-ups. Who he actually was has never been satisfactorily resolved but whoever he was he started a trend. Soon there was an influx of Shadows, including Owen Glyndwr Evans, who was deported to England in 1931 after serving two years for a series of about 100 burglaries. Then there were wannabes such as Herbert Granville, who pleaded guilty to a number of burglaries and left a note behind in a car he had rifled. It read: 'Beware of the lone wolf and the grey shadow.' But no one believed he was the Shadow himself.

Another claimant was Clarence Jones, who told one victim, Ethel Molloy, that he was the real thing and that a man arrested earlier was not the Grey Shadow. When Jones came to court the magistrate was not impressed. 'Grey Shadows and Blue Shadows are becoming so common that they are a nuisance to the public,' he said, sentencing him to three months for stealing a motor car. The charge of attempting to obtain money from Mrs Molloy was dismissed. Shadows were indeed becoming a hazard. One victim, William Tory, became so traumatised after a Shadow attacked him that he tried to commit suicide. Black Shadows, as well as grey and blue ones, were also becoming a menace. A man claiming to be the Black Shadow bailed up three taxi drivers in quick succession in September 1929.

As one Grey Shadow disappeared, another emerged. The previous month a man claiming to be the real Grey Shadow held up Arthur Hunt, the licensee of a Darling Road wine saloon, his wife and a friend, stealing a little under twenty pounds. Hunt later told police that the man had boasted 'there was not a detective clever enough in Australia to catch him and that he was itching to shoot someone'. If it was indeed the Shadow, he was remarkably indiscreet because he also told Hunt he was a timber worker and was married with four children.

Hunt's attacker may have been laying a false trail because the man thought most likely to have been the original Grey Shadow was a 29-year-old salesman, Thomas Herbert Skinner, who was arrested after robbing shopkeeper Richard Woods in Rozelle in early 1930. Chased by the police, Skinner shot one constable in the groin and got away but he was caught after a fingerprint on the lens of some spectacles—dropped in the robbery—was identified as his. Skinner fought it out, claiming he had been at the cinema with Vera Lee and that the whole case against him was a frame-up. He was sentenced to ten years with hard labour. Whether he was the real Grey Shadow or the fad had simply run its course, incidents with robbers wearing grey dusters faded away into the night.

Another man whose name had come up as the Grey Shadow was the career criminal Joseph Harold Ryan, who in August 1929 was acquitted of beating and robbing eighty-year-old Henry Wheale of twenty-seven pounds and James Stewart of fifteen pounds. Ryan may not have been the Shadow but he was certainly in the frame for what became known as the Mudgee train robbery. At about 11 p.m. on 8 April 1930, two masked and armed men entered the brake van after the train left Emu Plains on Sydney's outer west and held up the guards. The thieves jumped off just before the train, travelling at about 30 miles per hour, entered the tunnel on the Glenbrook side of Sydney, taking with them 4600 pounds' worth of bullion and another 13000 pounds in cheques. At first it was thought that Australians were not capable of such a daring robbery and that American criminals must have been involved. For a time it was even suggested that the D'Autremont brothers, who in 1923 had robbed a train in Oregon, had been responsible. This was always highly improbable, even given lax prison security, for, at the time, the brothers were serving life sentences in the United States. The always suspect Italians were also considered but, when it came to it, it was good old Australian planning.

In May the next year the Canberra mail train was robbed at Queanbeyan and this time 10000 pounds was stolen. It was a very different affair. The Commonwealth Bank had sent the money to Canberra in a mailbag. The train stopped at Queanbeyan at 4.15 a.m., when the bag and other sacks were unloaded and left on the platform for transfer. When the train reached Canberra, it was found that the Commonwealth sack no longer contained the cash but was packed with telephone directories.

On 30 April 1931, Ryan was charged with both of the train thefts, and James Caffrey and Arthur Collins were charged with receiving from the Canberra mail theft and also with a well-planned and -executed robbery of jeweller Samuel Cohen. Everyone was given bail and Ryan made the most of this unexpected opportunity to abscond. The papers thought he would soon give himself up and *Truth* was at its most eloquent, writing of an elderly, grey-haired mother sitting in her darkened room awaiting the return of her son. Over the years there were various sightings of him in and around Sydney and on one occasion he gave a statement to the press that he had absconded because the police had 'smoked' his principal witness.

Then, in June 1935, a firm of solicitors received a letter from Ryan—who had apparently been in England and was suspected of a gold robbery in Birmingham—asking them to arrange a meeting with a Detective Inspector Quinn so that he could give himself up. At 7.15 p.m. on 19 June he was rearrested. 'I have come back from abroad to give myself up to the police to meet the charges against me. I have always had a complete defence,' he told Quinn, adding that a man who had owed him money had failed to come through so he was left without funds to pay for his defence. By then, another man, Lancelot Lynch, had been acquitted and Arthur Collins had pleaded guilty to concealing knowledge of the Canberra robbery. Ryan, somewhat optimistically, thought that having done the decent thing and given himself up he might receive bail again. The argument cut no ice with Judge Curlewis.

The Canberra robbery was tried first and much of the Crown's evidence came from an informer, thief and forger Percy Jacobs, who in 1928 had received two years for a 1200-pound fraud. Jacobs gave detailed evidence of Ryan's pre-planning, but at crunch time, denied being personally involved, although Ryan had promised him 1000 pounds. This produced an outburst from Judge Curlewis: 'Why you were to get 1000 pounds I do not know. You did nothing to earn it,' adding, 'I do not know if the jury will convict on this man's evidence alone.' In fact, Jacobs was supported by George Morris (known, because of his size, as 'The Ambling Alp'—in reference to the giant boxer Primo Carnera), who had driven Ryan and his one-time friend Collins from the Mudgee robbery and had buried the cash on his farm. Morris claimed that Ryan had been standing over him because of a conviction some eight years before, which, if it came out, would lose him his job as a part-time postmaster. But there was clearly more to Morris than was apparent at first glance. Yes, he knew a man Jenkins but, no, he had never shot him nor had he placed a bomb in his car. (Jenkins was the receiver Percy 'Snowy' Jenkins, who had been shot and whose shop was bombed in a Melbourne gangland feud over either car re-birthing or drugs.) Morris also knew Alexander McIver and Francis Delaney, convicted of bombing the Greek Club in Melbourne in 1928.

Ryan's counsel, mixing his metaphors nicely, made a splendid attack on the evidence: 'The rotten house the Crown has built you would not hang a dog on.' And the jury declined to do so.

On 8 October, Ryan went on trial for the Mudgee robbery. This time Arthur Collins, who had done amazingly well for himself in plea bargaining—a bind over for the Mudgee robbery and an order to leave the state for his part in the attack on the jeweller Cohen— was there to put his old friend away. Morris was again on hand to give evidence that he had collected Ryan and Collins after they had made their way from the track and had taken them back to his farm where the money had been buried, to be collected by Ryan later. Collins was there reluctantly, demanding before he said a word that he be given assurances he would not be prosecuted. By the end of his evidence he was being treated as a hostile witness.

Ryan, making a statement from the dock which meant he could not be cross-examined, claimed that Morris and Collins were lying and trying to put their crimes on him to save themselves. Invited to account for his wealth, he ingeniously did so. His savings in the name of George Brown had been put together years earlier and came from betting; those in the name of Thompson were used to give to his mother. Thompson had kindly allowed him to use his name. He also called alibi evidence that he had gone to the funeral of a taxi driver—the same Thompson—and had been at the widow's home with two other drivers on the night of the robbery. After deliberating for twelve hours the jury announced they could not agree.

At the retrial Collins clearly thought he had had enough and failed to appear to give evidence. On 2 December 1935, after the jury retired for rather less than an hour, Ryan was finally acquitted of the Mudgee train robbery. Veteran crime reporter Greg Brown told Larry Writer, author of *Razor*, that he thought Ryan was the best of the Sydney hardmen of the period, far superior to both Chow Hayes and his offsider Joey Hollebone. 'Always impeccably dressed, very quiet … but if you told anyone that Joe Ryan was looking for them, they'd go bush.'

It was by no means the end of the matter, however. On 5 April 1932, William Cyril Moxley attacked Dorothy Denzil and her boyfriend Frank Wilkinson while they were in their car parked near Liverpool. Moxley, a good-looking Sydneysider with black curly hair of which he was intensely proud, had been declared a habitual criminal in 1925 and subsequently became a police informer, in the pocket of Superintendent William Mackay. When the talented safe-breakers Andrew Duncan and Edward Devine would not let him join them on an expedition, he dobbed them in. After their acquittal, they kidnapped him in Parramatta, gave him a bad beating for his trouble and then shot him in the face. He escaped near Homebush and dobbed them in again. He had no luck with that either because once more they were both acquitted.

It seems the masked Moxley had first demanded money from the courting couple. When Wilkinson tried to fight him off and partially tore off the mask, Moxley beat him unconscious. He then raped the girl and killed the pair, burying their bodies in a shallow grave where they were discovered a week later. Moxley's fingerprints were found in the area and he was caught on 21 April, still in the vicinity. On 16 April the enormously popular *Smith's Weekly* had described the case as 'The Most Fiendish Murder of a Generation'. Moxley made a long confession to Superintendent (later police commissioner), William Mackay personally. In return Mackay gave evidence at the trial to say that Moxley's behaviour had deteriorated since he had been shot by Duncan and Devine.

Unfortunately, on 30 July *Smith's Weekly* was duped by an ex-constable into printing that not only had Wilkinson been the driver of the getaway car in the Mudgee train robbery but that he was a pimp and blackmailer who was the victim of a gangland execution. Specifically, the article alleged, Wilkinson had been with Barney Dalton when he was shot in Kings Cross; Moxley had been there with the killer and Wilkinson had been blackmailing him. Other newspapers attacked *Smith's Weekly* but the paper took a statutory declaration from the constable and maintained its stance. On 31 July *Truth* came up with a letter from Moxley, which it published, headed 'Clears dead man's name'. *Smith's Weekly* took another fortnight before it retracted the story, describing its informant as 'Wicked Beyond Belief'. It was too little and too late. The public never really forgave it and the grave error substantially contributed to the decline of the paper.

Moxley was hanged on 28 August. Although his conviction was seen as one of the highlights of Mackay's career, it has since been suggested that the evidence against him was fabricated.

* * *

One pre-war robbery whose ramifications ran for several years was the bail-up of the Cleveland Street pawnbroker and fence Nathan Segal by Robert Sydney Jones and Eric Kelly on 20 March 1939. In the raid Segal was shot. There was no doubt about Jones's guilt but there was considerable doubt about Kelly's, whom Jones had exonerated at the trial. Both received life for shooting with intent to murder, and throughout his sentence Kelly continued to maintain his innocence. He managed to obtain an inquiry under section 475 of the Crimes Act and, although Segal said he might have made a mistake in his identification, and another serving prisoner Leslie Lang said he had been with Jones and fired the second shot, the judge reported there was no doubt of Kelly's guilt. His efforts lasted until August 1946, when the High Court finally rejected Kelly's claim and the Minister of Justice refused to intervene.

As for Jones, on 7 November 1941 he escaped from East Maitland jail, north of Newcastle. Along with William Burney, declared a habitual criminal at the age of twenty-four, Jones had hooked a rope to the rail on the perimeter wall. Burney was caught three weeks later in Darlinghurst, but Jones hid out, waiting for a boat to take him to South Africa. An arrangement was made to put him in a cabin trunk and load him onto the boat, where a crew member had been paid to look after him. Unfortunately he was dobbed in for the reward money and the scheme was aborted. On 7 January 1942 Jones was eventually run to ground in Elswick Street, Leichhardt, and, at the end of a gun battle with the police, he shot himself with his last bullet. As a result of the escape the jail's governor was demoted and several warders were dismissed.

The trick for the escaper is not necessarily the escape itself, which is often relatively easy, but managing to stay out afterwards. The pitfalls are many, the pleasures often few, and then only very temporary. First, there should be reliable contacts outside the prison to provide transport and safe houses. Unless these are relations or very close friends these people will require payment, often at extortionate rates. Money left in safekeeping with supposedly trustworthy sources often disappears during years in jail. A continuing life of crime is almost inevitable for an escaper without vast resources or the ability to get out of the country. It's the same the whole world over. The British Great Train Robbers found that most of their money evaporated in payments to those who looked after them for a few weeks, and there were more payments made to ensure they were not dobbed in.

Over the years, some escapers have managed to get quite a long way. One of the furthest was the baby-faced and ruthless John Brendon Parker, who ran a little team of robbers with his long-time girlfriend Elsie Bowden as the getaway driver. From a middle-class family, Parker started his career in 1918, when he appeared in the Children's Court for stealing, and from then his record was of breaking, receiving, standover and robbery under arms. He was also suspected of being a high-class safebreaker. The team was caught on 14 June 1928 after they ransacked a tailor's shop in Hurstville, stealing 600 pounds' worth of cloth. One of the team had dropped out and dobbed them in. Sentenced to four years and declared a habitual criminal, the diminutive Parker escaped from the Darlinghurst lock-up in August while awaiting transfer to prison. Using a fretsaw, he stood on the shoulders of other prisoners as they covered the noise of his sawing by singing 'There's a long, long trail a-winding'. Parker then broke a plate-glass skylight, clambered over a roof and lowered himself to the ground. He stayed in Sydney for some time before, disguised as a woman, he obtained a passport and stowed away for Europe on the German steamer *Mosel*. Again he was dobbed in and when the ship docked at Bordeaux on 26 October he was arrested and was brought back to Australia in February 1929. His career continued into the 1950s, when he served a three-year sentence, again for breaking, and once more was remanded at the Governor's pleasure.

When Parker was nearing the end of his career, Darcy Dugan, one of Australia's greatest serial escapers, was at the peak of his. On 15 December 1949 he and William Cecil Mears escaped from Sydney's Central Police Court. It was Mears's second successful escape, Dugan's fourth. At the time they were serving ten years for the robbery of an elderly woman in Paddington. Mears was at court to give evidence on behalf of Dugan, who had also been charged with possessing a pistol. During the lunch adjournment they cut through the cell bars with a hacksaw and ran into Central Lane where they boarded a tram.

They had both escaped three months earlier while on remand at Long Bay. Dugan had also escaped on 25 January 1946, when he forced his way out of a moving police van. He did not last long on the outside but in March that year he had cut a hole in the roof of a prison tram on its way from Long Bay to Darlinghurst Police Station and was off again.

This time he and Mears were arrested in Alexander Street, Colloroy, on 14 February 1950. They were now charged with assaulting and robbing the well-known jockey John Thompson as well as shooting and wounding Leslie Nalder, manager of the Ultimo branch of the Commonwealth Bank, on 13 January 1950. They made one final escape bid at the committal proceedings. Dugan slipped his handcuffs and made it through the court doors before being recaptured. At their trial they were sentenced to death but this was commuted and Dugan was released in 1985. He died in 1991 at the age of seventy-one.

In March 1999 John Killick escaped from Sydney's Silverwater prison in a helicopter organised by the Russian-born 41-year-old Lucy Dudko. Killick, a career criminal regarded by his fellow professionals as a gentleman, had first been convicted in 1960 and then served eight years for a series of TAB robberies committed in 1977 and 1978.

In August 1984 he had escaped in Brisbane while being taken to the Princess Alexandra Hospital for treatment of an injured eye. His then girlfriend, twenty-year-old Jacqueline Hawes from Adelaide, wearing an auburn wig, brought him a pistol and he held up his guards at gunpoint. While on the run he wrote to the *Brisbane Mail*, saying that everything he had done had been for the benefit of his nine-year-old child. A year later Hawes received two months for aiding and abetting the escape. Killick was sentenced to six years for three armed robberies committed while on the run.

In October 1998 he had robbed the Commonwealth Bank of $32 000 and three months later held up the Bowral branch of the National Australia Bank, shooting at an off-duty police officer in his escape. Now, charmed by Killick, Lucy Dudko, who left her scientist husband Alex for him, hired the helicopter for what the pilot thought was to be a joyride over the Olympic Games site.

Instead he found himself ordered at gunpoint to land in the prison exercise yard. He was later found bound with radio wires. The pair were thought to have left the state but were recaptured in a cabin at a caravan park six weeks later, on 9 May. Two pistols were found under Killick's bed. He had apparently devised the escape after reading Robert Lindsey's novel *The Flight of the Falcon*.

On 21 December 2000 Judge Barry Mahoney handed Killick the maximum sentence of twenty-eight years for the helicopter escape and some related matters, rejecting submissions from a solicitor and a CSE case manager that Killick could reform. It was argued that he had been well on the way to rehabilitation in the early 1990s when, after a series of personal reversals, he slipped back into a life of crime. Killick will be seventy-three when he can first apply for parole in 2014. Lucy Dudko, who was sentenced to a minimum of seven years, was released in May 2006. One of the conditions imposed on her was that she could not visit Killick.

One of the great robbers and escapers, who more or less operated solo, was Bernie Matthews, who began his career in October 1969 when, at the age of nineteen, he was arrested and charged with two armed robberies and possession of a sub-machine gun. It immediately established him as a cut above the average. He escaped from the Court of Appeal in June 1970 and, on his recapture, received ten years, plus six months for the escape. In November that year he escaped from Long Bay jail. Perhaps he was not that successful an escaper because, during his years in prison, he made some fifteen failed attempts. This time he was recaptured seven weeks later, by which time he had robbed two banks and a payroll office. One was the Rozelle bank in early December, which again was a solo effort. Armed with a sawn-off .22 automatic, Matthews jumped on the counter, yelled at the staff and customers, had his bag filled and was away, taking with him something in the region of $3000, which can probably be multiplied by ten today. The money went on gambling, women and liquor. Matthews later said of career bank robbers, including himself: 'They've got no respect for money, you know, because it's easy come, easy go, so you might have $100 000, you might have $10 000, there's no respect there because you haven't earned it … It's the adrenalin rush of getting it.'

After his sentence Matthews made an effort to start his own business and settle down. Then, on 20 February 1991, he was arrested in Sydney by members of Task Force Magnum of the Sydney Major Crime Squad over a Brambles security van robbery at Sunnybank Hills in Queensland on 3 April the previous year. Petrol had been poured over the driver and staff to force them to open the back of the van, and $694 000 was stolen. The evidence against Matthews was from a police informer, and a police inspector who alleged Matthews had made a verbal confession to him. Committed for trial, he remained in custody until, on 26 October, Garry Sullivan, a former Rugby League international, and William Orchard were arrested for an armoured car robbery the day before. They put their hands up and admitted to the Brambles robbery. Matthews was released two days later and the charges were finally dropped. His efforts to obtain compensation for his wrongful imprisonment came to nothing. After his release he began a highly successful career as a journalist, but that came to an abrupt halt when in April 2008, then aged 58, he was arrested in Sydney on drug and gun charges. In the autumn of 2011 he was still awaiting trial.

* * *

One of the dangers of working in a team is not only that you might be dobbed in by a mate who thinks he can cut himself a deal with the police but also that you might be killed by your offsider. Take Louis (or Lory) de Barbarezz as an example. At the end of December 1969 the body of the 31-year-old conman and thief (who was Yugoslav-born but claimed to be French) was found in a grave in Brighton-le-Sands, along with the mattock and steel wrench that had been used to kill him. His leg was hacked off. He had been missing since the previous September. Paul Arthur Barnhart, in Long Bay, told the police that de Barbarezz had been condemned by a kangaroo court held in Kings Cross, perhaps with kingpin Lennie McPherson presiding, after a feud over the spoils of a series of robberies. The police thought there were possibly six others who had been killed and buried in the preceding eighteen months, either because they were informers or because they had quarrelled over the proceeds of robberies. One victim had been buried in a forest, the second was de Barbarezz, a third dumped in the sea in concrete, a fourth buried in a cemetery, a fifth thrown in a river and a sixth put in a garbage dump. The seventh was still missing.

More information emerged in June 1970, when Barnhart pleaded guilty to being an accessory to murder and received ten years. He then gave evidence against Barrie Ronald Bruce Levy, saying that he had lured de Barbarezz to Kyeemagh near Kingsford Smith Airport with the promise of a safe-blowing exercise. Barnhart claimed that Levy then attacked de Barbarezz with a Stillson wrench, yelling that de Barbarezz had nearly got him killed over an incident with John Stuart (later convicted of Brisbane's Whiskey Au Go Go murders) in Long Bay. Certainly Levy and de Barbarezz had known each other and had in fact worked together in the theft of seventy-five furs from Mark Foy in May 1965. Levy, who consistently denied his guilt, was sentenced to life imprisonment and, with escapes from custody and breakings when on licence, was still in prison in 2000 when Justice Dowd set a minimum term which enabled him to apply for almost immediate parole.

Another robbery that brought pain, suffering and death to the protagonists, this time from outsiders, was the Mayne-Nickless robbery on 4 March 1970 in Sydney. The raid itself was a simple one. Incredibly, the guards regularly parked in the Guildford shopping centre while they ate their lunch inside the van before making a delivery to the Commonwealth Bank. When one of the guards opened the van door to put the rubbish out, in came the robbers and out went $587 890.

The pain and suffering came in the form of the much-feared Sydney-based Toecutters Gang, named for their tendency to amputate the toes—and other parts—of criminals to convince them to share their ill-gotten gains. Frank 'Baldy' Blair had his toes cut and testicles torched to persuade him to reveal where he had deposited his $90 000 share of the robbery. Blair died from his injuries and his body was thrown into Sydney Harbour in the belief that it would be eaten by sharks. It was not and it washed up in Botany Bay. The blame for that misapprehension was laid at the doorstep of the red-headed Jake Maloney, who was later shot by fellow Toecutter John 'Nano The Magician' Regan on 23 November 1971. According to underworld legend, just before Maloney was killed, Regan said, 'Sharks, hey Jake, I'll give you bloody sharks, you idiot.'

Meanwhile the Toecutters attacked the docker Stephen Nittes, who was also on the Mayne-Nickless raid. He handed over a substantial part of his share. Another robber Alan Jones escaped their attention but both he and Nittes received sixteen years for their part in the theft. Leslie Woon, the talented organiser of the robbery, left the country and went to Europe when he heard the Toecutters were interested in his share too. It was many years before he returned.

Former robber Mark 'Chopper' Read has a story about the Toecutters that tells how they kidnapped a robber to question him over a theft of $75 000. On his back the man had a tattoo of an eagle fighting a dragon and, with a pair of pliers, the Toecutters slowly ripped it off. The man died halfway through the operation. They then took the view that no man would die in such pain for the sake of the money and reasoned that his wife must have it. They promised her they would return him if she paid over the money.

It was only after she had done so that they told her she could have his body.

Another story is that the corrupt copper Fred Krahe, often suggested as a leader of the Toecutters, recruited Kevin Gore (another suggested leader) and Jake Maloney to retrieve the Mayne Nickless money on his behalf. In turn, the Melbourne hardman Brian Kane was dispatched by leaders of the Painters and Dockers' Union to deal with Gore and Maloney.

Much of the information on the Toecutters is speculative and some accounts claim the gang was led by an Englishman, Linus or Jimmy 'The Pom' O'Driscoll (or Driscoll), who was said to have grey-ferret eyes and to have been the personal bodyguard of the IRA deputy leader Joe Cahill, as well as serving in the Congo under 'Mad' Mike Hoare and being a friend of the Kray twins. Driscoll was convicted of the Maloney murder but was released on appeal and later deported after being convicted on a weapons charge. It appears, though, that he was completely rehabilitated and was allowed back into Australia in the 1990s.

* * *

It was the fear that she might dob in bank robber and ex-French Foreign Legionnaire Fred Harbecke and his offsiders, James Patrick Thornton and Alan Stanley Dillon, that led to the death of Helen Paunovic. She was shot as she left a coffee lounge in Kings Cross on 29 December 1967. The men had all met at Grafton jail where they were labelled as 'Intracs'.

One of the more violent of the quasi-independents, who regularly tried to shoot his way out of the slightest of troubles, was James Edward Smith, brought up in the Colac district of Victoria and who, because as a teenager he was apprenticed to a trainer, was known as 'The Jockey'. Early in his criminal career Smith, regarded as a bank robber's bank robber, teamed up with Ronald Ryan, who would become the last man to be hanged in Australia after killing a guard in an escape from Pentridge. This time, however, it was Smith who tried to shoot a police officer when the pair were caught burgling a shop in 1962. On this occasion, fortunately, the gun jammed. In 1973 the situation was repeated when a police constable, Russell Cook, was searching a car. Smith again tried to shoot and once more the gun jammed.

Charged with a string of robberies in Sydney, despite his earlier escape attempts Smith was given bail. He skipped and was found in Melbourne. Sent to Pentridge, he was there only a matter of weeks before he obtained a visitor's pass and walked out. One thing he was good at was dealing with horses and now he combined the names of two of the country's top trainers, Tommy Smith and Bart Cummings, and set up as trainer Tom Cummings. He did well at country tracks but the life of a small trainer has never been an overflowing cup. In 1976 he shot and injured Jerry Ambrose in a robbery in Sydney and on 13 June the following year he killed bookmaker and crime associate Lloyd Tidmarsh at his home in Kogarah. It was said to be a robbery but the $200 in the safe was left untouched. This time he was arrested in Nowra and tried to shoot Detective Bob Godden, who saved himself by putting his thumb between the breech and the trigger of the gun. In December 1977 he was charged with Western Australia's then biggest hold-up, the Taxation Department's $176 000 payroll snatch in Perth in May 1975. Smith was given a life sentence, of which he served fourteen years, for the attempted murder of the detective and on appeal was acquitted of the other charges after allegations that his confession had been fabricated.

He was released on 12 February 1992 and a day later was shot in the chest and left for dead outside his home in Curlewis Street, North Bondi. Dr Crozier, who was on duty the day Smith was brought into St Vincent's, recalls:

When he arrived he had multiple gunshot wounds to the chest and abdomen; he was barely alive. We split him from the chest to just above the penis, a big mid-line incision. He'd been shot through the liver, bowel, but it hadn't hit the heart or aorta, so he survived ... He left the indelible impression on me that with the right combination of good luck and good treatment a person can survive multiple gunshot wounds.

This is a far cry from the 1920s and 1930s when the victim was likely to develop peritonitis, which must be a great comfort to today's wannabes.

Smith declined to help the police, who said that he was another with so many enemies it would be difficult to say who might have shot him. He was in hospital for a month. Then, on 12 June, one of Smith's offsiders, former boxer turned standover man Desmond Anthony Lewis, was shot at Bondi Junction on his way home from the Nelson Hotel where he had been watching a Rugby League Test. It was thought the killing was linked to Smith's shooting as well as standover man Roy Thurgar's death the previous year.

For a time, Smith made good money dealing in amphetamines and it was said he was so mean he would 'bite the head off a shilling'. But, over the months, according to his flamboyant solicitor, the column-writing Chris Murphy, he became something of a recluse. In November 1992, breaking the rule of never shoplifting for oneself, Smith tried to steal kitchen equipment from Grace Brothers in Erina. Stopped by the store detective, he yet again produced a gun and hijacked a couple to drive him away. He hid in the bush for a while and later teamed up with Christopher Dean 'Badness' Binse—another escapee from Pentridge—in plotting a series of armed robberies.

Smith died on 5 December 1992. About 8 p.m. he was seen speeding by Senior Constable Ian Harris, who followed him to the Farmer's Arms Hotel in Creswick, Victoria. Asked for his identification, he pulled a gun on the officer, and when Darren Neil, a bystander who had seen the incident, approached, Smith fired a shot into the ground. Neil retreated, drove his car a short distance and dropped off his children. He then drove the car at Smith, distracting him. The constable pulled his own revolver and shot Smith three times in the chest.

* * *

If outsiders and one-time offsiders didn't harm you, you could do a great deal of damage to yourself. In the late 1930s the standover man and professional shoplifter Charles 'Kicker' Kelly turned to safebreaking. He should have stuck to what he knew best. Instead, in one early outing, he put too much gelignite in a safe lock and blew both it and his leg off. In July 1947 William Chitten went one worse, killing himself when a gelignite bomb exploded in his pocket as he tried to blow the safe in a Surry Hills factory. He had lost the sauce-bottle top, which should have covered the makeshift detonator.

That is not to say that over the years there have not been singularly spectacular robberies organised with military precision. One of the earliest of the major post-war robberies was at Cockatoo Docks when, at about 10 a.m. on 13 April 1946, three men armed with a Thompson machine gun and automatic pistols robbed five waterside employees of 12 000 pounds. The money had just been collected from the Drummoyne branch of the ES&A bank and the armed employees were in the launch to take them to the wharf when they were held up by a machine gun–wielding masked man and his colleagues. The robbers left the waterfront in a highly polished stolen black Buick, which was later found in Kalgoorlie Street, Leichhardt. Despite the offer of a reward of 1000 pounds and a free pardon to any informant provided he had not actually been on the robbery, the underworld remained staunch and no charges were ever brought. It was the first robbery in New South Wales in which a machine gun was used.

One of the great non-violent robberies, known as the 'Chinese Takeaway', which may be the biggest ever in Australia, took place on the evening of 2 January 1988 when three tankmen (the underworld term for safebreakers), squeezed through a gap in the wall of a construction site next to the Haymarket branch of the National Australia Bank in Sydney's Chinatown. A window had been left open and, with a 10-metre light extension ladder, they climbed through it to begin a systematic raid on the eighty-two safety deposit boxes in the bank. They were lucky because when they tried to blow a cash vault they had tripped a wire but security guards thought it to be a false alarm and did not check the basement.

Quite how much the thieves took will never be known because only half the people renting the boxes came forward to detail their losses, which were mainly in gold ingots and bars and jewellery. At the time gold was selling legally for $670 an ounce and estimates of the total haul have been put between $10 million and $100 million. Almost certainly much of it went abroad to Hong Kong and Singapore. The mastermind was often said to be robber, launderer and drug importer Michael Hurley, who, in December 1980, had been charged—along with his younger brother Jeffrey—over the theft of the Golconda d'Or, a $2 million diamond dating from 1793. It had been on display at Sydney Town Hall and the police believed a team of four switched the diamond for a fake after picking the lock on the case. Because the brothers looked almost identical the witnesses could not make a positive identification and the charges were dismissed.

Michael Hurley died on 23 January 2007 awaiting trial on a massive drug importation. He had been suffering from cancer.

The War Years, 1940–1945

5

When the first seven vessels containing 2100 American troops arrived in Sydney in 1941, an estimated crowd of half a million greeted their arrival with streamers, confetti and petals. And among those who gave the men the greatest welcome was the underworld.

War is a good time for criminals. Frankie Fraser, the London villain and friend of the Kray twins, whose career spanned half a century, thought that war made criminals out of everyone. While Australia may not have had the looting that followed the bombing of London or the rationing that so damaged Britain, it did have soldiers—visiting soldiers, deserting soldiers, soldiers on leave—all to be catered for and, particularly in the case of visiting soldiers, there for the plucking.

As the war progressed, American troops arrived in their tens of thousands, causing a wholesale boom in sly-grog shops, gambling and prostitution at all levels—from escorts for the top brass to street walkers and low-class brothels. There were pregnancies to be terminated and venereal diseases to be cured. There was the opportunity to work variations of the ginger game and the even greater opportunity to steal from drunken clients.

The Americans were sold cigarettes filled with cabbage leaves, and cold tea and tobacco water passed off as beer and whisky. They were overcharged by the girls and mugged by their pimps. Business expanded to fill the opportunities available, and now, to add to all the other enterprises of the underworld, a new market developed in forgery and black marketeering—making available not only papers for deserting troops but also items that were rationed.

Sometimes the ginger game turned out very badly. In May 1942 the 5-foot, 15-stone prostitute Barbara Phyllis Surridge (who worked under the unfortunate name of Stella Croke) was involved in the death of Ernest Hoffman, a chef at the Royal Sydney Golf Club. She took him to a ginger joint in Langley Street, Darlinghurst, and while there he caught her and another woman going through his pockets. When he struggled with the women, two men rushed in and beat him unconscious before dumping him in an allotment in his shirt and singlet. He died in St Vincent's Hospital ten days later, but not before identifying Surridge. She, her husband William and the other man, James Harris, known as Skinny Jones, were all convicted of murder. They were sentenced to death, but were later reprieved and given life imprisonment. For a time Phyllis Surridge was in the prison next door to her husband and they were allowed to meet once a year in the men's chapel. After her release from prison in 1956 she returned to prostitution and the ginger game, but died a year later as a result of an infected cut on her finger.

In July 1940 the Empire Club, a sly-grog shop on George Street, was closed by the authorities. It reopened in September and within a month the proprietor, Maltese-born Anthony Pisani, whose convictions for sly-grog selling went back to 1929, was sentenced to six months' hard labour and fined 100 pounds for selling beer without a licence. What was really up the nose of the authorities was that it was a hangout for black servicemen and white girls, many of whom were drunk. In September 1940 a magistrate called it 'One of the worst conducted clubs in Sydney'.

Two years later, in October 1942, Phil Jeffs's 400 Club was shut down and from then on he lived off his substantial investments at Ettalong, where he had built a library consisting mainly of philosophical works and where he surrounded himself with these as well as a series of good-looking women.

But no sooner had one club closed its doors than another opened, very often on the same premises. Some were ritzier and longer lasting than others and some established their owners as kings of the nightclub and underworld scene.

The war was the making of the small, dapper Abraham Gilbert Saffron, one of five children of a draper in Annandale. His mother wanted him to become a doctor but from an early age Saffron showed he had a head for business, selling cigarettes to players at his father's poker games. Educated at Fort Street High School, whose other alumni included the New South Wales premier Neville Wran and James 'Paddles' Anderson, a leading figure in the East Coast Milieu (an all-powerful, loosely linked association of criminals), Saffron left at the age of fifteen and began work in his father's shop. He was, however, destined to follow his uncle, Mr Justice Isaacs, in a career that involved many appearances in court, albeit as plaintiff and defendant rather than as advocate and judge.

In 1938 he acquired his first bookmaking conviction and the next year he was sentenced to six months' hard labour, suspended provided he join the armed forces. Over the years there were few prosecutions and even fewer convictions, and of those a number were overturned on appeal. When in 1940 he was convicted for possession of stolen car radios, Saffron had identifiable assets of ten pounds. Despite this he was able to open a number of clubs, often owned in partnership with his offsider Hilton G Kincaid (originally Hilton Maccossa). Among them was the Roosevelt Club at 32 Orwell Street, which catered for resting American troops and was described by Mr Justice Maxwell, who ordered its closure in 1943, as 'the most notorious and disreputable nightclub in the city'.

Saffron moved north to Newcastle, where he obtained a bookmaker's licence from the less than demanding Newcastle Jockey Club, and also took a licence on the Newcastle Hotel in the city. By the end of the war he was one of the biggest illegal liquor dealers in Sydney, owning a string of clubs and hotels and often using his relations as fronts. By the early 1950s he owned public house and hotel licences worth more than 84 000 pounds.

Sadly, some old friends did not see out the war. Henry Slater, once a friend of Snowy Cutmore, did not even last the first year. Since his run-in with Squizzy Taylor's offsider Harry Stokes in the fight for control of the Melbourne underworld twenty years earlier, and his self-imposed exile from that city, Slater had become something of a peripatetic villain, gravitating between Sydney and Adelaide, living by theft and the standover of SP bookmakers. Now, in a somewhat prosaic end for one of Sydney's senior standover men, Slater was shot at La Perouse near the Yarra Bay shantytown after he had left his home to catch a tram. The shooter pumped two bullets into him and then rode away on a bicycle. At the inquest into his death the coroner was told that Slater had been shot by a poulterer, Christopher Ransome, who had stood by the body and said, 'You won't worry me or anyone else again.' Ransome had allegedly shot him because, over the years, Slater had been calling him a pervert. By the time of the inquest Ransome had been committed to an insane asylum. Appearances are deceptive, though, and not everyone was convinced by the official account.

Another survivor of the Razor Wars went down around the same time. In July 1940 the body of 39-year-old William Smiley (sometimes Smillie), gunman, razorman and SP bookmaker with convictions going back to 1910, was found in a lane off Butt Street, Surry Hills, lying next to a dead cat. In 1928, at the height of the wars, he had received five years for slashing, and was acquitted of the attempted murder of Thomas O'Brien, shot in Surry Hills, when O'Brien refused to identify him. Undeterred, in 1935 Smiley had slashed a man at a party held by Kate Leigh and as a reprisal was shot through both feet a few days later. Harry Barker (also known as Harry James) was charged with that shooting and acquitted. That was a bad period for Smiley's legs: in September 1935 Kathleen McLennan was charged with shooting them and indeed wrote out a confession that she had borrowed a repeating rifle from a neighbour to do so. But if the police thought this would be sufficient to obtain a conviction they were wrong. She was acquitted after telling the court that she only made the confession after she had spilled Lysol, which she had intended to drink, over her body. She had, she now said, been at her mother's when Smiley was shot and witnesses were called to support her. Smiley behaved like a proper gentleman, telling the court he had been shot by a 'big man' and that McLennan had not been there. The next year, when he was found in Elizabeth Street shot in the thigh, he refused to help the police, saying, 'If I had the Town Hall clock in my pocket. I wouldn't tell you the time.'

Now John McIvor, regarded as one of the city's top safecrackers, and George Dempsey were charged with his murder. On the day of his death Smiley had come into a shop, run by a Mrs Sadie Pinn in Devonshire Street, and fired at Dempsey. Pinn ran upstairs and later heard another shot. Smiley had been shot four times with a .32 and his body had been carried to the lane. It would seem that he had attacked Dempsey in the past and had been standing over him. On 7 September the police prosecutor entered a *nolle prosequi* against both men.

* * *

As World War II went on, the demand for after-hours drinking establishments increased. They had, of course, maintained a regular trade before the war but now there was much more money around to meet the increased prices. Breweries were required to provide beer for the troops and for four years from March 1942 a quota system was imposed. The importation of Scotch whisky was also prohibited from the beginning of the war and both beer rationing and this ban created a ready black market. In 1943 the licensee of the Wentworth Hotel was charged with selling whisky at a price ranging between four and six pounds a bottle, yielding him an overall annual profit in the region of 30 000 pounds.

There was also the opportunity for a certain amount of freelance pimping. In August 1943, 46-year-old Westbrook Walter Turnbull, described as an invalid pensioner, and his younger brother, the 43-year-old John Alexander, pleaded not guilty to charges of procuring girls for the purposes of prostitution. They met many of the women at the Ziegfeld Club, but toured other clubs and amusement arcades for suitable women. Their girls worked in a house in Bondi and were paid three pounds per customer, half of which went to the brothers. Two months later, found guilty, the Turnbulls each received three years and three months' imprisonment. Then, in December, their convictions were quashed and a retrial ordered. The trial judge had ruled that it was immaterial whether the brothers knew or believed the girls were under eighteen. The Court of Appeal, however, said it was a material fact. It did them no good whatsoever. At the retrial they were again convicted and this time sentenced to four years.

Considerable attention was paid to morals, with clergymen in disguise investigating Sydney nightclubs, hotel lounges and dark doorways. In November 1943 the president of the New South Wales Temperance Alliance claimed that the police were prevented from cleaning up Sydney because the state government was controlled by liquor traffickers.

During the war racing was reduced to one afternoon a week but this did nothing to curtail gambling; more money was wagered on a Saturday afternoon. Bets of 1000 pounds by Americans in Thommo's Two-up School were not uncommon. The SP business still boomed and operators still paid for protection—if they complained they could expect visits from heavies. Mechanics installed gadgets to kill a telephone in the event of a police raid. When the prime minister, John Curtin, asked for a telephone call to be put through one Saturday afternoon to discuss the situation in Japan he was told there were sixty bookmakers ahead of him in the queue for connection.

With sly-grog, doctored spirits and prostitution, and taxi drivers cheating and robbing servicemen on leave, there was work and money for everyone. American servicemen roamed the city looking for recreation and the city roamed looking for the soldiers. There was a special brothel, the Tradesman's Arms Hotel in Palmer Street, for the black servicemen. Police officer Lilian Armfield wrote in her memoirs: 'We found it necessary to not only turn a blind eye, but to give tacit approval, to the existence of a brothel which catered exclusively to American Negro Servicemen.' This was putting it a little delicately. The military police were employed to keep the queues in the street in order and moving along, as if the patrons were buying tickets for the cinema.

When the Booker T. Washington club was formed for black servicemen in Sydney, there were not enough working girls to entertain the members. A screening test was established to check all women who wished to become members and they were required to provide their particulars and a photograph. Many of the women preferred the black servicemen, who paid better, and it was shameful to the white folk that they went with the black servicemen voluntarily. And worse, that some of them were married women or young girls. Armfield commented: 'It was like a knife through the heart when we found that one Sydney girl, only twelve years old, was in the bed of a Negro serviceman.' In January 1944, *Truth* was seriously unhappy: 'Not much has been said, outside the courts, of the spreading depravity involving our white women and visiting coloured men.'

There was mayhem in the other brothels too. Some servicemen did not seem to recognise the time limits imposed and, when one refused to get off a girl in one of Tilly Devine's houses, the girl began to scream and Tilly, to the rescue, hit him over the head with a bottle and fractured his skull. She was charged with grievous bodily harm and duly acquitted. Devine was an early casualty when she was ordered to leave Sydney and remain away for a period, under penalty of forfeiting 250 pounds. It did not seriously trouble her. This was her heyday and by the end of the war she was a rich woman.

* * *

During World War II Bondi was the place for the back-street abortionist, there to deal with women pregnant by visiting servicemen. The police targeted abortionists who did not pay them protection money and the women were arrested as they left the clinics. Often there was a police photographer in attendance to complete their humiliation. Obtaining co-operation from the police was therefore a must for the clinic operators.

A man who had no troubles in that area, and who had been on the fringes of the underworld from the 1930s, now emerged as a leading figure during the war. Last heard of being thrown out of his own club, the 400 in Phillip Street, he was the very dubious Dr Reginald Stuart-Jones. Born in London as plain Jones, he had arrived in Australia with his parents at the age of nine. A fine sportsman, Stuart-Jones played for Sydney University at cricket, football, tennis, athletics and rifle shooting. Once he graduated he returned to England where he married his first wife, Sheena, heiress to a chain of cinemas. He then returned to Sydney where he set up practice in Macquarie Street as a gynaecologist.

There appears to have been a louche streak in him for his constant companions were criminals. He carried a revolver, which he liked to fire into the ceilings of bars in Surry Hills, and in 1939 he was arrested for drunken driving. For a time he held interests in several nightclubs of varying degrees of quality. At the one end was the Lido at Bondi Beach and at the better end, certainly financially, was the 400 Club.

An interest in a nightclub or two can provide an endless stream of patients for an abortionist and he went into partnership with the former bouncer Richard Gabriel Reilly, the man who in 1937 had shot Clarrie Thomas. With the proceeds Stuart-Jones became a great racing man, owning, quite successfully, thoroughbreds, trotters and greyhounds. One of the horses, the grey Blue Baron, won sixteen races for him and Stuart-Jones was, at one time, president of the New South Wales Coursing Association.

His decline began when he appeared before the courts charged with 'unlawfully using an instrument for a certain purpose' in 1944. When the police raided the second floor of 229 Macquarie Street they found Stuart-Jones gowned up, preparing to operate on a girl who had paid his secretary forty pounds. He was duly acquitted.

That year he married his second wife, Mary Kathleen Ryan, having divorced Sheena in 1936. His second marriage was not a happy one either, particularly when he found her in a flat in Leichhardt wearing the pyjamas of the welterweight Cliffie Thompson (who boxed as Cliffie Thomas). He sued for divorce but before the decree was made absolute they were together again.

Then came one of the stranger episodes in Stuart-Jones's fairly extraordinary career. Just before midnight on 31 October 1944 he was kidnapped from outside his house, Casa Grande, in Bellevue Hill. He was asked by two criminals he knew to look at a man they had in their car. When he reached it there was his old sparring partner Cliffie Thompson along with a man he didn't know, Alexander 'Scotty' Jowett. He was taken at gunpoint to Maroubra and told he would be shot and his body thrown over the cliffs. Indeed just after midnight Jowett shot Stuart-Jones in the chest, hitting him in the lung. The doctor then, amazingly, seems to have talked his captors into dropping him off at the Vassilia Private Hospital in Randwick. He survived.

The resulting trial was all the press and public could reasonably hope for. There were details of Stuart-Jones's drink, drug and abortion dealings. There was the story of Cliffie Thompson's love for Stuart-Jones's wife and Thompson's wife's love for Jowett. Both men were convicted of the attack on Stuart-Jones and sentenced to death but the sentences were commuted to life imprisonment. In the end they each served a relatively short period.

* * *

Before, and in the early part of the war, furs from Canada were favoured smuggled goods, along with silks from Japan and China; silk stockings from America, England and Europe; and miniature radio sets from various countries. Since the duty on furs was 70 per cent and on stockings and perfume between 50 and 60 per cent, the potential profits for the underworld were enormous. Before National Security Regulations stopped people from boarding ships, two or three women would visit 'a friend' on board and come off wearing furs and several sets of underwear. Some would come off re-dressed from head to toe. Asian seamen donned ladies' underwear as they left the boat. Silk stockings and lingerie were hidden in boiler tubes, coal bunkers, false bottoms of cabin lockers and in lifeboats. Once on the black market at seven shillings and sixpence a pair, stockings fetched two pounds ten shillings at the end of the war.

In 1945 the black market in cigarettes and liquor was regarded by the underworld as more profitable than robberies. When a shortage of cigarettes followed the exodus of American servicemen, the prices rocketed. There was a black market in vegetables and there were premiums on potatoes, carrots and onions as well as on car tyres, often taken from vehicles stolen for the purpose. In nine months in 1944 more than a million smuggled cigarettes were seized. There was also a revolving market in liquor, with whisky bought at three to five pounds and sold in battle areas at up to twenty pounds. The profit was then invested in cigarettes bought at three shillings and fourpence a carton and resold at up to thirty shillings, which was again reinvested in liquor. There was a black market in homemade cigarette papers and one enterprising outfit began manufacturing the papers using toilet paper soaked in starch. The trade broke down when a newspaper kindly published the recipe.

It was now that opium began to arrive in 10- and 12-pound lots. By the end of the war it came generally from India and was smuggled in the heart of packs of butter, inside sausage skins and in the carcasses of sheep. Cooks took the drug from their ships in kerosene tins purporting to contain dripping.

Towards the end of the war, a figure emerged in black-market circles who in later years would have a devastating effect on crime and politicians alike. The 35-year-old Richard Gabriel Reilly, now euphemistically described as an electrician and still a friend of Stuart-Jones, was supplementing his income as a standover man and abortionist by running a forged clothing coupon ring from Roslyn Road, Elizabeth Bay. When it was broken up and nine people were arrested in February 1945 the police seized 250 clothing coupons and Reilly's wallet. It held 632 pounds—approximately two years' wages for a working electrician. He had built up a substantial operation collecting forged, stolen and otherwise illegally obtained coupons and selling them on to retailers. It was only part of his expanding empire.

By the end of 1944 there was a good clear-up rate in Sydney for murders generally, with only sixteen killings (down from thirty-two in 1940), and the authorities were quietly congratu- lating themselves on keeping crime under control. In 1944 there had been a total of forty murders in New South Wales; sixteen murderers committed suicide and only two cases remained unsolved by the end of the year. The first was a rather curious affair. On 8 February Joyce Pattison from Bourke Street, Darlinghurst, had gone with another girl and two black American servicemen to

Centennial Park, where she was found dead on the bank of a lake the next morning. There was at least one witness who said she saw Pattison being kicked to death but the coroner returned an open verdict. Bernard Shaw, who was arrested in Victoria on a charge of abducting a fifteen-year-old girl, falsely confessed to the Pattison murder to get himself out of the clutches of the Melbourne police. In the wash-up he was never charged with the murder but received two years for bigamy.

The second murder, on 29 March 1944, was that of an old friend from the Canberra and Mudgee train robberies, George Morris. He was found shot dead in his car, which was parked by a block of flats at Millers Point, almost directly above where Reginald Holmes had been shot a decade earlier in the shark-arm case. Six bullets had been fired into his head. Morris had, the papers said, 'been put on the spot'. A man had apparently telephoned him and asked him to be at Miller's Point at 9 p.m. At first it was thought he had been killed in a dispute over crime proceeds — Morris was on bail at the time, along with Cyril Humby and Arthur Jordan (both of whom had convictions going back twenty years), awaiting trial on a charge of stealing a safe containing about 2500 pounds in jewellery, coins and cash.

Nevertheless the person in the frame for the killing was none other than Joe Ryan, whom Morris had dobbed in over the train robberies. In fact, so far as the police were concerned, his was the only name in the frame. Ryan was charged and, at the inquest, Jean Evans, a girlfriend of Morris, alleged that Ryan had wanted him to help out in bailing up a baccarat game that Siddy Kelly was holding to raise funds for the defence of the financier John Walcott Forbes, then awaiting trial on fraud charges. Kelly had put a good amount into Forbes's companies and realised the only way he might possibly get it back was if Forbes was acquitted.

By this time, however, Ryan was associated with the waterfront and he produced an alibi to say he had been on a night shift on the docks when Morris was shot. Although Ryan was committed for trial, the Attorney-General issued a *nolle prosequi*. Afterwards Ryan claimed that Kelly had sooled Evans to give evidence against him, and he was most probably right. Given his reputation as a dobber there were plenty of people who would have been happy to see Morris dead. In due course Humby and Jordan were acquitted of the charge of stealing the safe.

Veteran of the Razor Wars, Siddy Kelly had by now emerged from the shadows to establish himself as one of the great crime bosses of this, and indeed many another, period until his death in 1948. With his 100-pounds-a-night profits from his baccarat clubs, he was, from an early stage, able to secure the assistance of the police, and his clubs were rarely prosecuted. Apart from raids early in 1944 there seem to have been none until an abortive one in 1947. Then there had been a tip-off and all the police discovered was a game of gin rummy.

The year 1945 began on a positive note with an announcement by Vice Squad Inspector Thompson that 'Sydney is freer of vice and illegal gambling than any other city of its size in the world.' In 1944, 851 women were charged with vagrancy in the city compared with 885 the previous year. An explanation for this might, however, have been that 258 had been arrested in the suburbs compared with 100 in 1943. There were 6225 arrests of men and 336 women under the Gaming Act.

The police may have had great success clearing up run-of-the-mill murders but what they could not clear up were the gangland murders and the weekly shootings. They may have known full well who was responsible, but proving it was a wholly different thing. Witnesses were there to be threatened and bribed by the friends of the suspect. Even on the rare occasions when a man was seen almost literally standing over a corpse with a smoking gun and there was a witness prepared to say so, then, as now, juries were happy to find self-defence.

One reason for the proliferation of gun crime in the period was the number of thefts from the army. As a result a .38 could be purchased for twenty-five pounds, Berettas and Lügers for thirty pounds, and ammunition was five pounds for 100 rounds. Every criminal—from the bosses of a baccarat game to (much more dangerously) the back lane sneak thief—carried a gun. By 1947 prices had fallen further. A .38 or a Beretta now cost ten pounds and a Lüger five pounds more.

There was also a fresh outbreak of the Basher Gangs, the equivalent of the old-time pushes. In the late 1920s and early 1930s the Basher Gangs were said to be Communist-organised gangs who randomly beat up men in work, but now they were youths operating in small gangs in Paddington and Darlinghurst, committing street robberies and molesting young women. Others were used as muscle by black marketeers to intimidate trade members trying to restrict their practices.

One man died when, running away from them outside a cinema, he tripped and hit his head on the paving stones. Now Commissioner William Mackay seconded young police officers to chase and deal with the youths at street level rather than take them through the courts. It was not a tactic that appealed to everybody, but ultimately it proved effective.

When it came to it, however, 1945 was something of a vintage year for gangland murders and deaths in Sydney. The first to go had actually been on New Year's Eve 1944, when Chow Hayes shot and killed Eddie Weyman. There had been bad blood between them after Weyman kept 1200 pounds for himself in a deal over stolen cigarettes. Later Hayes stole 3800 pounds from Weyman's safebox, which was kept in the cistern of his outside lavatory, but he still did not regard this as adequate compensation. On Christmas Eve, Hayes met Weyman in the London Hotel and demanded repayment of the 1200 pounds. Weyman promised it but that afternoon Hayes shot him at his home, hitting him in the shoulder. When he was released from hospital Weyman repaid the money but, according to Hayes, Weyman would not shake hands and had been saying there would be reprisals.

On New Year's Eve, racketeer and standover man Donny 'The Duck' Day threw a party at the Paddington Town Hall but Weyman went to another in Newtown and then home to Surry Hills. Hayes had put in an appearance at the Day party and then was driven to Weyman's home, where he shot him before returning to the Town Hall.

Hayes was acquitted after witnesses said he had been at the Day party all night. His costs were paid for him by his old friend Kate Leigh.

The Duck did not last the month. In the early hours of 29 January a woman telephoned Darlinghurst Police Station to say the black marketeer, who had recently purchased a car from Stuart-Jones, had been shot in a house behind a shop at the corner of Crown and Foveaux streets. By the time the police arrived they found indeed he had—a bullet hole through his cheeks and nose and two wounds in his chest. The witness claimed that earlier there had been a fight in the house when a man was kicked in the groin. Two stolen revolvers were found.

Day was another who had been a jockey but had been disqualified for life. At the time of his death he was on bail for unlawful possession of tyres and was appealing his conviction. He was also awaiting trial on a charge of conspiracy over black market liquor. The Duck's wife, Renée, and salesman Keith Kitchener Hull were arrested and charged with his murder. The case against Renée was dropped and the 27-year-old Hull was acquitted after telling the jury that he had fired in self-defence. Stuart-Jones's wife took the opportunity to drive another nail into the good doctor's reputation, telling the press in some detail just how close he and The Duck had been and just what they had got up to together. The cause of Day's death was probably his association with Dulcie Markham.

The day the Duck died Stuart-Jones's attacker, Cliffie Thompson, was found slumped in his cell at Long Bay jail. A warder heard a shot at around 1 p.m. and there was Thompson with a chest wound. He would not say how the gun came to be in his possession but it had probably been smuggled in at the instigation of Scotty Jowett.

Shortly before that, on 9 January, Cyril Norman (also known as Thomas Couldrey) held up a gunsmith's in King Street. He invited the manager, Maurice Hannigan, to show him some guns. Norman loaded one and shot him dead before he escaped with a total of six guns, ammunition and 164 pounds in cash. For a time the police thought that Hannigan's killer was Stephen Henry Cunningham, who later shot himself after a siege with the police when they went to arrest him over an assault; they were wrong.

The day after killing Hannigan, Norman returned to his more usual trade of stealing passengers' luggage at the city's stations. It would be his undoing. He picked up two suitcases at Woolloomooloo and found they contained American army officer uniforms. He had them altered and, now posing as the American, went to the country town of Blayney where he booked a room in the Exchange Hotel. He was caught on 12 January by pure mischance. While he was showering, a maid looked in his room and saw the guns on the bed. She reported this to the manager, who said that it was perfectly all right as they belonged to an American officer; nevertheless, she told the police.

Constable Eric Bailey and another officer went to investigate and at first they were convinced by the story Norman told them. They said, however, they would take him to the station to check it out. Norman panicked and ran. Bailey tackled him and cuffed him to his own wrist but, as he did so, Norman shot him. Bailey collapsed on Norman, pinning him to the ground. When reinforcements arrived, Bailey was sitting on the kerb. 'He has shot me, don't let him get away,' he told the officers. 'I had a go. I didn't squib it.' Sadly, Bailey died and was awarded a posthumous George Cross.

Norman was sentenced to death but then reprieved. One version of Bailey's killing is that it was a contract killing gone wrong, and that Norman had shot the officer mistaking him for another who had been closing down sly-groggers and SP bookmakers.

Joe Taylor, the proprietor of Thommo's Two-up School, was more fortunate. In February that year at Hawkesbury Races he quarrelled with the bludger and drug addict Joe Prendergast, brother of John who had been shot dead fifteen years earlier by Kate Leigh. The evening after the quarrel Prendergast shot Taylor as he was standing in Reservoir Street outside his school. It seems that Taylor would not allow revenge to be taken because he feared that if Prendergast was murdered the police would use it as an excuse to close The Game. It would have been enormously expensive for him if they had; the house rake-off in two-up games in Sydney after the war was four shillings in the pound and it was thought the turnover of the big game was 40 000 pounds a week. To divert attention from his school, the report was that Taylor had been shot at his home by an unidentified man. Prendergast prudently absented himself to Melbourne for some years.

Tilly Devine had long divorced Jim and her last major criminal case came later that month. The previous year she had been acquitted of threatening a butcher with his own knife—she claimed he had sold her bad meat. Now, on 18 February, she was charged with shooting Eric Parsons with intent to murder him. She said that she was in bed at the time that he had been shot on the street. Four days later, when he failed to recognise her as his assailant, she was acquitted and, to show there was no ill feeling on either side, the pair married. The papers described her as a 'plump thin-lipped blonde with marble-hard features and an expensive perm'.

After the War Was Over

6

Working in illegal gambling could be as dangerous for the bit players as for the principals. The year 1946 began with what might be called a 'good' murder, one where there are rival theories over the killer and the motive, and doubt as to the guilt of the accused.

Between 3 and 3.30 p.m. on 2 January, Jean Wicks was strangled with a rope and battered to death in her tobacco kiosk in York Street. The 45-year-old woman—who had two lovers, neither of whom knew of the existence of the other—was a cogwheel in SP betting and regarded as a queen of the baccarat tables. At the time she was holding a large sum of money to settle bets after the Tattersall's Cup meeting. Neither lover was implicated by the police but the next month a *Daily Mirror* reporter, Douglas Ronald Morris, was charged with her murder. Initially he denied being at the kiosk but when his bloodstained clothing was found in the ceiling of his Rose Bay home, he admitted he had found the body and left in panic. A last-minute witness, Sylvia Cantrell, gave evidence that she had seen Morris, whom she had known for some years, in a café at the time screams were heard. Morris, who owed money in gambling debts, claimed that he had told a known criminal, Joseph Patrick Morris (no relation), and a reporter at the Journalists Club, that Jean Wicks kept a lot of money and would be easy to rob. On 10 May, after Cantrell's alibi was produced, the jury acquitted Morris in twelve minutes to loud cheering—'Good on you, Morris, you beaut'— in the courtroom and on the street outside. Morris drifted away from journalism, buying a residential and then a wine bar. He died from a heart attack, aged thirty-six, while cleaning his car in March 1956. Apart from the jury no one had any real doubt about the identity of Jean Wicks's killer.

On 28 March 1946, 32-year-old Face McKeon, the pre-war killer of Harold Tarlington, was found dead in Rose Street. He had been shot as he drove along the street, and his car crashed. He was said to have had more enemies than friends but there were sixteen cars at Rookwood Cemetery for his funeral.

Raymond Emmett Bollard, Thomas Esmond 'Ezzie' Bollard and Harry Wyndham were arrested but by the time the trial was heard at the end of June the prosecution's case was in ribbons. The only witness was 72-year-old Edward Atkin, more or less a derelict known as 'Okey Doke', who had around eighty convictions, including robbery with violence. He told their committal hearing that he had seen the men drinking together in the Darlington Hotel and they had all gone off in McKeon's car. Unfortunately he later wrote to the men in Long Bay saying he was sorry he had told lies at the earlier proceedings. They were all acquitted on the direction of the trial judge. Chow Hayes says that McKeon was indeed shot by Hayes's cousin Ezzie Bollard. He does not say why Bollard thought the world was better off without the Face, but there were suggestions McKeon had been selling black market cigarettes, which contained too much sawdust, at 200 pounds a case.

One survivor from the 1930s who was among the most dangerous of his time, and has perhaps never received sufficient recognition for his exploits over a thirty-year period, was William 'Joey' Hollebone. In 1935, aged nineteen, he was sentenced to ten years for the manslaughter of Leslie Archibald Hobson in King Street, Newtown. Hobson had come out of a newsagent's to find Hollebone, along with James Charters and Edward Smith, about to steal his bicycle. In the ensuing fight Hobson was knocked to the ground and the trio kicked him to death. It was while he was in

Parramatta jail that Hollebone teamed up with Chow Hayes in a partnership that would last until his death.

After their respective releases Hayes and Hollebone became minders at Joe Taylor's two-up school but in 1946 Hollebone was sent to prison for possessing an unlicensed pistol. While he was inside, Alfie Dawes went to his home and took all his clothes. When Hollebone's wife, Hazel, complained, he hit her. On his release, on 29 August Hollebone undertook a short but lethal shooting spree in Mary Street, Waterloo, killing nineteen-year-old Marjorie Nurse, Douglas Graves and Alfred Dawes junior and wounding four others. Nine other people apart from the dead and injured were in the two-room cottage, described by the prosecutor in Hollebone's subsequent trial as a 'squalid shack'. The level at which they lived can be gauged by the fact that, after the shootings, Mrs Elizabeth Dawes had no sheets to cover the corpses. The police borrowed three from her neighbour and later Mrs Dawes quite properly washed and ironed them and quite improperly popped them at Grace's Pawn Shop in Chippendale.

The evidence against Hollebone came from Noreen Miller, who was there when the shooting took place, and Mrs Dawes. His barrister, George Amsberg, spent a good deal of time at the inquest asking Dawes how much she had to drink each morning. At the trial he asked what had happened to the sheets and she said that she was sure she had returned them to her neighbour, just as sure as she was that Hollebone had killed her son. Amazingly, Hollebone was acquitted. In 1953 he was shot in the chest, which he attributed to his own carelessness, and the next year he received thirty months for carrying an unlicensed pistol. In 1956 Hollebone's reputation faltered when he was badly beaten in Long Bay jail by the housebreaker Roy Dowden, a man described as a 'pie-eater' compared to the great Joey. The fight was said to be over an 'affair of the heart', and Hollebone set upon Dowden the moment he saw him, king-hitting him with an iron tub. To his surprise, Dowden got up and proceeded to give Hollebone a good hiding. Some years later Hollebone put a cut in his wife's face that required nearly forty stitches. He died following a cerebral haemorrhage in 1960.

* * *

By the mid-1940s, the veterans of the Razor Wars were, unsurprisingly, ageing and dying off. The number of men with holes in the sides of their noses—caused by the Dutch courage of cocaine, which not only blew their septums but sometimes burned a hole through the flesh—thinned over the years. But they had successors. When Siddy Kelly became ill in 1947 he turned to his offsider Joe 'The Pig' Sinclair, who had been acquitted of the slashing for which Kelly had received five years in 1934. He brought Sinclair from Melbourne to run the games at his baccarat school in Castlereagh Street and it was the pair of them who employed the young, up-and-coming Perce Galea. When Kelly died in 1948 his net estate was slightly under 3000 pounds but the police and tax authorities believed he had left up to 100 000 pounds, possibly in a safe-deposit box. He was known to have won 15 000 pounds on horseracing in Brisbane earlier in the year and it was rumoured that he had left 30 000 pounds buried in Centennial Park where he lived. The park was promptly invaded by treasure hunters, who dug up tracts without success. Later his wife and executrix, Theller Omega Kelly, complained that Sinclair and Galea had never accounted to her properly for the money owed to Kelly.

In 1949 the good doctor, Stuart-Jones, divorced Mary Kathleen and an Adelaide beauty queen, Adeline Morick, became his third wife. Life was, however, becoming increasingly difficult for him. After losing a tax case, in which he had run the usual and almost invariably unsuccessful defence that his wealth had been acquired through gambling, he was obliged to sell his home Casa Grande. For some time he had been suspected of being involved in horse doping and race fixing and in 1958 he was disqualified by the Queensland Turf Club after his horse, Kingperion, had run oddly at Bundama Racecourse. He turned to managing a middle-of-the-road boxer, Norman Valentine Gobert, whom he also employed as a driver. After Gobert went to work for Sammy Lee's 417 Club, Stuart-Jones, on the face of it, again employed Richard Reilly, of whom he was clearly in some awe. In reality Reilly simply relieved Stuart-Jones of any substantial sums of money he carried with him and the doctor could or would do nothing about it. In December 1960 he received another tax bill, this time for 186000 pounds, and again he claimed his wealth was from betting. Six months later, in June 1961, Stuart-Jones died suddenly, following a heart attack. After his death, Richard Reilly went into partnership with the confidence trickster Ivan Markovics in an abortion clinic in Bellevue Hill. Markovics also ran a scam, arranging that, for a substantial fee, suitable people (including Perce Galea) could become Knights of Malta.

By 1948 Tilly Devine had become something of a grande dame. Over the years she had more or less patched up her quarrels with Kate Leigh but her temper could still be roused. When she was refused permission to take a chicken and some cauliflower to the murderess Stella Surridge, then still in prison, she threw the bird at a prison warder and the vegetable at the prison gates. In November 1951, despite advice, she returned to Victoria for the Melbourne Cup and was promptly arrested on an outstanding consorting charge. She served five weeks before being released on the grounds of ill health. By now she was suffering from cancer.

Then, thirty years after the Eveleigh Robbery, Shiner Ryan returned to the life of Kate Leigh. Over the years he had become something of a celebrity, not because of his robberies (for which he was usually caught) but because of his ability to escape. When in 1923 he escaped from the Adelaide Stockade, he declined to tell the police how he had managed it. Instead he sold his story — delivered through the 'Prisoner's Post Office' — to *Smith's Weekly* to raise some money for his mother. The article glowingly described him as a 'misfit genius'. By the outbreak of World War II, Ryan was fifty-four years old and had racked up what the paper saw as an Australian record of sentences totalling forty-three years. In 1947 he and Kate Leigh began corresponding and he sent her a painting he had done, of Christ holding a black lamb named Shiner outside Fremantle Gaol. On his release he went to Sydney, where their engagement was announced shortly after Kate and the press met his plane.

It would be pleasant to record that these two old villains found happiness but it would not be accurate. After their wedding, Ryan pined for Western Australia. He stuck it out for three weeks and was off. Some little time later, Leigh tried to claim three pounds a week maintenance from him. Ryan resisted, saying he would rather go to prison, where he would at least get treatment for his asthma. When he died in 1954 she paid him his due tribute. He was, she said, a brilliant man, who could open any lock with a wire coat-hanger, even with his hands behind his back. She also placed a little poem in the Sydney papers:

> Shiner, we cannot clasp our hands sweetheart
> Thy face I cannot see
> But let this token tell
> I still remember thee.

In October 1950 the tax authorities issued a list of jockeys, doctors and businessmen who had under-declared their tax. There, along with the great and the good (which included a clergyman who had understated his income for five years), were the illegal baccarat club owner Henry Stokes and Leigh. He had underestimated his income by more than 12 000 pounds and was penalised 257 pounds. She had underestimated hers by 11 000 pounds and was fined 1000 pounds. Sometimes Leigh was justified in thinking she was being picked on.

Both Kate Leigh and Tilly Devine were finally brought to earth by their continual failure to file proper tax returns. Leigh was made bankrupt shortly before she died in February 1964, after choking on her tongue. Devine survived her tax battles, although she claimed to have been ruined by them. Lawyers still in practice today can remember her, ravaged but dressed in furs and finery, going shopping at the local supermarket almost up until her death. Like so many of her kind she was thought to have taken to religion. The 'Queen of Woolloomooloo' died in hospital in Concord on 24 November 1970. She left a little over $11000 to be divided between her adopted son, John Eric Parsons, and a niece and nephew in London. It is said that when a toast to her memory was proposed in a bar in Kings Cross no one could be bothered to lift their glasses.

* * *

Chow Hayes was still in full flight after the war. In 1948 he had been running a home-invasion racket reminiscent of the bushranger Edward 'Jew Boy' Davis. On 19 August he and five others burst into the house of George and Joyce Great in Surry Hills, sat down to eat and drink and, after threatening to shoot the son, threw out their unwilling hosts. They then ransacked the house, taking with them 600 pounds of jewellery and a pianola. Found guilty on 4 November, Hayes received five years and Joey Hollebone three. Hayes also received a two-year concurrent sentence for pulling the wig off the head of Joyce Great, leaving her, as he delicately put it, 'bald as a baby's bum'. The Court of Appeal quashed their robbery sentences in December, so Hayes just served the two years for assault. Hayes's defence was probably paid for by Kate Leigh, who attended court throughout the hearing.

Hayes's career as one of Sydney's top standover men effectively ended on 29 May 1951, with the shooting of another hardman and film extra, William John 'Bobby' Lee, in the Ziegfeld Club before an audience of hundreds. The quarrel that led to Lee's death had begun some months earlier over a complex misunderstanding in arranging bail for two other criminals, Seppi Allen and Johnny Flanagan. Under the pretext that Allen and Flanagan were trying to stand over Thommo's two-up game, Lee and a number of ex-boxers gave them a bad beating. Hayes decided to involve himself and after he had quarrelled with Lee in the London Hotel, he knocked him down and gave him a good kicking.

On the evening of 1 May 1951 Lee waited outside Hayes's home in Thomas Street, Ultimo, and watched him, his wife and daughter leave the house to go to see the film *Annie Get Your Gun*. Lee had been drinking and mistook the male with the two women for Hayes's son. Their nephew Danny Simmons, once a promising boxer, had remained in the house and Lee, compounding his error, shot him twice in the back of the head, believing it was Hayes. Hayes and Joey Hollebone now began a search of Sydney for Lee. On 29 May they learned through their offsider Sydney hardman, Jackie Hodder—who would himself be killed in March 1965— that Lee would be eating in the Ziegfeld later that evening with Hodder's brother Walter.

Hayes and Hollebone went to the club with their wives. Hayes was all for killing Lee on the dance floor but the more prudent Hollebone wanted them to wait until he went outside. Eventually Hayes went to Lee's table and sat down. Lee asked if bygones could be bygones and Hayes pretended to go along with things until Hollebone came over and began to quarrel with Lee over the Allen and Flanagan beating. Hayes then wanted to go outside but Lee thought there was safety in public. He was wrong. Hayes shot him twice in the chest and then three times more. Hayes and Hollebone grabbed their wives and ran from the club. Hayes threw the gun off the Harbour Bridge but instead of falling into the water it landed on a grass patch, where it was found the next morning.

A variety of people were charged and discharged, including the Hollebones and Hodder's brother Walter, but when it came to it Hayes and his loyal wife, Topsy, bore the brunt of things. Witnesses came, lied and went but Hayes's principal trouble was the evidence of Detective Ray Kelly, who claimed that Hayes had said, 'What else could I do? There were a lot of people there, and they saw me shoot him. I think I was entitled to shoot him … I got in first … The police didn't catch anyone for shooting Simmons, so I decided to do things my own way.' Hayes maintained that Kelly had verballed him, and made a speech from the dock saying that he was at Lee's table talking to him when the shots were fired by a man standing beside him. He called Hollebone as a witness, who denied he knew how guns worked. There was enough confusion for the jury to disagree after a five-hour deliberation, leaving Hayes to face a retrial.

At the retrial, much of the focus was again on Kelly's evidence. There was also a newspaper reporter who said he had called at Hayes's house three days after Simmons's shooting. Hayes had shown him a gun saying, 'And that's what I'll use.' Again the jury could not reach a verdict and the Crown announced there would be a third trial. This was most unusual. The only time it had happened in recent years was in 1950 when, on the third round, the radio announcer John Brian Kerr was convicted of the murder of a girl on a beach in Melbourne.

Now the judge was Mr Justice McClemens, who banned the use of nicknames, saying it resulted in the 'oblique glorification of crime'. He summed up against Hayes, and the jury was out only an hour before convicting him. Hayes said he hadn't expected anything else after the summing up and that he hoped Ray Kelly would 'die of cancer of the tongue'. It was one of the many cases worldwide in which the defendant is guilty but the evidence is embroidered to secure a conviction.

The case against Topsy Hayes for aiding and abetting her husband was heard in June 1952. In less than an hour, at the close of the prosecution case, the judge ruled there was no evidence to go to the jury. Hayes was sentenced to death and was reprieved. In Parramatta jail he ran an SP bookmaking racket and doubled up as a prison snitch. In July 1967 he was paroled, one of many criminals who apparently had only a matter of months to live. He had cancer in his remaining kidney with a life expectancy of eighteen months. But the prognosis was wrong: Hayes was made of sterner stuff. Later he admitted that, as everybody knew full well, he had indeed shot Lee. In October 1970 Hayes received a further five years for glassing petty crimial Gerald Hutchinson in the Prince Alfred Club opposite the Royal Prince Alfred Hospital. Hutchinson lost his eye as a result of the attack. On 14 February 1977, then aged seventy, Hayes was paroled again. This time there were no more court appearances before his death in 1991.

More and more of the old players from the 1930s were decaying or dying, often both. Leslie Eugene Francis Xavier 'Lair' Brown was one of the dying. Over the years this relic from the Razor Wars had run up nearly fifty appearances in the courts of New South Wales, Victoria, Queensland and New Zealand, charged under a variety of names with a variety of offences including assault and robbery, possession of explosives, housebreaking and bribery. Now, on 1 August 1962, he was shot by George Jacobsen and died ten days later in Parramatta Hospital. He had gone off with Jacobsen's wife, Marlene, but when she returned to her husband, Brown would not leave well enough alone and threatened to kill Jacobsen. On the night of 31 July, Brown turned up at their home in Seven Hills with a gun, shouting insults and breaking a window. Jacobsen shot him in the back. The charges were later dropped but it cost Jacobsen 120 pounds to prove his innocence and he was made bankrupt the next year.

Frank Green, who had fought Guido Calletti for so long and hard over the favours of Nellie Cameron, was decaying before dying. He had female breasts tattooed on the outside of his right arm, was now going bald by his fifties and was reduced to working as a cockatoo for a Woolloomooloo SP betting shop on a Saturday while doing house painting during the week. He was now living with, and abusing, Beatrice Bowes, known as Bobbie Hackett, a saleswoman in a city department store, and he had acquired a disconcerting tendency to pawn anything within reach. In October 1965 Bowes left him and he took up with a prostitute. In turn she left and in early April 1966 Bowes succumbed once more to Green's blandishments and returned. He continued to be violent towards her. On 26 April he was squabbling with her while she was cutting up liverwurst with a 12-inch knife. A struggle developed and the knife went into Green just above the heart. She ran into the street for help but by the time it arrived he was dead. An autopsy showed there were eight old bullets in his body. Apparently he used to say you had to be unlucky to be killed by one. In October that year, after telling the jury Green had stabbed her twice and she thought he was going to do so again, Bowes was acquitted of his murder.

For much of the 1960s, standover man Richard Gabriel Reilly was regarded as one of the most powerful men in Sydney crime. His police and political contacts had ensured that he avoided any prosecution after 1952 and now, with his offsider Ronnie Lee, he ran two baccarat clubs, the Kellett and the Spade Room. Lavishly furnished but illegal casinos had replaced the earlier, shabbier baccarat schools. Their profits were enormous, even after $15 000 had been paid out monthly to a police bagman. 'I personally wouldn't be surprised if some police officers in Sydney have shared as much as a million dollars out of graft over the years,' a former detective told *The National Times* in 1973. Money was paid in cash at a pub or in a car on a monthly basis. Even at the time of Reilly's killing the profits were rising but they were insufficient for him. He was also still standing over abortionists and prostitutes.

His murder—which created the most interest and, ultimately, unrest in the community that year—came a month after standover

man Ducky O'Connor's death. On 25 June 1967 Reilly was shot as
he left the Double Bay flat of his mistress Aileen Margaret Glynn.
The killing seems to have been part of a wild takeover bid by the
gunman and rival baccarat operator John James Warren, who
had been banished from the Kings Cross area by Reilly. Said to
have a backer who was never named, Warren planned to control
gaming by eliminating his rivals—including the formidable Lennie
McPherson—one by one.

Although he clearly had grandiose schemes, Warren, a man
who never grew out of a love of comic books, seems to have been
relatively small time. He had been in a youth gang in Annandale
with Leonard 'Ray' Brouggy, and they progressed via stealing car
radios to a theft-to-order business—the items ranging widely from
radios to pianos. In 1951 their lock-up store was found to contain
7000 pounds' worth of stolen goods and Warren received four
years, Brouggy half that.

By the early 1960s the pair were reunited. Brouggy's career had
not exactly prospered: he was known as 'Chooky Raffles' because
he had taken to running a number of chicken raffles in hotels. At
first they ran a small-time baccarat game in William Street. Warren
then moved to Macleay Street and it was then that Reilly ordered
him out. Warren transferred his centre of operations to Liverpool
and also began a highly successful operation—said to net $2000
a week—with his girlfriend Glory McGlinn, stealing from poker
machines at the South Sydney Junior Leagues Club.

Warren, along with McGlinn and a 'Joe Smith' who was never
named and who became a Crown witness, waited behind a stone wall
until Reilly left the flat in Manning Road at 7.30 p.m. and walked to
his blue Maserati. Warren had initially planned on torching Reilly's
car but changed his plans to a shooting and had undertaken several
dry runs. On the day, however, Warren's aim went slightly awry.
Intending to hit him in the stomach, he shot Reilly in the throat
and chest and the club owner managed to get to his car and drive

away into the hilly New South Head Road, where he collapsed. The car rolled back fifty yards and crashed into the window of a dress shop. Within an hour the *Sydney Morning Herald* received a call: 'Tell them that was for O'Connor and there's going to be more.'

An ecstatic Warren went straight to the South Sydney Junior Leagues Club to establish an alibi. The success was celebrated in some style, with doughnuts and coffee in a local café. 'Smith' received the less than magnificent sum of $500 for driving the getaway car.

Warren was questioned briefly, gave his alibi and was released. Then, on 25 January 1968, the police received an anonymous call from 'Joe Smith' about the reward then on offer. Warren's name was again in the frame. It was James Cyril 'Johnny' Walker and Charles Edward Rennerson who appeared in the dock charged with having conspired with Warren to kill Reilly. They were said to have been paid $12 000 for the death of Reilly and offered a further $8000 to kill Claude Eldridge, a gambling operator, who was shot at Neutral Bay.

Brought to court with heavy security, 'Joe Smith' gave his evidence with the public excluded. He wrote down and then printed his real name and told the court that Warren had been 'the best friend I ever had'. Warren, he said, had told him that the retired millionaire who had commissioned the killings was doing it as an act of public good. 'He's only having people killed who have killed other people.' 'Smith' had not exactly done well out of the killing of Eldridge either. On that occasion he had received $50.

Rennerson and Walker had the case against them dropped when in January 1968 Warren shot and killed his girlfriend, the man he claimed to be her other lover, Brian Bowman, another person and then, fortuitously, himself. It may not have been quite so neat, though. Shortly before his death, Brouggy wrote a series of letters to strip-club manager Frank 'Tubby' Black, indicating he had carried out the quadruple killing.

But who was the informer 'Joe Smith'? To those capable of working out the simplest of codes it cannot come as a great surprise that it was none other than Leonard 'Ray' Brouggy himself. Possibly he had nursed a grievance that he had been relegated to the position of doorman at the baccarat club or over the paltry wages he received.

What, however, caused the trouble was not simply Reilly's death but that he left behind him a series of black books containing 389 different telephone numbers, including (as might be expected) those of leading criminals and (as perhaps might not be expected) those of politicians, senior police officers and lawyers, along with details of money payments. Commissioner Norman Allan liaised with Premier Bob Askin to ensure that most of the contents were kept secret but two of the names that were leaked, to their great embarrassment, were those of former justice minister Norman John Mannix (ALP, Liverpool) and Albert Ross Sloss (ALP, Kings Cross).

The 1970s

7

Immediately after World War II, Sydney did not really have gangs in the same sense of the pre-war gangs. Rather, there were a series of individual criminals who came together on a regular or irregular basis, as the need arose, for standover and robberies. Then in the 1970s the face of organised crime changed exponentially. While the so-called East Coast Milieu had once made its money from the standover and illegal gambling, now its members turned their attention to drugs, expanding their empires and forging links with police, politicians and criminals both at home and in the United States and the Far East.

And so the East Coast Milieu began its inexorable rise that would last for nearly a quarter of a century. Who were its members? The first among equals, until his death in January 1985, was undoubtedly Frederick James Anderson, known as 'Big Doll' or 'Paddles', the latter because of the size of his feet and, he said, from his days as a kid in the swimming pool. Paddles sadly never kept to his promise—made to his barrister after being acquitted of the murder of Melbourne standover man John Abrahams in 1940—to stop mixing with undesirables. Four months later, he appeared in court on a charge of consorting with criminals in William Street, for which he received a month, and then, in quick succession, he was acquitted of standing over a bookmaker and fined for assaults on two police officers and obtaining a motor licence by false pretences.

After Ray Kelly's death in 1977, Anderson took over the ex-detective's interests in his brothel and abortion rackets. He also had business interests with the Chicago Mafioso hitman John Marshall Caifano. Late in his career Anderson was said to have hung a leading Sydney jockey out of a window by his ankles for winning when the money was not down. A traditionalist, he believed the rise in Asian crime was bad for Sydney and generally declined to work with men he regarded as newcomers. Before his death he is reputed to have philosophised, 'There's a bit of bad in the best of us and a bit of good in the worst of us.'

George David Freeman, Anderson's successor, was a late beginner, who did not begin to flourish until the mid-1960s. He was born in the poor area of Glebe–Annandale in 1935 and rode out for a racehorse trainer. He was tall for a jockey, standing at 174 centimetres, and at one time he sported a variety of tattoos, including a heart, a dagger, 'Mother' and 'Maria' on his right arm and a dagger in a scroll on his left. 'True Love' was tattooed on the backs of his fingers.

During his life he racked up nearly fifty convictions, most of which amounted to little more than petty theft, evading train fares and the like. His one serious conviction appears to have been in 1954, when he received three years' hard labour for breaking and entering. His metamorphosis came in the early 1960s, when he realised that to move out of the stultifying circle of petty offences he needed to forge links with some of the top men of the time.

Number 2 in Richard Neville's *Oz* list of Sydney's villains, and that of most other people as well, was Lennie McPherson. Born in Balmain in 1921, he did not receive the acclaim he deserved until Mr Justice Moffitt's 1973 Royal Commission into the infiltration of organised crime into the clubs of New South Wales, in which he was described as a 'vicious and powerful criminal'. By then he had been before the courts seventy-three times, the last serious charge being in 1955 when he received twelve months for possession of an unlicensed pistol.

McPherson left school at the age of twelve and worked as a driller at Morts Dock, helping to turn out sloops during the war. From there he drifted into crime, beginning his long career as a standover man working for Paddles Anderson. By the 1960s he was a man to be feared and was regarded as having that little bit extra, which elevated him above his contemporaries.

Another senior member, though slightly lower in the pecking order, was Stan 'The Man' Smith, who was born in Balmain in 1936 and had a police record dating back to 1954. Other members of the Milieu naturally included Abe Saffron, who went to the same school as Anderson but a little later. There was also Karl Bonnette, and the corrupt solicitor Morgan John Ryan. Bonnette had a variety of names, including Graham John Alleman, which he adopted by deed poll to facilitate his entry into the United States. Born in Melbourne in 1935, he was a great traveller who first became known to the police in 1954. Ryan, another who had worked as a jockey in his youth, was rather older. Born in 1920, he qualified as a solicitor and opened his firm Morgan Ryan and Brock in the early 1950s. It was he who would inadvertently bring down the liberal and highly regarded Justice Murphy to the ranks of convicted criminal. Certainly down the ranking was Milan 'Iron Bar Miller' Petricevic, born in 1938 in Croatia, a debt collector and standover man for Paddles Anderson who once volunteered his services (declined) to the authorities to deal with Vietnam demonstrators.

While criminals in the Italian community often favoured bombs, up until the end of the 1950s killings in traditional non-ethnic crime were generally face-to-face or back-of-the-head matters. The killing in July 1960 of 59-year-old William Joseph Thompson, who ran a gambling school in Palmer Street, East Sydney, was certainly a traditional affair. Thompson, supposedly under the protection of greyhound trainer and pre-war standover man Charlie Bourke, was found slumped across the front seat of his car near his home in Macdougall Street, Kensington. He had been shot at close range; the bullet penetrated the back of his head. It cannot have been a case of robbery because the sum of 1000 pounds was found on him.

Three years later, on 8 July 1963, a change came about when Robert 'Pretty Boy' Walker, an associate of Thompson, was shot dead in Randwick. Walker was nearly cut in half when two men in a stolen 1960 Holden with false plates drove slowly past him and fired eleven shots—six of which hit him. What made the killing a first was that an Owen sub-machine gun was used.

As is usually the case, a number of explanations for the killing were on offer. Walker had been involved with gangs of safebreakers and burglars and had also controlled prostitutes, and it was thought that his death might have resulted from this connection. The theory was eventually discarded in favour of a reprisal for an earlier shooting, at Walker's home in May that year, of Stan 'The Man' Smith, now described as 'an associate of some of the most vicious criminals in this state'. There had been some sort of a row between Smith and Walker, or possibly between one of Smith's friends, Gordon Reilly, and Walker in which Reilly suffered a broken leg. Instead of a simple stand-up between them, Smith went to Walker's home with a number of colleagues and was promptly shot in the chest with a .303 rifle. He survived. Walker was duly arrested and at first did not apply for bail, for fear of further reprisals. According to the not always wholly reliable murderer Neddy Smith, it was arranged for a girlfriend to tell Walker that things had been patched up. He was given bail and then very prudently went into hiding in Randwick. The girlfriend then told Smith where he was.

The gunman most favoured for Walker's killing was the 29-year-old, up-and-coming standover man, psychopathic Raymond Patrick

'Ducky' O'Connor (also known as 'Captain Rats'), who was, unsurprisingly, a most reluctant and unhelpful witness at Walker's inquest. The killing was intended to be seen as an example to lesser members of the underworld that a new regime was now in charge. It could be said that in the winter of 1963 the East Coast Milieu grew up.

The Walker killing was followed shortly afterwards by the slaying of Charlie Bourke himself. After his conviction for a triple shooting in Queensland in 1930, Bourke escaped from Boggo Road jail in Brisbane and came to Sydney, where the authorities left him alone. A violent man, he shot a taxi driver who he believed was having an affair with his wife. In May 1939 Bourke was acquitted of the attempted murder of Jordan Eastaughffe, better known as George East, who was shot in the stomach in the hallway of his house the previous month. Sportingly, Eastaughffe told the court that when he said Bourke had shot him he meant a William Bourke. In turn Bourke remained staunch, refusing to talk to the police, when he was himself shot in the back in October 1943.

Bourke, who was still standing over Greek gaming clubs, was another who was machine-gunned to death. It was just before midnight on 9 February 1964 when up to twenty bullets were fired at him as he took out the front-door key to his bungalow in Randwick. No charges were ever brought but the shooting seems to have been over the running of his greyhound, The Stripper. The man holding the machine gun was probably baccarat operator and hoon for hire, John James Warren.

In March the following year another old standover man, Chow Hayes's friend Jackie Hodder, was killed at a dance at the Waterloo Town Hall. Hodder had been stabbed in a fight on the dance floor but his death had not interfered with the spirit of things. The band played and the guests danced on. Indeed no one saw anything at all, which mystified the trial judge. Along with his brother-in-law Maurice 'Barney' Ryan, Charles 'Chicka' Reeves was charged with the murder, but in a most curious plea bargain Reeves copped to manslaughter and received three years. Ryan was discharged. In the underworld it was well known that the actual killer was the bludger Ronald Feeney, also known as Ronnie Royal, and that Reeves had taken the plea rather than risk a life sentence for murder. Sensibly Feeney absented himself to Queensland.

Throughout the latter half of the 1960s there was a series of gangland contretemps (if not wars) in Sydney with, as usual, a large number of casualties. The highly respected Robert Lawrence 'Jackie' 'Iron Man' Steele, who had served seven years for armed robbery and five for safebreaking, was shot near his home in Woollahra in November 1965. He was not a difficult target. Most nights of the week at about 8 p.m. he tended to walk to the Lord Nelson for a drink. On his way back he was followed by a car with the false plates CIB 1, its passengers wearing hats of a style favoured by the detective branch. Steele thought they were police, after him for money, but in fact the men were sent by Lennie McPherson. Pinned in the headlights, Steele received up to fifty pellets and bullets. He staggered the 300 metres to his home and climbed two flights of stairs to his flat before collapsing. His wife and daughter went into hiding. When questioned by the police Steele said he had no idea who was responsible: 'I didn't think I had an enemy in the world.' He had. McPherson was displeased that Steele was claiming the Number 1 position in Sydney and had been buying up and distributing copies of the *Oz* issue which labelled McPherson as a 'fizz' (an informer).

It was not for nothing that Steele was known as the Iron Man. In October the next year he survived a second attack when he and two others were badly beaten by a nine-man gang in Macleay Street, Kings Cross.

The week after the Steele shooting another standover man was in court. The up-and-coming but vicious Graham Leslie Moffitt, who had already served almost four years in Adelaide for robbery, was sent to prison for six months after pleading guilty to possessing two firearms at Annandale in November. He claimed they were for his and his family's protection. He had also been badly beaten in Kings Cross by men with iron bars shortly before he bought them. The police said the weapons were not connected to the Steele shooting.

Moffitt was right to be scared. On 31 March 1966 he apparently blew himself up while experimenting on the ignition detonator of a stolen 1964 Holden. Given Jackie Steele's noted skill with explosives, Moffitt's death may have been more complicated. In any event it was certainly fortuitous. Moffitt had been using excessively forceful debt-collecting tactics, and had savagely beaten a well-known doctor and his wife. The doctor had complained to the Milieu.

The unofficial, and indeed official, suspect in both the Walker and Bourke cases was Ducky O'Connor, who died on 26 May 1967 in what were unusual circumstances, even for that period. Shortly after 3 a.m., O'Connor went to the Latin Quarter club on Pitt Street and stood by the table of Lennie McPherson, near which Detective Sergeant MJ Wild and a colleague were sitting. At around 3.25 a.m. a shot was fired but because at that very moment people were leaving, Wild did not get a clear view of what happened. As soon as he heard the shot he went to McPherson's table and found O'Connor lying on the floor with a bullet in his head. Two pistols were beside him. By then they were clear of prints. Wild asked what had happened and McPherson told him that O'Connor had approached his table, pulled a gun, said 'Here's yours' and, as he was about to fire, one of the men at the table had grabbed his arm. In the struggle, McPherson said, O'Connor 'sort of' shot himself. A woman sitting at a nearby table said she had seen McPherson drop a gun to the floor but as no charges were preferred she must have been unsighted.

At the time of his death, O'Connor was on bail, charged with the murder of Shirley Bowker, caught in the crossfire in a blue after a junior VFL game in Melbourne. During the month he had been acting independently, collecting money at random from prostitutes, club owners and SP bookmakers. He was effectively out of control and was becoming a considerable liability to the Milieu. His wife, the talented shoplifter Grace O'Connor, was later killed in London by Tom Wraith, a fellow member of the so-called Kangaroo Gang. Her body was never found.

Earlier in the year, at about 9 p.m. on 15 January, nurse and standover man 'Big' Barry Flock was shot five times in the head in the grounds of the Scottish Hospital, Paddington. His body was found the next day in the undergrowth. One bullet had gone through his hand as though he had raised it to protect himself. He had been running a massage parlour for a Thelma Coyle, to whom he owed $800, and had received threatening telephone calls, probably from a group who wished to take over control. He was thought to have been talking too loudly about the parlours and to have had financial problems. He had told police he was scared and thinking of leaving Sydney. One of his associates was Johnny Regan, known as 'Nano the Magician', because he could make people disappear, who was never quite a wholly paid-up member of the Milieu, and Flock's killers almost certainly included him, possibly acting for McPherson. Standover man Ross Christie, who was a partner with Regan in a dress shop opposite one of the massage parlours, told Coyle he knew who had killed Flock. In short order he too disappeared.

* * *

What had the other leading members of the Milieu been doing during the period? They had been expanding in Australia and forging links with crime figures in the United States and the Far East. By the mid-1960s George Freeman had given up petty crime, bought a house with his safebreaking proceeds and in 1963 became an SP bookmaker, working first for 'Melbourne' Mick Bartley. From then on his fortunes changed. By his own account, Freeman was never more than a vastly misunderstood racing identity. The *Sydney Morning Herald* took a slightly different view, regarding him as holding no lower than the Number 3 position in Sydney crime for the twenty years before his death.

In 1965 both Freeman and Paddles Anderson became involved with Joe Dan Testa, from the Chicago Crime Syndicate, and later visited Las Vegas using a false passport and accompanied not only by his minder, Stan 'The Man' Smith, but also by his physician, Dr Nick Paltos, there to administer to his pneumonia. Just what real intention lay behind the association with Testa, who set up Grants Constructions Pty Ltd with Freeman, is unclear but the installation of the Bally Manufacturing Company's poker machines in clubs was the most likely topic of conversation. In his book *Disorganised Crime*, Richard Hall rather discounts any serious mafia influence in Australia, pointing out that not only did the development company soon go bust but that Testa was not exactly a key player. Perhaps Hall was wrong. Testa was certainly significant enough in the United States to be worth blowing up. Nor does the fact that a company goes bust mean that many have not made a good deal of money out of it. Freeman also moved around Australia and, in the mid-1960s, acquired a conviction for theft and receiving in Perth and later one for possessing explosives.

Over the years Lennie McPherson had also led a busy life. In July 1959 George Joseph Hackett was shot dead in Elswick Street, Leichhardt. Hackett had had an interesting career outside his day job on the docks. In 1951 he was acquitted of the murder of Albert Flarrity in a case known as the 'Body in the Brisbane River'. There were suggestions that the jury had been got at by McPherson. A list of potential jurors was found in an envelope bearing his name; it had 'To Be Collected' typed on it. McPherson and a solicitor were questioned but no charges were brought.

Five years later Hackett was again acquitted, this time of the murder of ex-boxer and standover man John William 'Joey' Manners, who was shot as he walked out of the Australian Hotel at Millers Point. At first it was thought to be a contract killing by a Melbourne gunman, and various reasons were suggested: Manners was a dobber; there was a quarrel over either a woman or the proceeds of a robbery; or it was simply revenge for a knockdown fight with another standover man earlier in the week. When it came to it, the prosecution opted for *la femme*, who they said was one Sue Henry. The key witness, the hotel barman Keith Craig, failed to turn up in court, and Ms Henry said she was not at all interested in Manners and never had been. Hackett was acquitted and Craig, who surrendered after the trial, was fined ten pounds. Unsurprisingly there were suggestions that witnesses had been nobbled.

A week before his death Hackett had been involved in a stabbing and it was thought his death might have been a reprisal. McPherson and his friend William Louis 'Snowy' Rayner were arrested the next day, prompting McPherson to remark, 'I suppose it's over the Hackett shooting last night. It's a funny thing that whenever anyone is shot in Sydney, the first thing they do is run for me.' McPherson ran the successful alibi that he had been visiting his sick mother in hospital and had then been discussing with two friends whether she should undergo an operation. Both he and Rayner were acquitted.

For McPherson 1960 was a particularly difficult year. First he was involved in one of the many Painters and Dockers' union power struggles and then John Joseph Unwin and another man were charged with attempting to murder him. They were acquitted—as was McPherson, not only of the murder of Hackett, but also of the attempted murder of his own wife and driving a car at Unwin with intent to murder.

McPherson often used intermediaries and it was through Wally Dean, on paper a Redfern barber, that he received a pension from one of Sydney's biggest illegal casinos, Michael Moylan's 33 club. The club paid Dean $600 a month for what was euphemistically called promotion. The casino had been highly successful during the life of English-born Michael Moylan senior but his son's gambling habit ruined it. In 1973 Moylan junior and his wife, Patricia, took to drug dealing and, in partnership with the bent ex-copper Murray Riley, imported marijuana and later heroin from the Far East and the United States using false-bottomed suitcases and a series of couriers. In July 1978, Moylan pleaded guilty to importing drugs, and the next month his wife and the lawyer Frank Lawrence were also found guilty. Both received eight years. In 1980 Moylan died in jail following a heart attack.

By the early 1970s much of vice and protection in Sydney was firmly in the hands of 'Nano The Magician' Regan, who began expanding his territory rapidly in 1973. He took over a string of brothels after contracting the killing of their owner, Eric 'The Monkey' Williams, who in turn had assumed the mantle from the late Joe Borg.

Regan's career had followed a slightly different path from those of his colleagues. Instead of relying on the help of the likes of Dr Stuart-Jones to avoid conscription, he desperately wanted to join the army but was rejected because of flat feet. Born in September 1945 and described as having cold eyes and a 'sort of hare-lip', Regan was involved in armed robbery by the age of seventeen; two years later he began work as a bouncer and by 1967 he was running a string of prostitutes. The previous year he had survived a shooting in Sydney by James Finch and when, in 1973, Regan was implicated when a Brisbane nightclub, the Whiskey Au Go Go, was torched and fifteen people died, Finch would be one of the defendants.

The next year Regan started trying to extort money from some of the upmarket casinos such as the 33 Club—and, not surprisingly, given the volatile state of the market, it may have cost him his life.

It was either that or his curious involvement in a quite genuine organisation, the Independent Action Group for a Better Police Force. Regan, taking time off from his everyday standover duties, began making statutory declarations denouncing high-ranking officers in the New South Wales police.

Among Regan's 'disappeared' was Robert Donnelly, who was spirited off the street in 1972. There was also the killing of Ross Christie, which the police sought to pin on Regan. Another to go was Kevin Gore of the notorious Toecutter gang, who was seen walking with Regan in Darlinghurst in the winter of 1972, but never again. Gore's colleague, William Donnelly, had disappeared only a few days before that. He had gone for a drive in Gore's car, which was later found burned out. A particularly nasty murder attributed to Regan was that of the death of Karlos, the three-year-old son of a friend, Helen Scott-Huie, whom he was babysitting. Regan told the police he had left the child in his car when he went to buy a paper around midnight in Taylor Square and on his return found him missing. The cognoscenti believed he had killed Karlos when the child began to annoy him.

By the time of his death, Regan was playing both sides, writing letters to the police naming those he claimed were trying to kill him. He had, he said, made known his intentions to close illegal gambling and to stop prostitution. This, said his enemies, was a blind in order to be able to extort more from them. With his other hand he was still busy denouncing police officers. Someone decided to end it all on 22 September 1974. After a picnic in Watsons Bay Park with Helen Scott-Huie—who seemed to have forgiven him for failing to mind Karlos, or for minding him all too well—Regan walked alone to an appointment in Marrickville. Three different .38 guns were used and some of the bullets were fired from as little as 8 centimetres away. The getaway car had also been used a month earlier in the killing of one of Regan's associates, John Edward 'Ratty' Clarke, shot in the Newington Inn in Petersham.

In his memoir *Catch and Kill Your Own*, Neddy Smith attributes the death of Clarke to Regan and that of the Magician to what he calls 'The Team' (the East Coast Milieu), acting in retaliation for the death of Clarke. In *Infamous Australians*, Andrew Dettre and his co-authors say Clarke was killed by Regan both to gain control of Sydney's inner and western suburbs and because Clarke had been bad-mouthing him. Writer Bob Bottom maintains that Regan's death was specifically in relation to a Marrickville club he wished to protect but which was already under Milieu control. One story that circulated was that Freeman fired all the guns himself, juggling them in turn, but even with his talents it is an unlikely one. Another theory is that his death was at the hands of the police, in the form of Ray Kelly.

* * *

The authorities had done nothing about the Apalachin-style meeting of the New South Wales Mafia held at Karl Bonnette's Double Bay home, in July 1972, by 'the boys playing cards' (as described by New South Wales police) or a 'summit meeting of criminal minds' (as described by Mr Justice Moffitt). Said to be present at the meeting—their names noted by an observant police officer—were Bonnette, Saffron, McPherson, Anderson, Freeman, Petricevic and others, including a Labor member of the state parliament, who denied that he was there. Confusingly, Bonnette denied that any of them were there. That the Australian meeting was undisturbed and unremarked upon by the police was not altogether surprising. The Moffitt Commission into organised crime found that three of the officers in charge of state investigations had deliberately or corruptly attempted to cover up organised crime links with a seemingly legitimate poker machine business. Indeed steps could be, and were, taken against pro-active police officers. In 1977 Tony Lauer—then a sergeant, later a commissioner—prepared a report that implicated Freeman in illegal gaming. His allegations were investigated but no criminal charges were brought, and for his pains Lauer was exiled to the Blue Mountains.

Following recommendations from Mr Justice Moffitt, a police operation, *Southern Comfort*, began tapping George Freeman's telephones. From the conversations it became clear that by 1976 he was supplying the Chief Stipendiary Magistrate, Murray Farquhar, with a series of almost infallible racing tips. A decade later Mr Justice Stewart reported that Freeman was involved in SP bookmaking, illegal casinos and the fixing of horse races. He also had improper relationships with three named police officers at inspector and superintendent level. As for the American connection, he was involved with Meyer Lansky's associate Danny Stein, who had given him a power of attorney on his account at the ANZ bank in Pitt Street. In September the following year it was closed and more than $56000 was transferred to Stein. Three years later Stein was back in Australia, where it was thought he was setting up a network for the importation and distribution of heroin both in Australia and in the United States.

It was Murray Farquhar who almost single-handedly put an end to the consorting laws. In 1969 McPherson was in front of him, pleading guilty to consorting with criminals. According to McPherson's barrister, he had been a motel manager for the past fourteen years and was highly thought of by his employers, earning $40 a week. Instead of sending McPherson to prison Farquhar fined him $100. It is well known that police forces can develop a collective anomie if they think their efforts are not being rewarded. Gradually, as fewer and fewer charges were brought, the law faded into disuse.

On 27 July 1977 it became apparent that Farquhar's relationship with Freeman was seriously unhealthy. Freeman was watched over a two-hour period and photographed as he sat in the members stand at Randwick with Farquhar and Dr Nick Paltos before being evicted by racecourse security. It was an afternoon that would have considerable repercussions for Farquhar and lead to another inquiry, this time conducted by the chief justice, Sir Laurence Street. What was alleged against Farquhar was that, because of the stream of winning racing tips, he had allowed himself to be influenced when he intervened in the trial of the then New South Wales Rugby League executive director Kevin Humphreys, who had pleaded not guilty to embezzlement of some $50 000 worth of funds from the Balmain Tigers. Despite what was a strong case for the prosecution, properly presented, the stipendiary magistrate, believing that he had instructions from Farquhar, dismissed the charges.

What was even worse was the other line of inquiry: that this intervention had indeed been made at the request of the premier of New South Wales, Neville Wran, from whom Farquhar said he received a telephone call on the morning of the hearing.

At the Street Inquiry, Freeman gave a highly entertaining performance, including a denial, despite a photograph, that he had been in the members stand at Randwick that fateful afternoon and his complaint that he had been falsely maligned by journalist Bob Bottom. At the end he made a plaintive little statement: 'Who am I to talk to? If I talk to the baddies, I'm in trouble; if I talk to the goodies, they're in trouble ...'

In the end Street found that Farquhar had influenced the outcome of Humphreys's committal proceedings but that he was not acting at the request of Neville Wran. There had been no such telephone call. The loser in all this was Farquhar. In March 1985, at the age of sixty-six, he was sentenced to four years' imprisonment on a charge of conspiracy to pervert the course of justice. On his release he went from bad to worse. In March 1991 he was somewhat surprisingly acquitted of receiving paintings he said he had bought from a man in a pub and, at the time of his fatal heart attack in December 1993, he was again on trial, charged with conspiracy to obtain false passports.

The decade ended with mixed results for Freeman. On 25 April 1979, he was shot in the head with a .22 pistol. He had been to dinner with Paltos when a gunman opened fire as he got out of his car at his home at Yowie Bay. The ill-aimed shooter was thought to be John Marcus Miller (or Muller), the father-in-law of robber and drug dealer Michael Hurley. Freeman had, it was alleged, debauched Hurley's wife while her husband was in prison. Hurley was unable or unwilling to do anything about it so, some claimed, Miller had a go instead.

After he recovered, Freeman went to Noosa Heads with his family. While he was there, on 7 June, Miller, then working as a casino doorman, was shot dead in Coogee. Freeman declined to answer questions when interviewed by the police and the coroner found there was no evidence to link him with Miller's death.

In January 1983 the police had a rare triumph, albeit a minor one, in their contest with Freeman. Meat was thrown over the wall of his home at Yowie Bay to distract his Rottweilers. The police then managed to gain entry to the house and as a result Freeman was fined $500 for illegal SP betting. Nor could it exactly be described as a major triumph for the authorities when, in April 1985, Freeman was fined the maximum $5000 after pleading guilty to more telephone betting offences.

On 20 March 1990 Freeman suffered a severe asthma attack and died shortly after he was taken to hospital. His funeral was a fine one, attended by such luminaries as McPherson and Freeman's solicitor, Christopher Murphy, who had assisted him with his autobiography. Dr Nick Paltos, who was unavoidably detained at the time, sent a wreath.

The reason for Paltos's absence was that he was in prison. Born Paltogou on 21 July 1940 of Greek parents, he came to Australia in 1947. His father died while he was young and he worked as an apprentice in a metal factory and drove a cab to support his family until he was encouraged by Joe Taylor, of Thommo's Two-up

School, to study. He qualified as a doctor in 1968 and became head of the casualty department at Sydney hospital. By 1976 his voice was turning up on intercepts of George Freeman. In 1978 he resigned from the hospital and set up practice in Woolloomooloo. Apart from Freeman his distinguished clientele included not only the magnate Kerry Packer, the chief justice and the entertainer Sir Harry Secombe, but also Farquhar, McPherson and the drug dealer Robert 'Aussie Bob' Trimbole. The latter combination was his final undoing.

After Trimbole fled to Ireland, Paltos assumed his role as a key figure in the Australian drug trade. Trimbole may still have made the decisions from abroad but Paltos was his willing lieutenant. By the time Paltos organised his final ruinous shipment in October 1983 the dapper figure pictured at the Randwick races with Freeman had long since blown up into a balloon. He was in debt to solicitor Ross Karp to the tune of $300000, hopelessly overweight, chain smoking and, worst of all, talking too much.

The end for Paltos, Karp and their offsider Graeme 'Croc' Palmer came with the anchoring, about 80 kilometres out of Darwin, of the 12-metre trawler the *Moray* on 23 February 1984. Some 1400 bags of Lebanese Gold had been unloaded from a mother ship, the *Gulf Frio*, which was then scuttled. Palmer was among the men who met the *Moray* as it sailed to an inlet north of Darwin, where its cargo was loaded into lorries and driven to Sydney. Stephen Nittes, the Painter and Docker from the Mayne-Nickless robbery, was used as an enforcer and drug distributor. The police, who had kept the load under observation throughout, swooped. In March 1986 Paltos received twenty years for conspiracy to import drugs, Karp and Palmer were both sentenced to fourteen years and, for his part in the deal, Nittes received seven years.

Freeman's death rather left Lennie McPherson holding the Mr Big title. He had mostly kept out of the limelight for much of the 1960s and 1970s, since the Moffitt Commission and Ducky

O'Connor's death at the gangster's table in the Latin Quarter nightclub. In 1973 McPherson was once more before Murray Farquhar, this time charged with being in possession of money extorted from the Pussy Galore nightclub in Kings Cross. Helpfully, Farquhar was not convinced that the $400 found on McPherson had indeed come from the club. He was acquitted.

As the years went by McPherson became more and more recognised as a leading figure in the Sydney underworld. In 1977, on a visit with two others to Manila, he was arrested—because, he maintained, the Australian police had sent advance warning that he was there to assassinate President Marcos—and he spent three days on death row in Fort Benefacio prison before being released.

The next year he changed his name to avoid unwanted attention. He became Leonard Murray, but his alter ego was short-lived and he soon reverted to his real name. By this time the press was seriously on his tail, as indeed were the politicians. In 1980 the Woodward Commission reported that perhaps McPherson had gone to Manila not to assassinate Marcos but rather to look after his interests there. The commission suggested that a wanted criminal, Martin Olsen, was his man in Manila, running his bar and looking after his prostitutes. It was also suggested that, during 1975, someone in the company of Danny Stein and George Freeman had been bringing back 'white powder' for McPherson, something he denied.

McPherson's final court appearance ended in 1992 with a sentence of four years for paying $20 000 to have the former general manager of his nephew's importing company beaten up. There had been a dispute when the man left, taking a substantial client with him—standard business practice, but it did not seem that way to McPherson. The beating was organised by strip-club owner Kostas Kontorinakis, known as Con Kostas. In a separate trial Kostas was imprisoned but the case against McPherson was endlessly delayed. McPherson dragged things out as long as possible and in the meantime took the opportunity to ingratiate himself with potential character witnesses by visiting a hostel for down-and-outs. A plea bargain was turned down by the prosecution and it seems that at the trial McPherson feigned illness, nodding off to sleep in the witness box. Neither the hostel visiting nor the illness benefited him, and he went to prison a broken man.

McPherson died in the recreation room of Cessnock jail on 28 August 1996. He had been speaking to his wife on the telephone when he collapsed with a heart attack. Aged seventy-five, he was due for parole the following year. At his funeral his daughter Janelle Olive told the congregation, which included many old friends and some relatively new ones (among them nightclub owners Sam and John Ibrahim), that her father had 'chosen a path in life that you or I might not have chosen but at least he was at the very top of his profession.' McPherson is interred in a mausoleum at the Field of Mars Cemetery, Ryde. The magnificent tomb is thought to have cost some $50 000. The full extent of his very substantial estate remains a close secret.

Tim Bristow—one-time police officer, casual journalist, private detective and sometime friend of McPherson (who refused to acknowledge the association)—died following a stroke in Pittwater on 10 February 2003. He was a major standover man in the building industry and gave evidence to the inquiry into corrupt practices. Once he explained the death of a union man who fell off a building as 'You can't help bad luck.' Bristow employed Jack 'Mr Fixit' Cooper, also known as 'Mad Dog' Williams—who was still on parole—to 'settle down' the industrial scene on behalf of Civil and Civic Properties. The Royal Commission into the building industry was told that, when action was taken to sack him, Cooper simply pulled a gun on a site superintendent at St Vincent's Hospital. A small-time identity with a liking for ballroom dancing, Cooper was shot and killed in a car park in Chinatown on 2 May 1991.

In 1976 Bristow was sentenced to eighteen months for assault and in the 1980s served five years for supplying cannabis. A more than marginal figure in the Milieu, he told a Royal Commission that a number of police had thrown him forty-nine packets of drugs from a window in the Chatsworth detectives' office; he caught them in a towel and drove away in his Mercedes with the booty. He was also a witness at the long-running inquest into the death of hitman Chris Flannery, where Justice Don Stewart, who had served with Bristow in the police, described him as 'a lumbering half-wit' and a 'nightmare'.

McPherson's passing really left only the reclusive Abe Saffron, who died in 2006, and Stan 'The Man' Smith as the last of the working old-timers—Karl Bonnette had rather faded away into respectability. Smith died in 2010. He had experienced some personal tragedy when, in 1979, his son Stan died of a drug overdose; some weeks later the body of a North Shore drug dealer was found at Narrabeen Lakes. He had been run over several times. Some seven years before his death, Smith apparently found religion, joining an Evangelical church and starting to read the Bible. Whether he had completed the Good Book by the time of his death goes unrecorded. Bonnette is now the last surviving member of the Double Bay meeting.

War in the 1980s

8

It was not until the Vietnam War, when Sydney was used as a home for servicemen on R&R, that the heroin trade really took off in Australia. Now there were drugs to go along with the booze and steaks served by Maurice 'Bernie' Houghton—shadowy CIA agent and Lennie McPherson offsider—at Harpoon Harry's, Texas Tavern, and the Bourbon and Beefsteak bar and restaurant in Kings Cross. But as late as 1966, with only a handful of known addicts in the country, drug possession and importation was a very low priority for the New South Wales Drug Squad.

It was a police officer who was among the first to take advantage of the vacuum. That year John Wesley Egan masterminded a high-grade heroin smuggling ring. A fine swimmer commended for his lifesaving, he was a member of the Police Underwater Diving Squad, which was asked by the Customs Department to try to recover some gold ingots thrown overboard by Chinese seamen. He duly located them but taped a number to a pylon for later personal recovery. After that Egan began smuggling watches, transistors and cameras which, he later claimed, were mainly sold to police officers. An unfortunate sale to a customs official blew the lid off the scheme and five officers resigned. It was then that Egan was introduced to the possibilities of heroin smuggling by a man connected to the Painters and Dockers, and he determined to make a million dollars inside three months then retire.

He learned of a potential customer, an ex-CIA agent in New York, borrowed money for home improvements, obtained compassionate leave to attend the funeral of an aunt in California and booked a flight to New York on Qantas with a kilo of almost pure heroin. He made $6000 from the run and was now up and flying. Four months later he resigned from the Special Branch and began a full-time career organising drug smuggling.

On that first run Egan wore a special vest that he had made for the purpose and now all his couriers—officers on leave from the New South Wales Police paid $2000 a run—were similarly kitted out, earning the group the name the Corset Gang. Six months later, with twenty couriers operating, he was netting $80 000 a week. The couriers were sent to Hong Kong, where they collected the drugs, which were then flown to the United States via London, Tokyo and New Delhi.

Egan's downfall came after a tip-off that there was to be a raid. He flew to Hong Kong to tell New Zealander Glenn Reid, in charge of buying from Chinese suppliers, to suspend operations. Unfortunately Reid kept 2 kilograms of heroin and, when he was arrested in Honolulu, he shelved Egan and arranged to set him up. Egan skipped bail, went to England and was arrested in Paris three years later. Extradited to the United States, he served just under half of an eight-year sentence. Back in Australia, Egan retired to the Gold Coast where in 1978 he was fined $1500 for illegal gambling. As sociologist Alfred McCoy points out, the exercise revealed the capacity for corruption within the New South Wales Police. Its tolerance for that corruption paved the way for a level of drug trafficking that would have astounded even Egan.

The first killing linked to the Australian heroin trade seems to have been that of the relatively small-time dealer and user Jan O'Truba. He became addicted at the age of fifteen while at school and in 1971 was arrested after breaking into a pharmacy. On his release he began to deal on at least a semi-professional basis but he was also willing to cheat his customers. On the day he died he was peddling heroin capsules at $20 each—friends said he had bought an ounce for $450 from a New South Wales detective. On 2 September 1972 his body was found against a tree on an embankment off the Wakehurst Parkway in Oxford Falls. He had been shot in the head three times with a .32 pistol. Despite a $10 000 reward, no charges were ever brought.

The next death was that of the much higher profile, 24-year-old fashion designer Maria Anne Hisshion, lover of solicitors, models and criminals, who lived in Rose Bay and was a darling of the drug users known as the Windsor Castle Set. On Christmas Eve 1975 Hisshion had dinner with her mother and was never seen alive again. Her body surfaced off North Head two weeks later and was identified through her jewellery. She had been shot in the head with a .32 bullet and tied to an anchor. Ten days later Barry Pyne, an associate of a group of dealers known as the Double Bay Mob, refused to answer any police questions about the suggestion he had borrowed a boat on the night of her disappearance. He was later said to have left Australia. It seems that Hisshion had become involved in the heroin trade reluctantly and wanted out.

After the deaths of O'Truba and Hisshion the killings came thick and fast. On 18 May 1979 the bodies of Douglas and Isabel Wilson were found in a shallow grave in Rye, Victoria. They had both been shot. They were two of the victims of Terrence Clark, otherwise known as Alexander James Sinclair, in his bid to eliminate leakage in his Mr Asia drug importing syndicate. On 9 June 1978 the Wilsons had been arrested by the Queensland Police in Brisbane and, although they were never charged, they spent some time providing information on tape about the workings of the Clark organisation. Through a dishonest solicitor's clerk, Brian Alexander, Clark purchased copies of the tapes for $25 000 and that was the end of the Wilsons. They were killed by James Bazley, also convicted in 1986 of the June 1977 killing of anti-drug campaigner Donald Mackay.

Also among Clark's victims, killed personally by him or ordered killed by him, were 'Pommy' Harry Lewis, Gregory Ollard, Julie Theilman and—the most high profile of them—Christopher Martin 'Marty' Johnstone, a founding member of the 'Mr Asia' syndicate, which imported and exported drugs worldwide.

Harry Lewis, on bail for drugs charges, reported to Customs House at Circular Quay on 21 May 1978 and was never seen again. It was believed he had gone with Clark to Queensland where he was killed within a few days. His remains were found in scrubland near Port Macquarie. Greg Ollard, another heroin dealer who was too keen on his own product, was shot in September 1977. He had refused a buy-out offer from Clark, who then simply eliminated potential opposition. His body was not located until 16 August 1982, when his remains were found in Ku-ring-gai Chase National Park. Three days earlier the remains of Julie Theilman, his girlfriend and a one-time brothel keeper, were excavated at Mount Victoria in the Blue Mountains. She had been shot in the chest.

Clark was born in New Zealand in November 1944 and began seriously dealing in cannabis at the age of thirty. Johnstone was then his supplier. The next year he bought a boat, the *Catana*, to bring heroin out of South-East Asia and by the end of 1977 he had become a major importer into Sydney with a distribution network across Australia. Johnstone, who was thought to have been the leader of the organisation, was in fact merely an executive officer and a dishonest one at that. For some months he had been skimming up to $100000 to set up his own organisation. He had also fallen out with the syndicate's Singapore supplier, Choo Cheng Kui, or Jackie Choo.

In 1979 Clark sent Johnstone to London and then on to Scotland under the pretext that there was a deal to be set up in Glasgow. With him, on 9 October, went Andrew Maher and a James Smith. Maher had already acquired ropes, weights and an axe. At Eccleston Delph, a flooded quarry in Lancashire, Maher asked Johnstone to take over the driving and, as they changed places, shot him twice in the head. Johnstone's hands were cut off but Maher forgot to remove a pendant with a Chinese 'long-life' symbol. The body was rolled into the water but caught on a ledge. Some five days later it was found by members of a sub-aqua club and Johnstone was identified through the pendant. After a 112-day trial Clark and Maher were convicted at Lancaster Crown Court and sentenced to life imprisonment. During the trial, held in the cavernous and draughty Lancaster Castle, one of the defendants complained he was cold. 'Not nearly as cold as Mr Johnstone,' remarked prosecuting counsel.

Clark died in Parkhurst Prison on the Isle of Wight after a heart attack. It was suggested he had been taking drugs in the hope he would be transferred to an outside hospital and so increase his chances of an escape. However Justice Stewart, who interviewed him in the prison during his Royal Commission inquiries, believed Clark might have informed on the IRA and that prisoners in Parkhurst had secured him with strips of blanket—so there would be no bruising—while someone sat on his chest until he died of heart failure.

Ten years after the deaths of Hisshion and O'Truba there was a full-scale drugs war in Sydney and reports that five gangs were struggling for control of both clubs and drugs in Kings Cross. Two gangs were said to be controlled by Chinese, another by Irish union toughs and the fourth by central Europeans. The fifth and most dangerous was controlled by a Melbourne hitman, Christopher 'Mr Rent-a-Kill' Flannery, thought to have been responsible for fourteen shootings.

In 1987 a witness at Flannery's inquest told the coroner that the line-up of gangs was slightly different. Roger Ford (a pseudonym—his name was suppressed by the coroner Greg Glass), the former right-hand man of bookmaker and dealer Barry McCann, claimed that there were only three main gangs. One was the famous alliance between Arthur 'Neddy' Smith and Detective Sergeant Roger

Rogerson, another was the Freeman–McPherson combination and the third an assortment of standover men including McCann, Tom Domican, Roy Thurgar and Vic Camilleri. Flannery, said Ford, was simply operating as an independent hitman in Sydney, available to the highest bidder.

Just who were all these new players? The greatly underrated McCann had operated a small illegal casino in Wollongong, which he closed after the death of Charles 'Chicka' Reeves—a murder of which McCann was rightly suspected, according to Neddy Smith. He then ran a small hotel in Kings Cross and began dealing in heroin in the early 1980s. McCann had almost certainly been involved in the 1985 death of another Sydney heroin dealer, his one-time partner Michael John Sayers, suspected of devising the Fine Cotton ring-in, and later an SP bookmaker and drug supplier to the Kings Cross clientele. The next year McCann was charged with harbouring an unknown gunman who shot and wounded Chris Flannery. The charge was dismissed but this led to fears in the underworld that he was a National Crime Authority informer.

Flannery, born in 1949, was a schoolboy swimming champion, had a tattoo, 'Lunchtime', on his stomach with an arrow pointing to his groin and a very changeable temper. He began his career as a basher and worked upwards. In October 1981 he was acquitted of the February 1980 murder of businessman Roger Wilson, whose body was never found, for which he was said to have been paid $35 000. One problem for the prosecution had been the disappearance of a key witness, Debbie Boundy, thought to have been killed in Melbourne by Painter and Docker Trevor 'Stretch' Anderson. As he left the court Flannery was arrested and charged with another murder, this time of Raymond Locksley, a Sydney massage parlour standover man, on 11 May 1979. After a retrial he was acquitted and became a hired hoon for George Freeman.

Career criminal Arthur Stanley 'Neddy' Smith had served a twelve-year sentence for a particularly violent rape. On 14 June

1967 he, Robert Arthur Chapman and two other men raped a young mother after they broke into her home. They threatened to kill her young child if she screamed and then to firebomb her place if she reported the matter. Smith was released on parole in March 1975 and in November the next year was arrested by Detective Roger Rogerson and charged with shooting with intent to murder, attempted armed robbery and possession of an unlicensed pistol. Eventually he was acquitted of all charges. It was then that he formed a close association with Rogerson and became his informer.

Smith had a wide variety of friends, including James White and Neville Biber, two members of the old Kangaroo Gang (White later disappeared and Biber was found dead in suspicious circumstances), Rugby league player Paul Hayward and heroin courier Warren Fellows, as well as a senior clerk in the prison service. As a result of a tap on Smith's telephones in the late 1970s the police learned that he was organising a heroin importation from Thailand. Hayward and Fellows were arrested and convicted there. Another of Smith's acquaintances, William Sinclair, friend of the disgraced ex-policeman Murray Riley, was acquitted on appeal. Smith himself was arrested on 12 October 1978 in Sydney and charged with conspiracy to import heroin. His brother Teddy Smith was later arrested; he pleaded guilty and became a Crown witness. It was not a success. Blood or fear was thicker than water; he retracted his evidence and on the second day of the trial the judge directed Neddy Smith's acquittal.

Smith had been returned to prison to serve out the remainder of his rape sentence and there he met Warren Charles Lanfranchi. Smith was released in October 1980 and Lanfranchi two months later. Meanwhile Rogerson had become the blue-eyed boy of the New South Wales Police, following, in almost every way, in the footsteps of Ray Kelly.

As for the standover alliance, Tom Domican, who was born in Ireland in 1943 and had been a bouncer in London, where he served a sentence for breaking and entering, came to Australia in 1968. In July 1980 he was seeking Labor pre-selection for Marrickville Council but he withdrew six weeks later. A fortnight after that he was charged with conspiracy and forgery, but the charges were dismissed in May 1982. Domican, along with career criminal Roy Thurgar, was acquitted of conspiracy to murder prison official Ron Woodham. Thurgar was later shot and killed at Randwick in July 1991. Domican's friend Vic Camilleri was more fortunate. He survived a shooting on 3 April 1985 at Kingsgrove.

The body count in this particular war totalled either eight or nine, depending who was counting. Two of the earlier victims were Brett David Hanslow, killed at Neutral Bay on 13 February 1983, and Kevin Arthur Browne, who was shot on 28 March that year. The hitman who killed these two drug dealers was thought to be Emil Rusnak, acting on the orders of Francis Michael Salvietti (also known as 'Stapp'), then one of Sydney's biggest independent heroin suppliers. Rusnak was himself shot and killed by the police as he interrupted their search of his house at Homebush. He had been suspected of sending a letter bomb to the Kings Cross restaurateur Stephen Novak. In turn Salvietti was shot at point-blank range in the back of the head at Concord on 19 March 1985. A Melbourne man, Stephen Allan Smith, was extradited for Salvietti's murder and convicted after a retrial. In 1977 he had received six years in Queensland for stealing in company while armed and, in December 1982, ten years for armed robbery. He had only been released two months prior to Salvietti's murder. The pair had quarrelled over the proceeds of the armed robberies for which Smith had done time and Salvietti had held the money. Smith received life imprisonment for Salvietti's murder, which was later reduced to seventeen years with a minimum of twelve and a half pre-parole.

Among the other casualties was Danny Chubb, killed on 8 November 1984. Chubb, known as 'The Brain', was shot dead at Millers Point as he left his new Jaguar carrying fish and chips for his mother's lunch. He had just completed another successful $2 million heroin collection from a group of Chinese businessmen. It was big money then but now this amount would rate him as little more than a bit player. At one time he had been the working partner of bookmaker Michael Sayers. They had split up and for a time Chubb worked with Nick Paltos until the good doctor went to prison. After that he worked with Brian McCauley, who was later sentenced to nineteen years in prison for drug trafficking. No charges were ever brought over Chubb's killing but it is generally accepted that the reason for his death was financial rather than personal. He was thought to have been owed more than $1 million by his distributors. Suspects have included Michael Sayers, Chris Flannery and Barry McCann, as well as everybody's perennial favourite Neddy Smith, who flatly denied any involvement.

On 17 August 1984 Frank Hing, one-time bus conductor and more lately the $1 million purchaser of the Goulburn Club from George Ziziros Walker (Police Commissioner Mervyn Wood's offsider), was attacked in the Empress Coffee Lounge, Kings Cross. Hing had come to Australia in 1973 and was named in parliament as an influential member of the Triads. George Freeman, Branco Balic and Tony Torok were arrested but Freeman was correct in his boastful prediction that no one would identify him and he was duly acquitted. The next year the premises were damaged by fire. The Empress reopened in December as the Wong Sing Kee restaurant and Rose's nightclub.

In January 1985 Flannery, his wife and children were sprayed with bullets from an Armalite rifle as they stood outside their home in Arncliffe. Happily, no one was hit. Three years later Tom Domican was charged with the attempted murder and sentenced to fourteen years' imprisonment. In 1992 the conviction was quashed and Domican was not required to stand trial again.

On 16 February 1985 Michael John Sayers, who had been using Chubb as his distributor, was killed. Sayers, a great gambler and now sampling his own product, had ripped off Barry McCann in a drug deal. He was on his way home to Hewlett Street, Bronte, when he was shot with a .22 rifle. A second man then shot him with a .357 Magnum. In 1988 Tom Domican, Vic Camilleri and Kevin Theobald were charged. They were all found not guilty.

In an effort to settle matters down, a meeting was called on 1 April 1985 by Louis Bayeh, the Lebanese-born sidekick of Lennie McPherson. Present at his home were Neddy Smith, Roger Rogerson, McPherson, the corrupt Detective Sergeant Bill Duff and possibly Flannery. It produced no great result because, on 3 April, Vic Camilleri survived a shooting at Kingsgrove and later that month, on 23 April, Anthony 'Liverpool Tony' Eustace, one of Flannery's close friends, was gunned down in Arncliffe as he sat in his gold Mercedes-Benz. Eustace, also known as 'Spaghetti', operated Tony's Bar and Grill in Double Bay. This time money was thicker than friendship. The killer was said to be Flannery, acting on behalf of George Freeman.

Flannery, by now a completely loose cannon said to charge $50 000 a job, was the next to go and the circumstances of his disappearance occupied Sydney's courts on and off for the better part of a decade. He was so hated and feared in the underworld that any of six people, including George Freeman and Lennie McPherson, could have been involved in his death. If anything is clear about his disappearance, it is that he was last seen on 9 May 1985 when, according to his wife Kathleen, he told her he was going to visit Freeman at his home at Yowie Bay. One reason for the visit was to pick up new weaponry supplied by McPherson. Flannery had with him a passport and a .38 pistol. It is possible he went to the airport; a taxi driver claimed that he took a very nervous Flannery there that afternoon.

Most of the conflicting theories are that he was killed either by the underworld or by the police; shot by a police officer at the Geelong racetrack; lured to Sydney Harbour and killed with a machine gun; shot by police at traffic lights; buried at sea; killed at a hide-out in Connaught; buried in Sydney's western suburbs; or killed by a biker and fed through a tree-shredder. Then there is a minority Lord Lucan–JFK theory that he was still alive a decade later. Possibly the best suggestion comes from ex-police officer turned author Clive Small, who believes that the only way to end the drug war in Sydney was to have Flannery eliminated and that Freeman and McPherson told McCann that, as an act of good faith, they would have it done. What is absolutely clear is that while the heroin war killings did not completely cease with Flannery's disappearance, there was a much greater survival rate among the remaining combatants.

One who probably did not survive was Flannery's close friend Laurie Prendergast. It is suggested that he and Flannery, who used to alibi each other for the various killings they undertook, botched the shooting of Tom Domican in early 1985. Prendergast disappeared in August that year. Neddy Smith has it that he was lured into a police car and driven away. In any event his wife found his car in the driveway with the driver's door open. In 1990 an inquest returned an open verdict. It was thought he might have faked his disappearance rather than face questioning over a number of murders, but the better view is that members of the Sydney underworld disposed of him when he came seeking revenge for the death of Flannery. After all, as Jackie 'Iron Man' Steele had found, the underworld was never averse to dressing up as police officers.

One who did survive was Neddy Smith himself. On 2 April 1986 he was run over outside his own hotel, the Iron Duke in Waterloo, managed by the now ex-police officer Bill Duff. Smith sustained broken ribs and a broken leg. An ex-boxer, Terrence Edwin Ball, was charged with his attempted murder and found not guilty.

Another who did not survive was Barry McCann, found dead near a lavatory block in Marrickville in December 1987. Recently

McCann had been importing drugs from Singapore, sending suitcases of drugs back to Australia as unaccompanied baggage which was passed through customs by a tame officer. McCann's fatal mistake was to deal in heroin with George Savvas, a one-time Marrickville council member. As Savvas's former associate Dr Peter Papapetros discovered when he tried to claim $160 000, Savvas was a dangerous man to know let alone do business with. The doctor's practice was firebombed and he left the country. Even public figures were not immune. When a Marrickville councillor suggested on television that Savvas should resign from the council, his car was firebombed within hours. When Savvas was on trial for fraud, one of the witnesses, Joseph Magros, was shot dead. Savvas was duly acquitted.

The arrangement between Savvas and McCann had been to sell some 3 kilograms of heroin in Melbourne but instead Savvas sold it in Sydney, undercutting McCann's normal distribution price. McCann announced he would be taking reprisals. On 27 December 1987 he went to an evening meeting at the HJ Mahoney Reserve. He was seen there at about nine o'clock by an off-duty detective walking with his wife and dog. Next morning McCann's body was found face down on a bench. He had been shot repeatedly.

In 1988 Savvas was charged with McCann's murder and conspiracy to import heroin. The immediate reason for McCann's death, alleged the prosecution, was that Savvas knew his partner was out to kill him and he needed to get in first. After a ten-week trial he was acquitted of the murder on the direction of the judge but was later sentenced to twenty-five years for heroin trafficking. In 1998, after an unsuccessful escape attempt, he hanged himself in his cell.

Another of the standover alliance, Roy Thurgar, was killed in Randwick on 20 May 1991. He was shot at point-blank range in the throat as he stood waiting for his wife outside their home in Alison Road. Garry Nye, a man with various convictions, including one for armed robbery, was arrested on the word of police informer and major con artist Danny Shakespeare, who once claimed to have shot Osama bin Laden in the foot while working for the SAS. Shakespeare, who gave completely specious evidence at the Flannery inquest, was a man known to supply false evidence to the police and one entry on his file read, 'He is an extremely convincing liar.' Shakespeare did not convince the jury. Nye was acquitted the following year and a decade later, when dying from cancer, was awarded $1.3 million for malicious prosecution.

The Roy Thurgar case never completely went away and there were suggestions the police might reopen it after the 1998 discovery of a shotgun that was forensically linked to the death of Sydney identity Desmond Anthony Lewis outside his home in Bondi Junction in 1992. It was also linked to two home invasions that took place some years later and to one of the top, if generally underrated, faces of the last thirty years, Robert Douglas 'Bertie' Kidd.

Until the end of the 1990s Kidd had only one conviction of any note: in May 1983 he was sentenced to four years' hard labour. Then, in his middle-sixties, Kidd led what might be called the Great Grandfather Gang and became a little careless. In July 1997 a raid on a Manly hotelier's home produced $275000 in cash and jewellery and, two months later, a raid on a Sydney motor dealer's home in Burraneer Bay netted another $14000 worth of jewellery. The next year the shotgun was found at the home of another veteran, Eric Leonard Murray, who was alleged to have been the driver in the raids.

In March 1999, in Brisbane, Kidd was sentenced to eleven years for striking with a projectile to prevent lawful arrest and in July 2004, then aged seventy-one, he was jailed for a minimum of twelve years for his part in the home invasions. Murray, two years his senior, was sentenced to three years for possession of the shotgun. Throughout the trial Kidd denied he had ever used the gun.

Right: Lennie McPherson,
the one-time Mr Big of
Sydney, was labelled as
a fizz in *Oz* magazine.
(© NEWSPIX/NEWS LTD)

Below: Writer Richard
Neville, editor of *Oz*,
who so upset McPherson
that Mr Big paid him
an unannounced visit.
(© NEWSPIX/NEWS LTD)

Left: Sydney hardman Chow Hayes is arrested by Detective Ray Kelly over the shooting of Bobby Lee in July 1951.
(© NEWSPIX/NEWS LTD)

Below: Abe Saffron's Ziegfeld Club the morning after the night before.
(COURTESY NSW POLICE FORENSIC PHOTOGRAPHY ARCHIVE, JUSTICE & POLICE MUSEUM, HISTORIC HOUSES TRUST)

Right: One of the great brothel keepers of the 1920s, the English-born Tilly Devine.
(© NEWSPIX/NEWS LTD)

Right: One of the most beautiful gangster molls of the 1920s, 'Pretty' Dulcie Markham, also known as The Black Widow because of the premature deaths of many of her lovers.
(© NEWSPIX/NEWS LTD)

Above: Kings Cross drug dealers the Bayeh brothers, Bill (left) and Louis (right). Louis is leaving Glebe Coroner's Court, where he refused to answer questions over the death of hitman Chris Flannery. (© NEWSPIX/STUART RAMSON, © NEWSPIX/BRENDAN ESPOSITO))

Left: Following his death, a bust of Bernie Houghton—CIA agent, restaurateur and friend of Lennie McPherson—was controversially unveiled in a park in Kings Cross. (COURTESY DOCK BATESON)

Above: Nightclub owner
John Ibrahim, the current
and undoubted king of
the Cross.
(© NEWSPIX/NEWS LTD)

Right: Abe Saffron, who
died in 2006, was king of
the Sydney club scene for
more than fifty years.
(© NEWSPIX/NEWS LTD)

Left: Disgraced former detective Roger Rogerson is released from Long Bay.
(© NEWSPIX/NEWS LTD)

Below: Bandidos arriving at the funeral of their members at Rookwood Cemetery after the Milperra Massacre.
(© NEWSPIX/IAN MAINSBRIDGE)

Sex and the Sydney Citizen

9

While 1860s Sydney might not have had the palatial premises of some of Melbourne's brothels, prostitutes of the time were still hard at work. A pupil of the late Professor John Woolley, conducting a rudimentary survey in 1873, found that prostitutes were mainly:

> women who have been in a state of menial servitude; and who
> from the love of idleness and dress, together with the misfortune
> of good looks, in some instances, have mostly from inclination
> resorted to prostitution for a livelihood ... girls were corrupted
> by idle and frivolous habits encouraged or contracted on board
> ship when not subjected to the most careful supervision.

His research showed that two or three girls would take a house together in Woolloomooloo or live in a boarding house run by a retired whore. Prostitutes mainly worked at the Prince of Wales Theatre before it was burnt down, at Belmore markets on Saturday nights, the Domain Gardens on Sunday afternoons and George Street on Sunday nights. Elizabeth Street provided an easy escape across the racecourse after they had robbed their clients. Some were as young as twelve; many were diseased. He also found there was a certain amount of homosexual prostitution, with a degree of cross-dressing. Then, as now, many of the city's cabmen worked hand-in-hand with the prostitutes.

New South Wales was late to implement prostitution-specific laws. Only in 1908 was the Police Offences (Amendment) Act passed. This criminalised soliciting, a male living on the earnings of prostitution, brothel keeping and leasing premises for the purposes of prostitution. Ironically, these legislative changes had almost the opposite effect of that intended, changing prostitution from a free-wheeling trade to an industry in which the girls were controlled by organised crime. The dynamics of prostitution changed and many prostitutes were forced to work in houses owned by criminal networks. Throughout the 1920s and 1930s prostitution was inexorably linked with sly-grog and cocaine traders.

Most of the immigrant Italian population of the era arrived in Australia in the 1920s and totalled well over 40 000 by the end of the decade. From the moment of their arrival they were blamed for most things criminal—demanding with menaces, living off immoral earnings, theft. However, the historian and author Richard Evans regards the suggestion of early organised Italian crime in Australia as an overrated concept. He believes that, at a time when the White Australia policy was an article of faith, the local population was bigoted and hostile towards a conspicuously male-dominated society in which few were married and most were law-abiding.

The Italians were also accused of running the white slave traffic for the benefit of the cane field workers in New South Wales, but they were not the only ones. *Smith's Weekly* ran an experiment, taking three girls to Chinatown to sell. Naturally, the reporters were obliged to witness scenes of degrading bargaining before they took the girls away unsold. What the girls had to say about things went unrecorded.

After World War I Kate Leigh and Tilly Devine may have been Sydney's brothel queens, but they were, putting it kindly, plain-looking. The two good-time girls who were stunningly attractive were 'Pretty' Dulcie Markham—described by the *Daily Mirror* as having seen 'more violence and death than any other woman in Australia's history' — and the flame-haired Nellie Cameron.

In all, eight of Markham's lovers died from either the gun or the knife. On her death the *Sydney Morning Herald* wrote rather charmingly, if ingenuously, that she had never been a prostitute; rather she had been a gangster's moll. A girl with the looks and poise of a model, from a respectable family, she was working the Kings Cross area before she was sixteen.

The first of her lovers to go was Cecil William 'Scotchy' McCormack. He wooed the eighteen-year-old Dulcie away from another standover man, the 21-year-old Alfred Dillon, whose mother ran what was euphemistically called a 'residential' in George Street. With McCormack promptly sentenced to six months for consorting with criminals — he ran a fruit stall with Guido Calletti — Dillon reasserted his charm. By 13 May 1931, McCormack had reclaimed his 'property' and that evening Dillon stabbed him in the heart with a stiletto in Darlinghurst. Dillon ran an alibi defence, and in September a first jury failed to agree. Then, acquitted of murder on 2 December, Dillon received thirteen years for manslaughter. Dulcie had done what she could for him, suggesting that McCormack had been in a quarrel with 'some Germans' and no, there was no reason for the men to be jealous of each other. Dillon's mother, Catherine Scurry, was unhappy with the sentence, telling the judge, 'I've done no harm and my child has done no harm. Why should I have to suffer judgement like this?' As a mark of respect, for a time Dulcie went about her business wearing a black wig. Dillon was released in October 1937. Time dulls official memory. The reason given for the early release was that McCormack had stood over Dillon's mother.

The next of her lovers to go was Arthur Kingsley Taplin (known as 'The Egg'), shot in a bar in Swanston Street, Melbourne. A peripatetic Sydney standover man, Taplin took over as Markham's pimp when she was working in a Melbourne brothel. He had no longer a life than her other lovers. Taplin was acquitted in 1933 of the attempted murder of Cedric Maher and on 15 December 1937 was in the Cosmopolitan Hotel with two friends when they began to stand over hairdresser Harcourt Lee, persuading him to buy them drinks. When Taplin threatened Lee, smashing a beer glass on his head, the hairdresser drew a gun and shot The Egg. Three days later an announcement that he was out of danger proved premature. He cracked and died on 22 December. On 16 March the next year Lee was acquitted. He claimed that he thought Taplin was about to draw a gun on him and so he used his own. After all, hairdressers often need to carry guns.

Dulcie was back in Sydney with Guido Calletti, said to have been connected with the city's Black Hand, when he was shot and killed at a birthday party held by the Brougham Street gang in August 1939. She had already married the mobster Frank Bowen, but the relationship did not last. He was shot dead in Kings Cross in 1940.

Markham had the particular ability of making men fight over her. In June of that year she took a trip to Melbourne with Paddles Anderson and it was there that another boyfriend, John Charles Abraham, was shot and killed. Anderson was acquitted of the murder but Markham was locked up on a vagrancy charge.

During the war she went to Queensland with her new de facto, Arthur Williams, who actually survived the association. In 1944 she defeated another vagrancy charge, claiming that she had been living with Williams for some six years—subject to interludes with Calletti, Anderson and others—and that, when they came to Brisbane, Williams had 600 pounds and he gave her money for the rent and groceries. She did not know the money came from sly-grog selling. In July 1945, back in Sydney, he was jailed for eighteen months for receiving 3107 ration cards and 1848 clothing coupons. Rather ungallantly, Williams attributed his lapse to his association with Markham, which had led him into bad company.

On 27 November 1944 Markham shot a soldier at her home in Liverpool Road, East Sydney. She took him to hospital and, despite the police finding his blood on her bed, said she had come across him in the Domain and, good Samaritan that she was, had tried to help. It all passed off nicely.

In January 1945 it was the turn of major-league standover man Donny 'The Duck' Day, who was shot and killed in a quarrel in Sydney. Back in Melbourne, in September, down went her standover man lover Leslie Ernest 'Scotland Yard' Walkerden. There followed six years of relative calm until in September 1951 two men burst into her home in Fawcett Street, St Kilda, where she was drinking with Gavan Walsh and his brother Desmond. All three were shot, she in the spine, but only Gavan died. The quarrel had been over some missing bail money, which had been held by Walsh. She was carried into court only to fail to identify the killers.

In December she married Leonard 'Redda' Lewis and they returned to Sydney where, despite the fact he was her husband, she was promptly jailed for seven days for consorting with a known criminal. Back in Melbourne in April 1952, Lewis was shot six times after opening the door of his parents' flat in Prahran. The gunmen returned an hour later and shot at the constable who was now guarding the flat. Apparently the incident was to persuade Lewis to return to Sydney. Three men were suspected of being involved in the shooting and the former boxer Meredith Hamilton, an offsider of major Melbourne identity Jack Twist, was charged with wounding with intent. But by the time the case came for trial Lewis was in smoke and, in June, Hamilton was discharged. Lewis was shot again in June the following year, this time in the back, but again he survived, which was more than he could say for the marriage.

At Markham's last court appearance, in 1957, her looks were described simply as 'gone' and at the end of her life she married a seaman. On 20 April 1976 she went to bed, lit a cigarette and, in turn, the bedding. She died from asphyxiation. She was sixty-three.

Although they shared the same lover in Guido Calletti (if not others), Nellie Cameron and Dulcie Markham never seemed to share the same enmity as Tilly Devine and Kate Leigh. Described as a 'filly who could easily run at Randwick', Cameron came from a good North Shore family. This did not stop her from becoming a prostitute at the age of fifteen in Surry Hills and Woolloomooloo, or being known as another Black Widow. For a time she also taught dancing at Professor Bolot's Academy in Oxford Street, around the corner from Sargents' pie factory.

After her brief fling with Norman Bruhn ended with his death in 1927, Cameron took up with both Guido Calletti and standover man Frank Green, who regularly fought over her. One battle in Woolloomooloo was said to have been watched by a crowd of 500 and ended only when both men were exhausted. In her turn, Cameron was a good girl with her fists. Said to be able to punch like a man, she easily saw off the much heavier 'Black Aggie' when they fought over the rights to a two-block stretch of Darlinghurst.

The Green–Calletti–Cameron triangle was the stuff of which whole television soap series could be made. A major standover man in Woolloomooloo whose career began at the age of nine when he was ruled to be an uncontrollable child, Calletti had appeared in the courts nearly sixty times, in three states, by the time of his death. On 16 November 1931 Cameron was shot in the shoulder but naturally she refused to identify her attacker. She was walking home with Billy Ralph and Ivy Rasmussen after visiting Frank Green in hospital. With Calletti in prison and out of the way, Green had temporarily become the man in her life but he had been shot in the stomach a few weeks earlier. The next year she received a two-month sentence for consorting with known criminals, including Green, becoming the first woman convicted under the new laws.

After that she undertook to leave Sydney for a year. In the autumn of 1933 Cameron had absconded her bail and the police were looking for her. Green stole a car, spirited her out of the

Newcastle Hospital and they drove to Sydney, where she was picked up by the police and sent to serve her one-month sentence for theft.

In 1934, while Green was in hospital after his right hand had been nearly severed, she married Calletti. They were still together in November that year, when Calletti joined the line of gangsters who sought to draw attention to themselves by bringing libel actions. In Brisbane he was awarded a farthing against *Truth* over an allegation that he had married Cameron to avoid consorting charges and was a 'cowardly, vicious and brutal member of the underworld'. He claimed he was a greengrocer and, for a time, he and Nellie did sell a little fruit. He was said to have framed the penny stamp the paper sent as his winnings. He later left Queensland but she remained, finding work more lucrative than in Sydney where there was a temporary crackdown on vice. But she was back in New South Wales by July 1937, when she was charged with shooting a Harry Roper in the ankle. She was acquitted, but mainly because the police could not find him, possibly because Roper had sensibly gone to Queensland. Quite what that was all about was never clear.

Cameron was away again, working in Queensland, when Calletti was killed in 1939. The next year she married the greyhound trainer and standover man Charlie Bourke after his escape from Boggo Road jail. In 1945, back in Sydney, she was ordered to forfeit 168 bottles of beer found at her home in Crown Street.

There were other lovers on the side. Ernest Connelly (also known as Hardy) paid dearly for the privilege. He was shot by Calletti in Womerah Avenue, Darlinghurst, in February 1929 after what was described as a 'wild night party'. His dying deposition was taken but Connelly, brave lad that he was, declined to help the police. Calletti's home, in the same street, was searched and five live bullets and an empty cartridge case were found, but no one was charged. Connelly survived the shooting and ten months later was sentenced to two years' hard labour and declared a habitual criminal after a conviction for housebreaking. He did not take it well, yelling at Judge Curlewis, 'Do you realise you have given me a life sentence?' 'Nothing of the sort,' replied the judge, smoothly. It was Connelly's twentieth conviction. The Court of Appeal would have none of it, describing the appeal as 'impudent'. It was certainly not a life sentence but it was a life sentence away from Nellie, who, by the time he was released, had moved on to the New Zealand–born Alan Pulley. Pulley was later fatally shot in Glebe by Florrie Riley, a Redfern blonde.

In March 1952 Cameron was shot in the spine at her flat in Darlinghurst by William Donohue, with whom she was living. In the operating theatre she was found to have a number of healed bullet wounds and part of her liver was removed. Donohue had actually walked into a police station and given himself up but, after she refused to identify him, claiming she had been shot by a stranger, they left court arm in arm. She was still living with Donohue when she gassed herself on 8 November 1953 after being told she had inoperable cancer. On the afternoon of her death, he took her adopted child, Janice, to a party and when he returned he found Cameron lying on the kitchen floor. More than 1000 people attended her funeral at Botany cemetery. The *Sun-Herald* wrote of her that she had 'exceptional sex appeal; she had nerve and would carry a gun for a lover; and she could be trusted with secrets. She was completely loyal to the criminal scale of values'. Not a bad epitaph.

* * *

Once upon a time the word 'brothel' conjured up the spectacle of ladies sitting in chemises and thigh highs, à la Toulouse-Lautrec, drinking champagne while a piano player wearing a derby hat, with a diamond in his tooth, played ragtime. In the 1880s Melbourne brothels may have conformed to this image but after World War II many houses in Sydney bore no resemblance to such fantasies. Once more *Truth* was on the warpath, reporting on the houses of ill fame around George Street. At the Crystal Residential, six shillings could buy a room for twenty minutes, and four shillings, a candle. The rooms were partitioned into blocks of four, with the walls just shy of the ceiling, so there was nothing to prevent a robbery. Others included the Weldon Residential and the Park View Residential, run by 'Scotty' Wilson. Jack Kops kept one at 152 Castlereagh and *Truth* claimed there were another twenty like them in the area. In its true campaigning style it complained the council would do nothing about them.

And when, in May 1952, a William McGrath claimed the Park View and the Crystal Palace Residential were brothels, he received very short shrift from Mr Justice Maxwell. McGrath had written to him:

> Derision, distrust and suspicion would fittingly describe the average opinion about the police and judicial system under which flourish such social cancers as brothels, clip-joints, sly-grog houses, baccarat schools and two-up joints. These places could not last one hour if the police were, to use a slang expression, 'fair dinkum'.

His Lordship was not pleased and threatened the unfortunate McGrath—who also complained he had been offered a reefer and then approached by 'male perverts' in Ziegfeld's—with a spell in Long Bay for contempt. In fact the only reason he did not commit him there and then was that he was not sure McGrath was responsible for his actions.

Although Tilly Devine still kept a number of houses, by the 1960s she and Kate Leigh were getting old and so the Maltese-born Joseph 'The Writer' Borg—gunman, thief, shop-breaker and pimp—assumed their mantle. There was nothing stylish about his houses. The undoubted claimant to the title 'King of Palmer

Street Vice', Borg arrived in Australia in the early 1950s and in June 1963 he opened his first brothel at Woods Lane, East Sydney. Four years later he owned a row of terrace houses as well as another twenty houses in the area. A man with an eye to business, Borg also opened the Maltese Club, which provided rest and recreation for the mainly Maltese pimps, giving them a place to drink and play cards while waiting for their girls to finish their shifts. He was, by some accounts, a good man to work for and was regarded as fair to his girls.

Borg earned his nickname 'The Writer' from the frequency with which he wrote to the police complaining of harassment. At the time of his death in 1968 he was due to appear on a charge of controlling prostitutes and was on bail while appealing against a conviction for attempting to bribe a policeman. Borg's troubles were not only with the authorities. He knew there was a serious challenge being mounted for control of Darlinghurst prostitution — an enterprise that was said to net him $10 000 a week — and consequently he slept with a loaded Beretta under his pillow. It did not prevent him becoming the first casualty of the 1960s Sydney brothel wars.

At 11 a.m. on 28 May 1968 he left his home in North Bondi, turned the key in the ignition of his van and was blown up. A massive gelignite bomb weighing up to 2.5 kilograms had been planted under the van during the night. Borg's right leg was severed and he died before he arrived at St Vincent's Hospital.

Devoted to his Alsatian Caesar and his four cats, Borg had bequeathed his property to the RSPCA. While the Victorian branch declined to accept the wages of sin, the New South Wales branch had no such qualms, sending a wreath, 'In Gratitude from all the Homeless Animals'. In fact, despite reports of his wealth, the charity did not do quite as well as hoped. While Borg did indeed own a number of properties, he had them mortgaged to the hilt. Three years after his death the RSPCA had only received some $25 000.

One theory was that Borg's death was arranged by another Maltese Paul 'King Joe' Mifsud because of The Writer's tendency to steal girls run by other men and also because he would not allow a greater share in his operations. Another is that Mifsud was not the prime mover and that certain members of Sydney's senior criminal hierarchy wanted him disposed of. They approached Keith Keillor, known as the 'Jitterbug Kid' because of his prowess on the dance floor in his youth, and in turn he recruited Mifsud and another Maltese Paul Attard. A variation is that they approached Keillor in the Maltese Club in April 1968 and he sought the advice and help of the experienced explosives expert Robert 'Jackie' Steele, with whom Borg had quarrelled badly. They had clashed in the Mediterranean Club in May when Borg had set Caesar on Steele, who had conveniently been heard by a prosecution witness to say, 'I will have that bastard put in orbit if it's the last bomb I make.'

When Mifsud and Attard were arrested they failed to play by the rules and dobbed in Keillor. In turn he let the police know that he would tell all and was given a reduced bail of $200, put up by Lennie McPherson. Mifsud and Attard received sentences of life imprisonment. Keith Keillor was given seven years for showing them how to make the bomb. Steele was also charged but died during the trial from wounds he had received when he was shot in 1965. Despite the convictions there were underworld rumours that the principals had not been arrested.

Within a matter of days Borg's houses were shut down and his rivals upped the money they required to allow their girls to operate to $48 a shift, more than double the price exacted by the benevolent Borg. Borg's offsider, Simone Vogel, left for Queensland where she set up a very successful string of 'rub and tugs' before she disappeared. After a series of attacks on her Palmer Street houses, Tilly Devine closed her brothels and left the area in the hands of another Maltese Eric 'Monkey' Williams, so called because

of his long arms and generally simian appearance. Williams—
an associate of Donny 'The Glove' Smith and John 'Ratty Jack'
Clarke—was a great success for a time, principally because he took
up with the formidable Julie Harris, Borg's de facto wife. He later
married her after he had served a two-year stretch at Long Bay. On
his own release, John Regan, who had known Williams in prison,
decided he would like to move in on the brothels. He engaged an
old Canberra criminal to carry out a contract on Williams, who had
declined to share the takings with him. Williams had a habit of
sticking to a set routine. He could generally be found in the Maltese
Club playing cards, waiting for Julie Harris to shut up the shop.
On one occasion when Williams went home alone, the contractor
knocked on the door of his house and, when Williams came to the
door, fired five times through the woodwork, hitting him every
time. Williams was unable to reach the telephone to call for help
and died in his hallway. Regan was never charged but Painter and
Docker Tony Aquilina was. After some weeks in custody, rather
shamefaced, the police admitted they had arrested the wrong man
and he was released.

Brothels were legalised in New South Wales under the
Summary Offences Act 1988, with street prostitution also legalised,
except near a church, school or hospital or near a school, church,
hospital or dwelling. There were also limited restrictions placed on
advertising, and living off the earnings of a prostitute was made
illegal, except in the case of persons who owned or managed a
legal brothel.

By mid-1999, brothel numbers had tripled in Sydney to
between 400 and 500. The vast majority had no licenses but
operated and advertised anyway. Pillars of society, such as a one-
time investment adviser to the media baron Kerry Packer, were
allowing their premises to be used for brothels in the hope of
gaining some of the profits to be made. According to a report on the

out-of-control industry by the *Sydney Morning Herald*, hundreds of brothels specialising in Asian women were set up, creating a huge industry out of the traffic in women.

In 1999, due in part to persistent lobbying by Project Respect, an amendment was made to the Commonwealth's *Criminal Code Act 1995*, which deemed slavery and sexual servitude a punishable offence, with jail terms of up to twenty-five years. But women are still being coerced a great deal to work in brothels. There have, in fact, been few successful prosecutions in New South Wales since the introduction of the anti-slavery laws.

The first jury conviction under the new Act was in Melbourne against Wei Tang, a Brunswick brothel owner who, in June 2006, was sentenced to a minimum of six years for keeping five Thai women as sex slaves. The next month Sydney brothel owners Yotchomchin Somsri and Johan Sieders were each found guilty of engaging women in sexual servitude. The girls had been recruited as sex workers in Thailand and entered Australia ostensibly as tourists. They were obliged to work off $45000 each before they could earn for themselves and were only occasionally allowed to accept a tip of up to $25 from a customer. It worked out that a girl would have to service 1500 customers in fifteen-minute shifts, or 563 men in one-hour sessions, to clear the debt. Somsri was sentenced to five years and Sieders to four. Appeals against both convictions and sentences were dismissed.

More recently, in July 2010, a 48-year-old Thai-born woman, Namthip Netthip, who became an Australian citizen in 1994 and had worked in the sex industry herself, was given twenty-seven months with a minimum of thirteen months. She had paid an agency in Thailand $20000 over a three-year period to supply eleven other Thai women, whom she sent to work in Sydney, Newcastle, Adelaide and Perth, using their earnings to pay the mortgage on a unit in Lakemba. Perhaps generously, the trial judge thought she would not offend again.

But illegal brothels still flourish; according to one 2006 report they outnumber their legal sisters by as many as four to one— two hundred to fifty—with a similar ratio reported in 2009. In 2007 the brothel black market was said to be worth $500 million a year. Illegal brothels and drugs often go hand in hand and can be dangerous places to work not simply for the girls but also for other personnel. On August 2003, fifty-year-old Joseph Attallah became the first person in New South Wales to be given two life sentences for trafficking, first $925 000 worth of heroin and then $2.1 million worth of cocaine. He had run a brothel in Bankstown, Total Eternity Services, and the women who worked there were expected to buy their drugs, particularly heroin, from him. Many of the girls were incapable of working without heroin to help them and Attallah supplied the drugs at between $150 and $180 for half a gram. The first half-gram was supplied on credit and, when a girl had worked off the purchase, she was then sold another half- gram. Heroin was also sold to street purchasers. The sales of drugs generally totalled a substantial $3000 a day, increasing to $4000, except during the Olympic Games of 2000, when it reached $10 000. In August 2005 Attallah's life sentences were varied on appeal to twenty-four years, with a minimum of eighteen to be served.

On 3 November 2000 Victor Zaccak was working in the brothel's office when he was shot and killed by Michael Eleter. Eleter had gone to the brothel mob-handed with other members of his family to sort out George Dib, who also worked there, after Eleter's brother Tony had been injured in a fight with Dib in a pool hall. He fired shots through the window, hitting Zaccak by mistake. It was after this that the manager dobbed in Attallah and his co-defendant, Nabil Youssef Sabbagh. In 2005 the Court of Appeal varied Attallah's sentence to twenty-four years with a minimum of eighteen to be served.

In a very different league from Attallah's premises was A Touch of Class, known as 'Toucha', at 377 Riley Street, Surry Hills.

It functioned as an illegal brothel for more than forty years until it closed its doors for the last time in the spring of 2007. There Kim Hollingsworth—the former stripper who caused Commissioner Peter Ryan so much grief over her claim to be allowed to continue to train as a policewoman—worked at $400 an hour. It was also where the National Union of Workers boss, Louis Jamieson, ran up a bill of $1320 on two visits in 1988. He resigned after his romps came to light in 2003. Before it closed, the brothel appeared to be in decline. It had not reopened during what other establishments said was one of their busiest periods: World Youth Day in July 2008, when thousands of Catholic pilgrims descended on Sydney for a weeklong celebration. There were also allegations of unpaid taxes. An effort to sell the premises for $6.5 million in 2007 came to nothing and it was temporarily reopened for the filming of the television series *Underbelly: The Golden Mile*.

In 2009 it was thought that there were more than 11 000 sex workers, working either in legal or illegal brothels, or independently. A statewide survey in the spring of 2010 showed around ninety illegal brothels in Sydney, at least that was the figure from the councils who responded—just over a third replied to the survey.

The Best That Money Can Buy

10

There is bound to be some corruption in any police force in any major city but, from time to time over the years, Australian forces in general and the New South Wales Police in particular really do seem to have raised it to an art form. Anyone who thinks that a high percentage of that force have in the past been rogues has the support of Sydney solicitor Christopher Murphy, whose father was himself an officer:

> Lennie McPherson and George Freeman may have been the Mr Bigs of Sydney crime but in truth the real Princes of the City were the police. When they came back from the Second World War the uniform seemed attractive. By the 1960s they had started networking criminals and they got lazy. In the end, by the late 1980s, they were using criminals to kill people.

Given the origin of the various forces around the world it is not surprising there have been continuing troubles. In London the police had initially been made up of ex-soldiers, and the commissioners there had troubles enough. In Australia convicts were encouraged to become constables and consequently there was a high turnover of personnel.

In the 1840s three consecutive chiefs of police in Sydney were dismissed in fairly quick succession for a variety of indiscretions. The first was Henry Wilson, who survived allegations of a relationship with a female convict but not those of using policemen to build his home and as liveried domestic servants. He was removed from office in July 1840. Wilson was succeeded by William Augustus Miles, reputedly the illegitimate son of William IV. In 1848 his accounts were found to be out of order and he was removed following allegations of insobriety, but retained his position of magistrate. He died three years later. The third, Captain Joseph Innes, retired because of 'irregular practices' when he had been a visiting magistrate at Darlinghurst Gaol, which was run as an early example of private enterprise by the governor Henry Kech, his wife and mistress. By 1850 the New South Wales police force was described as being at an all-time low, with scandals, drunkenness and bribery prevalent among the constables and with itching palms throughout the force.

Over the next sixty years things did not improve greatly. In 1915 Sydney physician Ralph Worrall gave evidence to the Select Committee on the Prevalence of Venereal Diseases that police were regularly accepting bribes from brothel keepers and were operating a de facto licensing system. Unsurprisingly the police denied this.

One of the best detectives of the New South Wales Police immediately after World War II was Ray Kelly. After his retirement, on 4 February 1960, the *Sydney Morning Herald* thought 'he deliberately made friends in all walks of life because he knew that was the way to be a successful detective'. Good detective he might have been but unfortunately Kelly was also probably one of the most corrupt policemen worldwide. He was a good friend of Tilly Devine, Kate Leigh and Dulcie Markham. Standover man Richard Reilly and East Coast identity Paddles Anderson were more than just his informants; they were his partners in abortion and other rackets, as was Dr Reginald Stuart-Jones.

For a time Kelly, born in New South Wales in 1906, worked as a jackeroo, but he craved excitement and in 1929 came to Sydney, where he joined the police. On 23 August 1930 he was on bicycle patrol in Newtown when he saw three men in a stolen car and followed them into a dead end. They tried to run him down and he leapt on the running board, grabbing the steering wheel. The car crashed into a shop window and the driver again tried to shake Kelly off by reversing at high speed. Instead Kelly shot all three, hitting one in the head and the others in the back. The eighteen-year-old Joseph Swan from Marrickville, already a known standover man, died in hospital.

The next year he worked with the Riot Squad and his skull was fractured in the eviction riots in Newtown. He recovered from his injuries, and from then Kelly's career was onward and upward. He went into detective work in 1936, equally at home with bankers and standover men, his colleagues said. Although some of the photographs of him appear to show a small, bespectacled, almost dapper little man, he was more than 2 metres in height and weighed nearly 90 kilograms. A keen golfer and surfboarder, he didn't drink or smoke.

On 15 March 1953 Kelly killed Lloyd Edward Day, who with two companions had spent a weekend dealing with the safe of Marcus Clark in Central Square. The police had heard there was to be a major job and Kelly and others had been on a seventeen-hour stake-out. When the men emerged, two got into a truck said to have been driven by Lennie McPherson, although he was never charged. The other three got into a car driven by Day. They were chased down College Street, Drummoyne, and Kelly called out for them to stop. When they didn't, Kelly, leaning out of the window, fired a number of shots, hitting Day.

He was involved in the repeated captures of the gunman and escaper Darcy Dugan, on one occasion in 1958 using his informants to tell him Dugan was waiting patiently in a 1.3 metre hole for the chance to move over the prison wall. That same year he confronted and disarmed James Hackett, who had fatally shot Marlene Harvey in her home and wounded two other men. The next year he was part of the team that tracked down Kevin Simmonds and Leslie Newcombe, who had clubbed an Emu Plains prison warder to death as they were searching for food following their escape. He was also in the Arthur Street, North Sydney, shoot-out with the cross-dressing Tony Martini and Edward Garland, for which the pair were sentenced to death and later reprieved.

That was Kelly's public, good side, but he was also quite capable of arranging for criminals such as Dugan to take the blame for some robberies he and his colleagues had set up—indeed that was said to be his speciality. He was one of three senior detectives who, questioning applicants for the plain-clothes division, asked them if they were prepared to load a suspect. If the answer was no, they would be rejected and Kelly was apt to remark derisively, 'Give him back to the Cardinal. He's no good to me.' The Cardinal was the incorruptible uniformed officer, Brian Doyle, a practising Catholic.

Kelly's retirement party on 3 February 1960, a five-pounds-a-plate buffet with unlimited drink, was attended by 874 people and included luminaries such as Premier Askin, Commissioner Norman 'The Foreman' Allan, judges, horse trainers, criminals and gambler Perce Galea.

Farewell dinners attended by politicians and criminals alike were common at the time. In 1950 James Sweeney, a retiring metropolitan superintendent, was feted by 600 vice traders at Sammy Lee's restaurant, where he received a cheque for more than 600 pounds. Inspector Noonan, Metropolitan Licensing Inspector, did rather better on his retirement, pocketing 1000 pounds at the Australia Hotel. The 1951 Royal Commission on Liquor Laws in New South Wales found that the practices were simply 'indiscreet' rather than illegal.

It was with Kelly that Fred Krahe groomed a young officer, Don Fergusson, to be their bagman in the abortion rackets of the 1960s. Krahe had joined the police as a cadet in 1940 and, although another good detective, he also organised abortion rackets, armed robberies and the extortion of prostitutes and criminals. In 1971 Krahe was exposed by Shirley Brifman, a working girl in the Kings Cross area, who said she paid him a regular $100 a week to be allowed on the streets. When she was arrested for allegedly procuring a fourteen-year-old girl, something she bitterly denied, she went public, maintaining that Krahe had helped organise a theft of bonds from a bank and that he and a Queensland officer 'exchanged' criminals—one of whom was Donny 'The Glove' Smith, shot dead in 1970 by club owner James Anderson in Abe Saffron's Venus Room—so that they could work in each other's state without fear of recognition.

Fergusson rose to be a detective superintendent and was at one time chief of the CIB. With exposure of the abortion business about to break, he was found dead in the lavatory of his office at the Police Administration Centre, in Campbell Street. He had been shot through the right temple. A verdict of suicide while suffering severe mental depression was returned but there were many who thought Krahe had held the trembling hand.

Shirley Brifman fled to Queensland where she was found dead in her Brisbane flat in March 1972. She died either of a heart attack or a drug overdose but there have been persistent rumours among the police that Krahe, either with or without the active assistance of a Queensland officer, forced the pills down her throat. Krahe was allowed to retire that year, at the age of fifty-two, with a thrombosis in the leg. He was later involved in the Nugan Hand bank affair and was charged with conspiracy to defraud the group but was acquitted on all counts. He died, aged sixty-one, in December 1981 from the thrombosis, brought on, said one admirer, 'by kicking too many people to death'.

During his career Krahe was involved in a strange case. In February 1972 Alan Burton, who had been involved in a huge car-stealing racket with the one-legged Reg Varley, disappeared. The Varley–Burton combo stole cars worth $1.5 million in seven months, the lion's share of which, said Varley, Krahe received. In January 1972 a series of raids began on the Varley chop shops and on the night of 7 February Burton disappeared. Varley was accused of paying two New South Wales detectives $5000 to dispose of his partner. Much of the evidence against Varley came from another member of the gang, Paul Hos, who told the Central Criminal Court that Varley said he went to Burton's house with some detectives, one of whom hit Burton with a cosh. Allegedly Varley then also hit him and the body was taken 320 kilometres down the coast and dumped at sea. In his defence, Varley told the court that Krahe had called on him that night and told him they were going to give Burton a hiding. Burton had, it was said, swindled Krahe and the other officers in the scam out of $20 000. When Varley protested, he was hit on the ankle of his one good leg and his aluminium crutches were smashed. He and Burton were taken for a drive and then Burton was pulled from the car and Varley heard shots. However, Varley was convicted of manslaughter and sentenced to fourteen years. He served nine and, after his release, he constantly tried to have his case reopened, claiming the kidnap had been organised by detective Cyril Edwards.

The case had a curious sequel. The next year Edwards was dismissed from the force and, although it was recommended that charges be brought against him, none were and he disappeared from view until March 1986, when 1100 Indian hemp plants were found at his chicken farm. He was charged with cultivating and, on 31 October, shortly before he was due to appear in court, his body—legs and hands trussed—was found in the sea at Mackenzie's Bay near Tamarama. He had been shot in the head. Before he disappeared, he had told his wife he had information implicating high-ranking officers and was going to see two detectives in Sydney to 'fix' the evidence against him. He had also taken out a life insurance policy and changed his will. Peter Collis, a company director, claimed he could produce evidence showing who had shot

Edwards, but he never did. Despite leaning towards a verdict of suicide, the coroner returned an open verdict.

If there was corruption in the senior or lower levels in the New South Wales Police during those years, it was not surprising. The corruption went straight to the premier's office and the belief is that both the commissioner of police, Norman 'The Foreman' Allan. and the Premier, Robert Askin, were on the take from illegal casinos, abortion rackets and prostitution. Askin died in September 1981, leaving something over $3 million. Could he have acquired this legitimately? There is little doubt that Allan acquired his money dishonestly but there is possibly room for a chink of doubt in Askin's case. He may just have been getting insider information on the stock markets.

In 1962, aged fifty-two, Allan had become the youngest ever appointed police commissioner. He was derisively known as the Mushroom, because he was kept in the dark and fed muck by his subordinates. On his debit side, apart from his relationship with Askin, he was also badly damaged by disclosures on the massaging of crime figures. His most disastrous act, however, was to ensure the promotion of Fred Hanson to commissioner in November 1972.

Under Frederick John 'Slippery' Hanson, the New South Wales Police became known as 'the best police force money could buy'. Hanson began his working life as a railway porter, joining the force in 1936. Two years earlier he had been rejected as undersized and had gone on a bodybuilding course. After the war he was a founding member of 21 Division, set up to deal with the young bashers who were causing general mayhem in the Sydney suburbs.

As commissioner, Hanson, who disliked his nickname, declined to go after casino owners such as the highly popular gambler and identity Perce Galea, said to be pushing $5000 a week all the way to the top. Unbelievably Hanson claimed the police did not have the authority to go into the clubs. His appointment coincided with the growth of organised crime in New South Wales and, if there is not clear evidence against him, there is the deepest suspicion that he protected identities like his duck-shooting friend Robert Trimbole, part of the Mr Asia drug syndicate.

By 1974 Hanson was slacking off, working only 47 per cent of his official hours, and in February 1976 he brought and settled an action against a newspaper which implied he had an interest in an illegal casino at West Gosford. But with the action his days were literally numbered. He agreed to retire early if he could appoint his successor and sat on the three-man committee to select his nominee, Merv Wood, overlooking the 'Cardinal' Brian Doyle, who would have been a far more suitable appointment and who might just have stemmed the corruption in the force. Hanson died of carbon monoxide poisoning in his car in October 1980, and many believe it was a suicide. The coroner dispensed with an inquest.

Mervyn Wood had had a most successful rowing career, representing Australia in the 1936 Berlin Olympics. He won the single sculls at the 1948 London Olympics and in 1950, at the British Empire Games, he won the single and the double sculls, this time partnered by another policeman, Murray Stewart Riley, later a convicted drug smuggler.

Indeed Riley was one of the earliest post-war senior officers to go astray in a very public way. He had been a police officer since 1943, resigning in 1962 after an incident in which he was alleged to have taken a communication to a serving prisoner. He then went into the security business and at one time was an adviser to South Sydney Juniors. He was convicted in New Zealand of attempted bribery of a police inspector to obtain bail for Sydney criminals who had been arrested in a pyramid-selling fraud, and was sentenced to twelve months' imprisonment before being deported back to Australia in March 1967.

In both 1973 and 1974 he managed to avoid being called to give evidence before the Moffitt Royal Commission into the Administration of the New South Wales Police Force. Despite regular reports of sightings in the neighbourhood, Riley could not be found by the police and Justice Moffitt recorded that he had been treated with undue favour by them.

From then on, Riley flirted with organised crime. He was with the Californian mafioso Jimmy 'The Weasel' Fratianno in San Francisco in November 1976. Two days later, his briefcase was stolen from his room while having lunch with the gangster. In June 1978 Riley pleaded guilty to the importation of 2.7 tonnes of cannabis, and received ten years. He had overloaded his boat, the *Anoa*, which was unable to make port. He had also been importing heroin from Thailand, bought at several thousand dollars a pound and, duly cut with sugar, selling it at several thousand dollars an ounce in Australia. In 1980 he received a further seven years on charges of possessing an unlicensed pistol and conspiracy to cheat and defraud the American Express Company of $274000. Shortly before his release in May 1984 he was made bankrupt, owing over $132000 to the Nugan Hand (Hong Kong) Bank, which was, by this time, in liquidation. In 1985 he was named in an inquiry by Justice Bredmeyer of the Papua New Guinea Supreme Court as being part of a ring to import $40 million of heroin from Bangkok.

He then moved to England where he was jailed in July 1991 at Bristol Crown Court after he and an accomplice were convicted of a plan to defraud British Aerospace of approximately $93 million by means of computer fraud. In 1990 they had applied to open a bank account on the Isle of Man but the manager became suspicious when Riley could not provide references. Less than six months into a five-year sentence he walked out of Spring Hill prison, Aylesbury, and eventually returned to Queensland.

Overall, Commissioner Mervyn Wood's attitude was one of live and let live and, until he was forced to do otherwise, that was the way policing was conducted. His first clash with Premier Neville Wran came in December 1977. At last, after years of tolerance, illegal casinos were to be closed but Wood stated publicly that he did not intend to close them before Christmas because of the hardship it would cause the 300-odd employees who would lose their jobs. The next and more serious blue came in March, when a report linking George Freeman and Lennie McPherson to the upper echelons of the American mafia was not passed to Wran. The third came at the beginning of May, when Wran appointed Bill Allen to the post of chief superintendent ahead of recommendations by Wood and did not inform him.

It was not a good winter for Wood. In the face of mounting criticism of the police, and leaked allegations—which he denied— he resigned on 5 June. The allegations included an association with casino owner George Ziziros Walker, who, along with 'Linus the Pom' O'Driscoll, was later charged with conspiracy to murder. The charges were dropped. Wood was also said to be associating with George Freeman and Abe Saffron and, more specifically, it was alleged that a senior policeman had been at the Wentworth Hotel on 7 November 1977 with a casino operator. It was there that two croupiers, Joanna Coman and Erica Scott, were killed by Coman's husband Walter two days later. There were also allegations, never proved, that Wood was linked to a drug conspiracy case with the one-time Chief Stipendiary Magistrate Murray Farquhar, the dishonest Sydney solicitor Morgan Ryan and a convicted drug trafficker, Roy Cessna. The case was heard in May 1979 and Farquhar dealt with Cessna most leniently. Originally he had been charged with the importation of cannabis valued at $1.5 million. In court the value was more amorphously given as 'some value'. Farquhar fined him a nominal amount. The allegations were that Morgan Ryan had pressed his old friend Wood for help.

Jim Lees, a devout Christian, was the next to be appointed commissioner, with Brian Doyle once again being overlooked. Doyle lasted only three months as Lees's special adviser before he resigned, maintaining there had been 'no row, no blue, no blow-up'. With, or particularly without, Doyle, Lees simply could not cope and lasted only two years. During his time, however, he had to deal with the corrupt Bill Allen still clawing his way to the top, and it was in November 1981 that the lid blew off. As was often the case, the problem arose over gambling and the plans for a casino at a time when Allen was the assistant commissioner for licensing. There was a separate allegation that on five occasions that year Allen had given Warren Molloy, then chief of the Special Licensing Squad, $500 cash in an envelope. There was also a problem caused by Abe Saffron's regular visits to Allen's office.

In May 1981 Allen, his wife and daughter had been in Macau, guests of the *Sociedade de Turismo e Diversoes de Macao*, run by the Yip family of the Macau Trotting Club. Then came the second freebie in as many months. On 6 June 1981 they all flew first class to Hawaii, where they met another of Allen's daughters and her husband. There they stayed free of charge at the home of Lori Yip. On 11 June they went on to San Francisco, staying again free of charge, this time at the Holiday Inn at Union Square, courtesy of 'representations' by the Sydney bookmaker Bill Waterhouse. Then it was on to Las Vegas where once again they were in luck because, this time, the tab was picked up by Jack Rooklyn, the head of Bally poker machines in Australia, a man who had come under heavy fire from Justice Moffitt. Not only had the Allens had their trip shouted but lucky Bill Allen also won $1000 on the machines. Allen was a man who liked cash. He told the inquiry into his conduct that he was a regular winner at the races. He bought his house with cash, paid off his American Express card in cash and, he said, kept $10000 in cash at home. In turn the inquiry told him that by accepting hospitality and associating with the likes of Abe Saffron and Rooklyn he had acted in a manner likely to discredit the police. By paying money to Molloy he had tried to compromise him. Allen resigned.

Tony Lauer, back from exile in the Blue Mountains (where he had been sent as a young officer after lodging a report that George

Freeman had been involved in illegal gambling), was appointed commissioner in 1991. He just could not accept that there was corruption in his force until it was too late for him to save his career. In the teeth of evidence to the contrary, he argued against a Royal Commission, claiming that reports that 'corruption was entrenched' were 'figments of the political imagination'.

* * *

By the mid-1980s, on any account, certain police officers were not only out of control but also, as it was said of Lord Byron, 'mad, bad and dangerous to know'. Once a shooting star, detective Roger Caleb Rogerson had aligned himself with career criminal Arthur Stanley 'Neddy' Smith and was taking an active part in the drug war that was running in Sydney at the time. It was during these drug wars that the police really appear to have come into their own, and Rogerson's career has to be set against the conduct of some of his superior officers of the time. He had caught the end of the Ray Kelly era and therefore served under both Fred Krahe and Donald Fergusson, and had a most unhealthy relationship with Smith, much of which would be revealed—along with a picture of Rogerson in his underwear—in Smith's book *Neddy*.

Talented but corrupt, Rogerson's association with a number of colourful identities would cause immeasurable grief to the New South Wales Police. He was born in January 1941 and joined the force in 1958 and the Criminal Investigation Branch four years later. He became a member of the Armed Holdup Squad in May 1974 and was there when the bank robber and murderer Philip Western was shot and killed in June 1976. The following year Rogerson shot and killed a man who was trying to hold up a courier taking money to the bank. He was an arresting officer in the high-profile Ananda Marga bombing case in June 1978 and in August 1979 he was there when Gordon Thomas, another bank robber, was shot and killed at Rose Bay. In 1980 he received the Peter Mitchell Award for the most outstanding performance in any phase of police duty. By now he was well on his way to what many thought would be a dazzling career, with words such as 'future commissioner' being bandied about. But he was far too close to Smith, who was rather more his partner than his informer, for that to happen.

Rogerson's career began to spiral downwards with the shooting of drug dealer Warren Lanfranchi, killed on 27 June 1981. The police wanted to interview Lanfranchi, and Neddy Smith, acting as honest broker, indicated to Rogerson that the dealer was prepared to pay up to $50 000 to avoid this unhappy event. Later Rogerson said he had been offered $80 000. Lanfranchi was then living with the prostitute Sallie-Anne Huckstepp and, according to her version of events, he left their home, unarmed and carrying $10 000, to meet Rogerson alone in Dangar Place, Chippendale. In fact Rogerson had discussed the meeting with his superiors, and at 2.45 p.m. that day some eighteen officers were in the area, with Rogerson and three others in an adjoining lane. Smith drove Lanfranchi to the meeting where, according to Rogerson, Lanfranchi pulled a gun that had been manufactured around 1900 and which later turned out to be defective. Rogerson shot him twice, once in the neck and once in the heart. The police said that Lanfranchi had no money on him. At the inquest the four-man coroner's jury found that Rogerson had shot Lanfranchi while endeavouring to make an arrest but specifically declined to say it was in self-defence. An internal inquiry headed by Superintendent Ronald Ralph, known as 'Click' because he said when he saw a criminal something 'clicked' in his mind, cleared the police of any misconduct.

As for Huckstepp, she was found strangled and drowned in Busby's Pond at Centennial Lake on 7 February 1986. She came from a Jewish family named Krivoshaw and had been privately educated when, at the age of seventeen, she married Brian Huckstepp and went to Kalgoorlie to work in the tin-shed brothels. A number of the usual suspects came into the frame for her death, including Neddy Smith, who maintained he had never spoken to her. However, in a conversation with a fellow prisoner, Smith apparently confessed that he had killed her, not because she was a police informer (which she undoubtedly was), but simply because he did not like her lifestyle. He later denied this. After a five-week trial Smith was acquitted in less than three hours on 12 November 1999.

In early November 1983 Rogerson recruited the Melbourne-based hitman Chris Flannery as another informer. By now, however, his career was slumping. The catalyst was the shooting by Flannery of another officer, the honest and talented Michael Patrick Drury, the following year.

In 1983 Drury had been working undercover to set up a drug bust involving Melbourne dealer Alan Williams, and a meeting was arranged at a Sydney hotel car park. Williams did not go through with the deal but Drury recognised him. To prevent the officer from giving evidence, Williams arranged for Rogerson to try to bribe Drury, an offer that he refused in September that year. In May 1984, Williams, who like so many criminals had a pathological fear of prison, then arranged with Flannery to murder Drury for a fee of $100 000, of which he claimed Rogerson would receive half.

Shortly after 6 p.m. on 6 June 1984, an attempt was made on Drury's life as he was about to wash up after his evening meal at his home in Chatsworth. He was shot though an open window in the stomach and chest. Fortunately, for once, Flannery had had an off day and Drury lived. Later Flannery would say he went to the hospital to try again but could not get past the police guards. It was believed that Drury would not survive and he made a dying deposition in which he said that Rogerson had approached him with a bribe and in November 1984 Rogerson was charged with trying to bribe Drury. The following June he was acquitted but the damage to his career had been done. For the next decade he was in and out of court.

Returned to uniform duties, Rogerson was made the subject of anti-corruption surveillance and on 1 July 1985 he was photographed closing two accounts in false names—not in itself illegal then. The sum involved was more than $110 000 and a fake contract was drawn up by Dr Nick Paltos and businessman solicitor Maurie Nowytarger to account for the movement of the funds. The next year, in April 1986, Rogerson went on television denying that he had ever taken a bribe and doubted he had ever had so much as a free lunch. On 28 July that year he was dismissed from the force after seven of nine counts of misconduct were found to be proved against him. He had been suspended for a time during the inquiry but he still interceded in a quarrel between drug dealer Louis Bayeh and Lennie McPherson, going to a meeting at Bayeh's home to try to help.

In February 1988 Alan Williams was extradited from the Northern Territory, charged with conspiracy to murder Drury. In June he pleaded guilty and was sentenced to fourteen years' imprisonment. Now he would give evidence against Rogerson on the same charge. At the end of a three-week trial the judge warned the jury that it would be extremely dangerous to convict Rogerson on Williams's evidence and on 28 November Rogerson was acquitted.

Next up was Rogerson's trial over the bank accounts. It was the Crown's case that the money in his account was from illegal sources and part of the evidence against him, strongly challenged, came from a woman who claimed that she had taken a bundle of money to Sydney airport on behalf of the Melbourne drug dealer Dennis Allen, 'Mr Death'. There she had given it to Rogerson in exchange for plastic bags of heroin. He maintained the money came from the sale of a vintage Bentley and successful gambling.

In March 1990 he, Paltos and Nowytarger were convicted of conspiracy to pervert the course of justice over the bank accounts and Rogerson was sentenced to eight years. Nowytarger received a minimum of four and Paltos, who was serving his drug sentence, another thirty months. On 11 December the Court of Appeal quashed Rogerson's conviction and, in turn, the then Director of Public Prosecutions, Reg Blanch, successfully appealed that decision. Rogerson finally served three years and was released from Berrima jail on 15 December 1995. He was just in time to attend an inquest into Flannery's death and appear before the Wood Commission into the New South Wales Police. The inquiry had begun the previous December and was by now in full swing as, week by week, ever more amazing revelations were made. Rogerson was not co-operative, saying, 'I don't care about this inquest and I don't care if you find out anything about Flannery at all.'

From then on his career has been one of short prison sentences interspersed with writing books and appearances with celebrity criminal Mark 'Chopper' Read and a former footy player in highly lucrative talks on the club circuit. But he has not entirely given up his pastoral work. In 2010 he could be found giving solace and support to the stressed Kings Cross nightclub owner John Ibrahim, whose family was currently under siege from the police.

In 1990 Rogerson's old associate, Neddy Smith, was given a sentence of life imprisonment for what amounted to the road-rage killing of trucker Ronald Flavell. He had stabbed the truck driver to death in a Coogee street after a day's drinking with Rogerson in 1987. In 1993 Smith went into segregated confinement as he became a principal witness at the Independent Commission against Corruption hearing conducted by Ian Temby QC, which led to the Wood Royal Commission.

Chaired by Justice James Wood, the commission sat for more than 450 days and heard 640 witnesses. Its broad terms of reference were to inquire into the existence of corruption and misconduct within the police service and into the efficacy of its Internal Affairs Branch. As an immediate result, eighty-two police officers were dismissed. It was, even its critics agreed, the most thorough and far-reaching of all the inquiries into the police.

The star witness was the corrupt former detective Trevor Haken, who had worked with the Commonwealth–State Joint Drug Task Force (JTF) for two years from 1983. At an early stage Haken had been persuaded to roll over and, provided with a mini-camera, taped and filmed his dealings with other corrupt colleagues. On 12 September 1995 he gave evidence about these dealings, including the New Year's Eve 1983 divvying up of $200 000 taken by officers from drug dealers.

As the weeks went by it was apparent that, when sufficiently armed, Wood was quite prepared to be ruthless with police officers who initially followed the golden rule that, provided they all stuck together, they would be all right. They were swiftly disabused of this theory.

On 11 December 1995, Wayne Eade, the former head of the Gosford Drug Squad, faced questioning by Virginia Bell, assistant counsel to the inquiry. Yes, he thought he was an officer 'of impeccable integrity'. No, he did not have an interest in child porn videos. Nor had he tried to buy ecstasy for colleagues; of course he knew that was an illegal drug. He had certainly never visited a witness code named GDU7, a former prostitute and drug dealer, while on duty.

It was a classic piece of cross-examination. Eade was then invited to look at a film taken when he was on duty at 10.40 p.m. on 27 August that year. Up on the room's television screens appeared a film of GDU7 pouring a line of cocaine on the officer's penis and then proceeding to lick it off. She then started to talk about a shipment of cocaine before they moved to a couch where he began masturbating and talking about buying ecstasy and a porn video of children. The screen went blank as GDU7 was about to provide more oral sex.

Wood asked Eade if he wished to see more of the film. He did not. Before the end of the day the man about whom there had been suspicions for the previous ten years and who had survived a number of internal investigations had been dismissed by the beleaguered Commissioner Tony Lauer. That half-hour broke the resistance of corrupt officers. Who could tell who was on film and in what position? No longer a question of solidarity, it was more one of who could be first onto the life raft. Eade was later sentenced to twenty-two months' imprisonment for inciting and procuring the supply of prohibited drugs and knowingly giving false evidence to the commission. In 2006 he was ordered to pay over $286 000 to the state, which had settled an action by a Michael O'Sullivan, who claimed that Eade had threatened to load him up with heroin.

Historically few investigations had gone further than officers being asked to resign and, if they did not, being dismissed. The commission was no exception. At the end of 1995 an amnesty was offered to corrupt officers if they agreed to tell all and provide evidence against their colleagues. This was, said Justice Wood, a once-and-for-all amnesty. Those who did not take advantage of it would not get a second chance. They had until 9 February 1996 to come out of the locker room. Resignation would be required but they would be allowed to keep their superannuation, pension and ill-gotten gains.

With the Wood Royal Commission winding down, in mid-January 1996 Lauer resigned as commissioner. Unfortunately not only had he been quite unable to recognise that there were corrupt officers in the force, but he was also given to making statements that would rebound on him. In 1993 he had said, 'In New South Wales we are at the cutting edge of policing as far as our ability to act on corruption among officers.' The next year there was another statement that would come to haunt him. 'It ought to be my responsibility that this service never again has working among it another Roger Rogerson.'

In June 1996 Peter Ryan, a lecturer at Bramshill Police College in England, was called in at a salary of $400 000—rather more than that of the premier—to drink from the poisoned chalice. The job had been hawked around senior officers in Britain and, although he had been chief constable of rural Norfolk, Ryan had never commanded a city force. From the start he was isolated and fed contradictory advice and information. At his first press conference on 11 June he asked, 'Who is Roger Rogerson?' The press conference came to a hurried end.

Some 200 officers were known to have criminal records when Ryan took over. It was proposed he should have power of dismissal without appeal. Unsurprisingly it was an unpopular move and on 20 November there were demonstrations with calls to 'send the Pommie back'. Seventy per cent of officers sacked for having criminal convictions won reinstatement at industrial tribunals. In fact, after the Royal Commission only one person went to jail.

When interviewed shortly after his appointment Ryan had been keen to dismiss suggestions that he did not have the depth of experience to deal with city detectives bent on hiding their misdeeds. 'People have overlooked the fact that there is a determination to clean up the act. It rests not only with me but with a widespread group of people.' There was now in place a Police Integrity Commission, established in January 1997 to root out corruption.

On 7 February 1997 Ryan launched a new code of conduct, including the banning of free gifts and drinking on duty, and the threat of dismissal for any criminal offence, including drink-driving. It did not go down well, particularly when it was immediately disclosed that he had earlier accepted a ticket from the New South Wales transport minister for the footy grand final and another for the opening night of *Crazy For You*.

On 28 June that year the drug dealer Ron Levi was shot by officers Rodney Podesta and Anthony Dilorenzo on Bondi Beach. He had been seen wading fully clothed in the surf brandishing a knife. In March 1998 the coroner decided the officers had a case to answer over his death but no charges were ever laid. Two years later Podesta admitted he had dealt in cocaine. His father, who ran a coffee shop in Kings Cross, had been named in two Royal

Commissions. Another problem arose when former stripper and prostitute Kim Hollingsworth was dismissed after eight weeks at the police academy. Some of her stripping performances had been for police smokos. Ryan was quite unwilling to let her stay but he was overruled. She later dropped out of the course.

Ryan announced in 2001 that his reformatory mission was now complete. In his earlier years in New South Wales he accepted he had faced a good deal of sniping on a professional and personal level but he believed he had weathered the storm. In his first months he had dismissed twenty officers and 150 had been suspended. 'When it was seen I was dismissing officers, there was a rush to hand in resignations,' he said. The force was now clean.

Unfortunately at hearings of the Police Integrity Commission that same year, *Operation Florida*, a three-year sting mounted by the force's internal anti-corruption unit, told a different story. Microphones and cameras had been planted in lavatories in Manly and the police were filmed as they met and dealt with drug dealers. A detective was filmed pushing banknotes down his trousers. He had found the money while searching the home of a cannabis dealer. Another clip of film showed three officers taking $40 000 and laughing as they chorused 'Happy Days'. Much of the evidence came from a former officer, known as M5, who had been trapped and persuaded to roll over. For six months he recorded what he did on a daily basis.

Vince Caccamo, a senior heroin dealer of the North Shore area, claimed he had paid a total of over $92 000 in bribes, including a weekly $1000 to Patison and Senior Constable Matthew Jasper in 2000. He was recorded complaining to his associate Anthony Markarian that he was being badly squeezed: 'Every cent I make goes to them.' Markarian thought it was like having a shop and paying rent. In another traditional police rort Jasper had arranged for a convicted burglar to rob the home of a man known not to be security conscious in return for a percentage of the proceeds.

Patison and Jasper received seven-year sentences with a minimum of five to be served and Caccamo received eight years with the same minimum sentence. Forty former officers and three serving officers were said by the commission to have been guilty of a variety of offences, but because of the lack of corroboration they were never prosecuted. One Sydney solicitor was acquitted of bribery and acting with intent to pervert the course of justice. Nevertheless, the Law Society cancelled his practising certificate. It was reissued in 2009.

Ryan, who had just negotiated a new $400 000-a-year contract, was said to be very angry, as well he might be. Putting on a brave face, he told his force to 'Wear your uniform with pride'. But on the roads, drivers stopped for speeding were asking the police, 'How much?' Ryan said that the operation showed his reforms were working. In fairness to him, a good deal of the evidence heard by the commission pre-dated his appointment. It was a long uphill struggle in which eventually he was totally isolated. He resigned on 3 April 2002 amid scenes of recrimination on all sides. He became the security expert of the International Olympic Committee.

* * *

In March 2010 former officer Wendy Hatfield, married and living in Victoria, attempted to obtain an order against the makers of the television series *Underbelly: The Golden Mile*, which had repeated allegations she had had an affair with John Ibrahim. She wanted to see the programs before they were shown to the public, claiming her life could be destroyed by them. She failed but continued to deny any involvement with Ibrahim. An appeal to the Court of Appeal was rejected and in May she began an action for damages against the television channels and the series producers.

It was that month that probationary constable nineteen-year-old Jessica Parfrey claimed unfair dismissal. Usually it is policewomen who complain that they have been sexually harassed by their male colleagues but this time the badge was on the other breast. She had told her married field supervisor she wanted to have an affair with him and offered another officer oral sex in a hotel lavatory and again in the car park outside. The Industrial Relations Commission also heard she had offered to lie, saying she had seen a man, found standing a hundred yards from his car, driving the vehicle when she had not. Ingeniously (or perhaps ingenuously) she argued that most of the harassment had taken place off duty and so could not be counted. She failed in her action just as she had failed two subjects in her associate degree in policing.

Bikers

11

In the beginning there were the Hells Angels. Imported from California, the club was formed in Sydney in 1967 and was officially inaugurated in 1973. By then the Rebels had arrived and were at war with the Angels. Then came the Finks, probably a splinter from the Angels, the Coffin Cheaters, the Gypsy Jokers, the Nomads, the Comancheros and the Bandidos, as well as a whole host of smaller clubs. And last but by no means least, forty years later came the recently formed quasi-outlaw motorcycle gang (OMCG) Notorious, sometimes described derisively as 'Nike Bikies', whose members wear T-shirts and tennis shoes instead of beards and leathers. 'They don't even ride bikes' is the comment often made about them. Notorious grew out of the Nomads' now-defunct Parramatta chapter, which died while its president, Sam Ibrahim, was on remand in jail. In the autumn of 2010 Notorious had around thirty members, many of them Pacific Islanders and Middle Eastern men from Sydney's West. Its logo is a turbaned skull brandishing twin pistols, with the motto 'Only the dead see the end of war', and Alen Sarkis, a former Parramatta chapter Nomad and close associate of Ibrahim and his brothers, became its first national president. That autumn the gang targeted the Comancheros, whose president is a Shiite Muslim, in contrast to Notorious's affiliation to the Sunni Muslims.

Given the high attrition rate—death, motorcycle accidents, drugs and arrests—estimating the number of OMCG members is not an exact science. In 2003 Professor Arthur Veno of Monash

University put the number at between 2000 and 3000 in Australia, down from 8000 in 1980. In 2006 a report by the Australian Crime Commission put the number at 3500 members, spread over thirty-five gangs. Ten gangs had recently opened twenty-six new chapters in all six states. Others have put the estimate far higher: the Rebels, currently said to be Australia's largest gang, may have as many as 2000 members. In 2009 the Crime Commission thought the figure had remained static, with around 3500 bikers in thirty-nine gangs. There was, however, a notable recruitment of Pacific Islanders, used by the clubs as bouncers, bodyguards and in the drug trade. In the early months of 2009, twenty-two out of thirty-two drive-by shootings or bombings in Sydney were linked to biker gangs.

Apologists for the OMCGs say there is little or no evidence that the clubs are involved in organised crime and that it is individual members who are the culprits. Whether that is sophistry or the clubs take a slice from their members' misdeeds, or even back them, is another matter.

Over the years there has been intense rivalry between gangs, both business and personal. In the early 1980s OMCG interclub rivalry in New South Wales reached a high with the notorious Milperra battle between the Bandidos and the Comancheros, originally a Texas-based club then ruled in a paramilitary fashion by William 'Jock' Ross. In 1983, tiring of Ross's autocracy, members led by Anthony Mark 'Snodgrass' Spencer formed the first Australian chapter of the Bandidos in a breakaway movement from the Comancheros. It was clear that there was bad blood between the groups and from then on the Bandidos became a predominantly New South Wales–based club. Apart from the insult to the Comanchero colours, there were problems over the control of drug and gun running and prostitution. By the middle of winter the next year, relations, which had always been fragile, had completely broken down. On 11 August 1984 the Comancheros barricaded their clubhouse and put an armed sentry on the roof. In their turn the Bandidos posted guards.

Representatives of the two gangs met and it was agreed that on Father's Day that year there would be a full-on confrontation in the satellite town of Milperra, 24 kilometres south-west of Sydney. The venue was the car park of the Viking Hotel, where a swap meet of around 1000 motorcycle enthusiasts was being held. On 2 September 1984, at the end of a twelve-minute gun battle, twenty people had been injured and seven killed, including four Comancheros, two Bandidos and a fourteen-year-old girl, Leanne Walters, caught in the crossfire.

The police charged forty-three men with the murders. Before the trial, charges were dropped against eleven, one of whom, Bandido Bernard Podgorski, turned Queen's Evidence. On 25 June 1987 nine were found guilty of murder and twenty-one of manslaughter. One biker was found guilty of affray. The Court of Appeal substituted manslaughter for murder in three cases. Nine received life sentences. Snodgrass Spencer committed suicide in prison before the trial. In 2009 former Bandido Caesar Campbell claimed that the real reason for the split in the club had been that Jock Ross was sleeping with another member's wife, which led to the mass defection.

For a time the Milperra Massacre, as it became known, seriously undermined the position of the Comancheros in Australia. It also brought drastic changes in Australian gun laws. As a result of the massacre the *New South Wales Firearms and Dangerous Weapons Act 1973* was amended to include the temporary banning of semi-automatic weapons.

By the end of the 1990s OMCGs had moved into what was euphemistically called security, which translates as protection and standover, and there was major feuding among the larger clubs over control of the standing over of cafés and bars.

Just before noon on 9 November 1997, Michael Kulakowski, the National President of the Bandidos, turned up at the Blackmarket Cafe in Regent Street, Chippendale, with his girlfriend Angela Konz, the Bandidos' Sergeant-at-Arms, Sasha Milenkovic, and members Rick De Stoop and Robin David. As the group reached the door of the nightclub/café, they were met by Rebel member Justin Culshaw, who sometimes worked there as a bouncer but was then off-duty. Soon after, Constantine Georgiou, another Rebels member, arrived in his Porsche with his friends Bruce Malcolm Harrison and Reid Kingston. Below the café's dance floor and bar area was a basement cellar and storage room not open to the public.

According to Angela Konz, the Bandidos group was still at the bar when Kulakowski was called away by Milenkovic. She saw the pair walk towards the basement door and within minutes gunshots were heard coming from the cellar. Seconds later she saw first Georgiou and then Harrison rush out through the front door of the club. Harrison, she said, was holding a gun.

Bandidos Kulakowski, Milenkovic and Rick De Stoop were all shot dead in the cellar that day. Robin David escaped with his life. The evidence implicated several of the Rebels in what the court said 'had the appearance of planned executions'. The confrontation had been over profits and the lucrative business of providing security for the café. Harrison, with a wound to his hand, escaped with Georgiou in the Porsche. Harrison was caught near Surry Hills and Georgiou was arrested two months later as he tried to leave on a ship bound for Japan. The two maintained at trial that they were at the café primarily as lookouts and that it was Reid Kingston and another Rebel who had been in the cellar for the meeting with the Bandidos. In April 2000, and again after a retrial in 2003, a 28-year non-parole period was imposed on both. Their appeals against conviction and sentence were dismissed.

The year 1999 was a very difficult one for the Rebels: three members were shot dead in an Adelaide ambush; their former sergeant-at-arms, Paul William Wheeler, disappeared; and another member Paul Summers died in a machine-gun ambush while asleep at the Rebels' clubhouse in Gosford. Two years later, on 19 November 2001, the first parts of the dismembered remains of convicted amphetamine dealer and Rebels' associate Terry Wallace Falconer were found wrapped in mesh and weighted with rocks in the Hastings river on the mid-North Coast. Over the next week five more bags containing bits of Falconer were dragged from the river. The final bag surfaced in September 2002. Falconer, who had survived a shotgun attack in 1981 when forty pellets were embedded in his face, had been serving a five-year stretch for manufacturing a commercial amount of speed. He was on day work release from Silverwater prison when he was abducted from a smash repair shop by three men posing as police officers. A chemically doused handkerchief was shoved into his mouth and he was led away in handcuffs. He was never seen alive again.

Despite a fourteen-month investigation and a number of arrests for drug-related offences, no one was charged with his murder for nearly a decade. Then, on 19 January 2009, Anthony and Andrew Perish and Matthew Lawton were arrested by undercover police officers dressed as plumbers at the Lavender Blue Café at McMahon's Point, and charged with Falconer's murder. The prosecution alleged his killing was related to the murder of the Perish brothers' grandparents, both in their nineties, who were shot and killed on 14 June 1993. Before he died, Falconer was due to give evidence at an inquest on the Perishes as well as informing on the Rebels, of which Andrew Perish was a member. The three deny the charges. Andrew Perish had vanished immediately after the deaths of his grandparents. He was only found by police in 2006, when he was living in an armour-plated room in a fortified house outside Sydney.

* * *

In 2003 the Australian Crime Commission reported that biker gangs were behind the flood of illegal amphetamines onto Australian streets and were suspected of forming alliances with other crime groups, such as ethnic gangs, to distribute amphetamine-type stimulants and ecstasy. Literally hundreds of secret drug labs were discovered or raided around the country and it was estimated that biker gangs controlled 75 per cent of the methamphetamine trade, with one in five clandestine laboratories directly linked to OMCGs. In New South Wales seventy-two labs were uncovered along with a seven-lab Nomad drug network which resulted in fifty-one arrests. OMCGs were also said to be involved in vehicle theft, car rebirthing, currency counterfeiting and fraud. They run guns and prostitutes, stand over bars and are contract killers.

That year a Hunter Valley amphetamine network of over twenty people linked to the Nomads came before the courts in Newcastle in one of the biggest criminal trials in New South Wales; it was certainly one that had serious repercussions for the Parramatta chapter. Club members obtained their methamphetamines from two Nomads: Tony Vizl supplied the pure drug to Johnny Skyrus, who cut and distributed it. Richard Walsh, who had joined the Newcastle Nomads in 1995, then began to help with distribution. When in 1997 Skyrus was killed in a motorcycle accident Walsh moved into his position as cutter and distributor, obtaining supplies from Vizl, who had moved to Queensland. Walsh soon after became the Newcastle Nomads' sergeant-at-arms.

Walsh and his de facto Melinda Love enlisted the assistance of dozens of others to help cut the drug or act as couriers or distributors. His new manufacturer from 1999 was Todd Douglas Little, who had premises, labs and storage sheds in and around Murwillumbah. They were found to hold containers of drugs, lab equipment, chemicals and liquids, firearms (including a semi-automatic handgun with a silencer) and over $145000 in cash. It was estimated that from September 1999 to September 2001 he had received about $2.5 million from Walsh. Between March 1997 and September 2001, Walsh purchased 50 kilograms (110 pounds) of about 77 per cent pure methamphetamine for around $50 000 to $60 000 per pound. After cutting it with other compounds, he distributed about 450 kilograms of the drug to some seventy-five Nomad members and associates. To give some perspective on the size of this operation, one kilogram qualifies as a 'large commercial quantity'. Walsh was also in the business of stealing trucks to harvest their parts, and rebirthing vehicles used in his construction work as a concreter.

Robert Zdravkovic was among the high-ranking Nomad members working with them, and Walsh's cleaner, Anne Chapman, and her husband, Paul, also got in on Walsh's business, as lab tester and courier respectively. Following a dispute, Paul Chapman lost his position. He and Melinda Love later became indemnified witnesses.

In 2004 some Sydney Nomads went to Newcastle to remonstrate with the local chapter over what they saw as its abandonment of Walsh after he received thirty-two years for the drug offences. The Newcastle sergeant-at-arms, Dale Campton, and member Mark Chrystie were beaten up and kneecapped. Sam Ibrahim, Scott Orrock and two others were charged with the assaults but in 2008 all were acquitted. However, while they were on remand in custody the Parramatta chapter of the Nomads effectively came to an end. Members drifted away, either to join other chapters or to patch over to Bandidos and Rebels. But a hard core, said to have been organised by Ibrahim's brother Michael, formed an OMCG for bikers without bikes, the highly militant and multicultural Notorious.

Meanwhile, back in Sydney, nightclub owner Sam Ibrahim had been trying to put an end to a bikers war between the Nomads and the Rebels. Around Christmas 2004 the Rebels had formed a Queensland chapter without consulting the local Nomads, which resulted in ill feeling. As president of the Nomads' Parramatta chapter, Ibrahim now indicated that he would fight Rebel leader Alex Vella, known as 'The Maltese Falcon', with 'guns or fists anywhere, anytime'. This would, he said, stop innocent members of the opposing clubs getting hurt. The police did not think this was a good idea and suggested they broker a peaceful meeting. Under Sam Ibrahim's leadership, the once all-white Nomads opened their doors to the ethnic minorities.

* * *

On the night of 11 February 2006, one of half a dozen bearded men told a bouncer at the Sapphire Suite in Kings Cross that they were Hells Angels. The bouncer made the mistake of refusing them admission and was promptly shot in the leg. A woman in the queue was grazed by a bullet. It was the first in a series of incidents involving rival biker gangs that autumn.

On 16 March, another shooting occurred, this time outside the Men's Gallery club in Pitt Street. The police claimed that the victim was a member of the Nomads, who had been shot by a former member of the Finks who had recently defected to the Angels. Police suspected that the shooting was a way of announcing that the Hells Angels, long dormant in Sydney, were back in town and ready to reclaim their mantle.

On 26 March, Showgirls, another men's club in Kings Cross, played unwilling host to a biker squabble which resulted in the shooting of the Nomads' national sergeant-at-arms. Although reports said the shooter was not a patched Hells Angel, and the dispute concerned a woman not turf, the incident was taken as further evidence that biker gang members were 'armed and dangerous' in inner Sydney.

On 20 April a group of Bandidos met up at Bar Reggio in East Sydney. They were waiting for their meals when an argument between two members—one current and one former office-bearer—spilled over into the street. In a lane behind the restaurant gunshots were fired, from a high-calibre automatic pistol, according to police. Bandido Rodney Monk was killed, and 39-year-old Russell Merrick Oldham jumped into a taxi to Town Hall railway station.

Oldham was a medical school dropout. He had been working in the clubs in Kings Cross as a doorman when he met boxing promoter, club owner and Sydney identity Phillip Player, who employed him as a bodyguard and doorman at his Bonnie and Clyde nightclub in Newtown, where the staff dressed as gangsters. Player used Oldham's middle name for the company Merrick Player Group Ltd; the convicted drug smuggler Duncan Lam was a fellow director. In time, Player moved to Darwin—where he was being investigated over his connections with drug dealers and money launderers—and later to China. Oldham joined the Bandidos and in 2000 was sentenced to five years for manslaughter following an ambush of two men in Bankstown. He was released in 2003.

In Oldham's absence Monk had been elevated to club president, deposing Felix Lyle, a friend of the Vincent family from Market Street known as 'Big F', on the grounds that he was of bad character. There was considerable ill feeling between Monk and Lyle and an internal feud was brewing over the murder of Milad Sande—the nephew of one of Melbourne's biggest heroin dealers. Sande, an associate of both the Bandidos and the Nomads, had been shot in the head and dumped beside a waterfront park in Malabar on 23 November 2005 while delivering $2 million worth of pseudoephedrine to other Bandidos. The buyers, who had ripped off Sande, then endured weeks of painful and expensive payback at the hands of the Nomads. Monk took the killing badly and the next year, when Lyle's 24-year-old son Dallas Fitzgerald was kidnapped and tortured, Monk was suspected of being behind it. Now, as president, Monk stripped Lyle of his gang colours. He also suspected Oldham of being involved in the drug rip-off and of breaking club rules by organising trysts with a female parole officer. Oldham was now facing expulsion.

After Monk's shooting, Oldham made no contact with his family, who had always been concerned for him. Then, on the night of 12 May, witnesses saw him wading into the water at Balmoral Beach, raising a gun to his head and shooting himself. Monk's funeral was well attended by the Bandidos and the eulogy was given by his older brother, Detective Inspector Brad Monk. In contrast, Oldham's funeral was private, for fear of reprisals. His former employer Player commented, 'He was a very intelligent, lovely bloke who lost his way over the years.'

* * *

In the mid-1990s, former police officer Ray 'Chopper' Johnson, the Bandidos' one-time sergeant-at-arms and friend of Roger Rogerson, had more than his share of trouble. First, he was charged with drug dealing. He was acquitted but while he was in custody he sent two drug dealers he knew to 'clean up' his home. They found $270 000 in cash and jewellery, along with a pistol hidden in his rockery and, unfortunately for Johnson, they took it all to the police. Understandably upset, Johnson took his Bandido friend Tony Olivieri to confront them, and was consequently charged with interfering with witnesses. He was convicted but in June 2002 his conviction and that of Olivieri for conspiracy to 'prevent, obstruct or dissuade witnesses from attending trial' were quashed.

Olivieri had his own troubles. In 2006 he was convicted of the contract killing of solicitor Tom Williams, whom he shot five times, and was sentenced to twenty-eight years. He had been hired by Burwood tax agent Mark Norman, who believed Williams was about to expose him as a swindler. Norman was also convicted and received a minimum of 29 years. Both indicated they would appeal.

In October 2002, Sean Lawrence Waygood, who later pleaded guilty for his part in kidnapping Terry Falconer, shot at Raniera Puketapu outside a central Sydney pub. He had mistaken the unfortunate Puketapu for either the disgraced former Bandido president Felix Lyle or his son Dallas Fitzgerald. Because of the exceptional help he had given in relation to the Falconer murder, and the resulting danger to himself and his family, Waygood received a mere fifteen-year minimum.

A high point for Lyle during his presidency was an acquittal on an ecstasy conspiracy charge but then things went steadily south. The New South Wales Crime Commission froze his $3 million Sydney property portfolio only to discover that he had inflated its worth by 100 per cent. After he was made bankrupt, the 57-year-old, who described himself as a 'project manager', claimed he had only $100 in cash and had been forced to move from the old Pyrmont dwelling (once the Bandidos clubhouse) to a Rozelle boarding house.

Lyle's name resurfaced in the civil courts in 2010 when he was alleged to have been involved with Terrence Reddy, one of many men known as the 'Black Prince' and once the right-hand man of conman Michael McGurk. Reddy was considering whether to give evidence against another biker, Alex Marcello, in a civil case brought by the Perpetual Trustees of Victoria over an alleged mortgage fraud dating back to 2005. Reddy said he feared Marcello, but during the case he was given a certificate of immunity from prosecution. At the end of the month lawyers acting for Perpetual Trustees announced that, although they intended to call Lyle, they had yet to trace him. The judge thought they might best start looking for him at the Gas Nightclub he was said to own. If not there then Lyle might also be found farewelling Jamie Vincent, of the well-known Sydney family, who was about to begin a prison sentence in November that year.

* * *

The Angels were not the only club moving into Sydney. One Comanchero who survived the Milperra battle was Raymond 'Sunshine' Kucler, who later deposed Jock Ross, the Comanchero founder and president. Two decades on from Milperra, the Comancheros were on the rise again. Reports were that this gang was recruiting around Sydney in 2006 and the members are younger and mainly Lebanese–Australian. The days when OMCGs were white supremacists are passing. Now relationships are being formed with Middle Eastern and Asian crime gangs and mafia-type groups.

On 15 March 2007 masked men broke into the Mr Goodbar Club in Paddington, fired shots into the ceiling and proceeded to smash up the bar. One of the assaulted men was Fadi Khalifeh, the bodyguard of club owner John Ibrahim. No money was taken and the police believed the attack was a move by rival biker gangs to establish control of the area.

Biker gangs often use bombs as warnings or weapons. Most clubhouses are fortified against bomb attacks from rival gangs, but this did not deter the firebombing of the Angels' clubhouse in Crystal Street, Petersham, on 4 February. The new kid on the block, Notorious, was believed to be behind the attack, in retaliation for the murder of associate Todd O'Connor. O'Connor was shot seven times in the body and three in the head in a park in South Street, Tempe.

In July 2010 a jury failed to reach even a majority decision at the trial in which ex-law student Hugo Jacobs (who had changed his name from Hashem Ibrahim but was not related to the Kings Cross nightclub owner's family) was charged with O'Connor's murder. It was perhaps unfortunate for the Crown that it was forced to offer alternative scenarios for the killing, claiming that either Jacobs had shot O'Connor with the help of another person or that he had hired two hitmen—two weapons were used—to kill the drug dealer and money lender to whom it was alleged Jacobs owed over \$300000. Just before the shooting Jacobs had been recorded by the New South Wales Crime Commission (who had a tap on O'Connor's phone) saying, 'I'm just in the park,' but he claimed it was a different park from the one in which O'Connor was shot.

On 27 February 2009 three members of the Nomads had been shot by masked gunmen in an attack on their Sydney clubhouse in Chalder Street, Marrickville. This was generally regarded as surprising—the ongoing war was thought to be between the Hells Angels and the Comancheros. On 7 February a year later a Comanchero was shot in the leg in Silverwater, allegedly by Hells Angels. That month, Angel Peter Zervas was also shot—in the shoulder, chest, abdomen and foot—when a gunman fired eleven bullets at him through the rear right window of his car. A police source has alleged that the shooting was orchestrated by the Comancheros.

Biker fights tend to be reported only locally if at all—but one that received nationwide coverage was a mass brawl on 22 March 2010. It took place at Sydney airport when members of the Comancheros fought with members of the Hells Angels. Peter Zervas's younger brother Anthony was killed. The trouble began when Hells Angel Derek Wainohu, then president of the Sydney chapter, ran into five Comancheros on a Qantas flight from Melbourne. Out came their mobile phones and members of both gangs were summoned to the arrivals hall. Things escalated when the Comanchero national president, Mahmoud 'Mick' Hawi, threatened and punched Wainohu, and the denouement came at the domestic check-in desk at Terminal Three. Anthony Zervas, among the Angels' reinforcements, attempted to stab Hawi. The Comancheros then beat Anthony Zervas with steel bollards and stomped on his head. He died from multiple fractures to his skull and stab wounds in the lung, liver and stomach. Ten Comancheros were charged and three Angels were charged with affray. In January 2011, Peter Zervas, said by psychiatrists to be suffering from post-traumatic stress disorder which a prison sentence would only worsen, pleaded guilty to affray. All others deny the charges. Two more Comancheros pleaded guilty to affray and one who received a nine-month sentence became a Crown witness, claiming he had only gone to the airport as a chauffeur. It was reported that the Angels then put a $100,000 contract on Hawi. Another report has it that Hells Angels leaders in America ordered their Australian club to shoot at any Comanchero they saw to restore the gang's image.

In July 2010 the police began their attempt to have the Hells Angels declared a 'criminal organisation'. Unsurprisingly, it brought a wave of support from other OMCGs, but also a challenge in the High Court by the chapter's now former president Derek Wainohu, who argued that the *Crimes (Criminal Organisations Control) Act*, passed in the wash-up of the airport brawl, 'undermines the constitutional integrity of the Supreme Court'.

It may be that Notorious, said to have links with industry and the police, will become the most powerful of the Sydney OMCGs. Some members might already have eyes on the interstate drug market. One reason is that in July 2010 in Western Australia the price of one ounce of methamphetamine—or speed—fetched almost double the price that it did in New South Wales.

In September 2010 the current head of Notorious, Alen Sarkis, was given a suspended sentence but in October he and the second-in-command, Sofe Levi, were charged with an assault on a Comanchero biker in Campbell Parade, Bondi, allegedly breaking his ankle. Their lawyer indicated there would be a plea of self-defence.

On 3 September 2009 Scottish-born loan shark and standover man Michael McGurk—who had been cleared earlier that year of assaulting two men he claimed owed him money and firebombing their houses—was shot at close range, killed in front of his ten-year-old son in the driveway of his house on Cranbrook Avenue. One initial suggestion was that he was shot by a former outlaw biker chief, hired by people McGurk had ripped off. Those whose debts McGurk chose to pursue could expect to be attacked with crowbars and their cars smashed. He was another whose victims of property deals and scams could have been said to be lining up to kill him. In October 2010 the former Australian featherweight champion boxer Lucky Gattellari, his business partner, former Bosnian soldier Senad Kaminic, Haissam Safwetli and twenty-year-old Chris Estephan were charged with conspiracy to murder. All have denied the charge. By the end of the month multi-millionaire businessman Ron Medich was accused of contracting McGurk's murder, which was said to have been worth $250000. And down the chain it is alleged to have gone, from Medich to Gattellari, on to Kaminic and in turn to Safwetli and Estephan, who, it is alleged, were present when the fatal shot was fired. Medich has also denied the charge. In November 2010 it was reported that some of the men charged with McGurk's murder had agreed to give evidence against Medich. In December he was given bail, with the judge declaring that the evidence so far presented against him was not strong.

Back in May 2007 Detective Superintendent Scott Whyte, appearing on ABC's broadcast on potential biker wars, had summed up the situation saying:

> I've got no doubt that in ten years the dynamics of outlaw motorcycle gangs will be very different to what it is today. I couldn't even speculate as to which way it will go. I think we just have to keep on monitoring it, keep on top of it, keep our eyes open, keep our minds open for the change.

Now, four years later, anyone foolish enough to think that outlaw bikers have cleaned up their image and are simply businessmen who go for rides at weekends or distribute toys for sick children at Christmas, as their apologists would have you believe, should think again. Certainly the New South Wales police did not think this. They believed a number of Kings Cross clubs, including The Tunnel and George David and Sonny Freeman's Lady Lux, were in danger of becoming biker haunts. Between November 2006 and August 2009 there were said to have been forty-one biker-related incidents at clubs, hotels and bars in the area. They included assault, kidnappings and the shooting of doormen, as well as the standover. Notorious was alleged to be demanding $5000 a week for protection. The police intend to try to impose conditions on liquor licensees not to allow in biker members. Failure to comply would carry a one-year sentence and an $11000 fine. There are also disturbing signs that outsiders are being drawn into the wars. Generally, provided they stay at arms-length from their clients, lawyers are safe, but one lawyer representing Notorious members was held at gunpoint by masked men who burst into her Hurstville home after midnight and rifled through her property. Others are understood to have been warned they are targets.

Notorious and the Comancheros do not get on, so it is not surprising if there is truth to the story that in the spring of 2010 Comanchero members kidnapped a Notorious drug dealer and tortured him until he revealed where some 70 kilograms of Chinese heroin was hidden. Employing the age-old trick of the red and blue lights used by police to pull the dealer over, the Comancheros then forced him out of his car at gunpoint in Rozelle. The drugs were said to have come into Sydney through Port Botany; 70 kilograms of it was sold to Notorious and 77 kilograms to the Comancheros but, after the raid, the Comancheros had the lot. The financial blow to Notorious members was said to be in the region of $25 million.

Towards the end of 2010 there were signs of further violence. In October there was a mass brawl between Comanchero and Notorious members in Kings Cross and another at a Bondi tattoo parlour. At the end of November shots were fired at the Ryde home of Armani Stelio, Sam Ibrahim's sister, and the next day Notorious sergeant-at-arms Saber Murad was shot in Doonside. Later in the month the tattoo shop of senior Comanchero Mark Buddle and national president Duax 'Dax' Ngakuru was torched.

And 2011 began badly or, viewed another way, it began well for Sam Ibrahim when he was shot in the legs in a drive-by at his mother's home in Merrylands. The police treated the attack as an attempted murder. There were reports that Sam Ibrahim had re-established the Parramatta branch of the Nomads. Ibrahim passed on a message to his attackers through his lawyer Brett Galloway: 'Bad luck.'

The bad luck continued. On 13 February 2011 two men connected to the Ibrahim family were shot during a fight on The Promenade, Old Guildford. One was thought to be Hassan Sayour, John Ibrahim's nephew.

Laws attempting to curtail illegal biker activity vary from state to state, so it is likely that the OMCGs will migrate from the states where they are viewed as criminal organisations to states where such laws have not yet been enacted.

The Drug Trade

12

'We're not the Anglo-Saxon country we were in the 1960s and 1970s,' said Superintendent Scott Whyte of the New South Wales Gang Squad in a television broadcast in 2007. And of course he was correct. From the 1970s onwards, two things changed the face of Australian organised crime irrevocably. The first was the huge expansion in the importation and manufacture of drugs, and the second, closely linked, was the repeal of the White Australia policy.

Originally drug trafficking was in the hands of the old-fashioned, blue-collar, white criminals, but things did not stay that way. One officer recalls: 'After 1970 there was the emergence of Middle Eastern and Asian criminals who lived in Australia and who realised from a commercial perspective that it was far more profitable to import the drugs themselves from people they knew and trusted, and they could take the lion's share.' And take the lion's share they did. Their involvement increased exponentially. During the late 1960s and early 1970s, crackdowns on secret societies gave Chinese criminals and gangsters in Singapore and Malaysia pause for thought— perhaps there were greener pastures not far south. It cannot have gone unnoticed that Australia, as yet, had no national police force and state forces were preoccupied with their own duckhouses.

During the 1960s Singapore's Triad gangs had been the subject of intense police scrutiny, and in the early 1970s Malaysian authorities followed Singapore's lead, conducting a similar crack-down. Triads closely resembled Mary's little lamb: wherever the

Chinese community went, they were sure to follow. By the 1970s some half a dozen powerful triad gangs were thought to be operating in Sydney and Melbourne — among them the Wo Yee Tong, Sun Yee On, Wo Shing Wo, 14K and the Big Circle from mainland China.

Interviewed in October 2005 for ABC Television's *Australian Story*, the corrupt New South Wales police officer Trevor Haken said: 'The Chinese in Chinatown were virtually a law unto themselves. They were involved in all sorts of crime, from video pirating right through to heroin importations, illegal gambling, prostitution.

By the 1980s law enforcement agencies accepted that ethnic Chinese were indeed the major organisers of heroin imports into Australia. The National Crime Authority's Chinese liaison officer in 1988 reported that the Chinese had been linked to every major seizure of heroin in the preceding two years; that seizures totalled 63 kilograms and of those 96 per cent were thought to be Triad-related. And while ethnic Chinese were primarily wholesalers, rarely involved at the local distribution level, they then also supplied other groups, often non-Chinese, who were distributors.

Of course the Chinese were not the only wholesalers. Lebanese gangs began to develop from the 1960s. Beirut — already a multicultural city, with Christians, Muslims and Druze living together in a melting pot — was seen by fun-seeking Arabs from strict Islamic countries as a vice-laden holiday mecca. The civil war in the 1970s forced Beirut's vice kings to close down their establishments and look further afield. Many operators moved first to Bombay and later to Bangkok. Australia was a short sail away for drug dealers who, instead of buying from Chinese wholesalers, now used their contacts in Bangkok.

By the 1980s the Lebanese-born Bayeh brothers, Louis and Bill, had built up serious businesses, money and reputations. Although initially hoons for Lennie McPherson, with bribes to, and help from, the police, they came to be the effective controllers of Kings Cross. With their colleague, the go-between and fixer Frank

Hakim, the Bayehs established a working relationship not only with the East Coast Milieu, but also with government figures such as Sir Rex Jackson.

Of the Bayeh brothers, Louis was regarded as physically bigger and marginally less bright but neither were thought to be really smart. Louis Bayeh's highest profile moment came when he gave evidence before the Wood Commission in 1995 claiming he had paid hundreds of thousands of dollars in bribes and naming the police officers involved. Two years later he was described by an acting judge as 'obese, illiterate, unable to find gainful employment, a hypochondriac, panic-stricken, of questionable morals and an author of his own misfortune'.

There were plenty waiting in the wings to take over his interests in the Cross. According to witness KX11 in the Wood Commission, Louis and Bill Bayeh had divided the territory between them but Alex Mattae and Russell Townsend were still controlling street operators, with Bayeh protégé Danny Karam operating on the fringes.

On 2 July 2000 Louis Bayeh was seriously injured in a shootout in the foyer of the El-Bardowny Restaurant in Narwee, south-west Sydney. Initially it was thought the incident was part of a power struggle and detectives, following reports of threats in the hospital at Long Bay prison, investigated the possibility that a contract had been taken out on Bayeh. Perhaps disappointingly, the shooting turned out to have been over a jacket. In January 2001, still suffering from his gunshot wounds, Bayeh pleaded guilty to standing over brothel owner Antoine Debruyne. He also asked for a similar offence involving John Hundy to be taken into account.

According to Bayeh, over the years $180000 had been shared with corrupt New South Wales police officers. On 27 July Bayeh limped into the dock to receive sentences totalling three years with a minimum of two to be served. On 26 February 2002 he was acquitted of charges relating to the shooting.

Louis Bayeh's explanation as to his wealth had been the usual one. His annual income of $36 000 was supplemented by his gambling winnings to such an extent that he was able to put $126 000 towards a $526 000 home in Gladesville. However, according to evidence given to the Royal Commission, Louis Bayeh acted as a standover man, earning $20 000 a week.

In May 1999 brother Bill had gone down on drugs charges and was sentenced to eighteen years. He and Karam had been keen to introduce heroin users to cocaine on the grounds that it was more profitable. By 2005 Bayeh could reflect from his cell that the use of cocaine was now rife among the general public and not simply the party-going rich. Under the Bayehs' regime things had been almost gentlemanly. As they faded, from then on things changed dramatically.

Karam, a former commando in the Lebanese Christian Army, had worked as a rigger after he migrated to Australia in 1983 but soon found drugs more profitable. Now he ran DK's Boys, a gang that organised the supply of cocaine to their own street-level runners but also stood over other dealers who paid them protection money, known as 'rent', so that the competitor dealers could operate without fear of harassment in the form of robberies, beatings and shootings. The rent collection business alone brought in around $30 000 a week.

DK's Boys were also encouraged to set up their own little networks of cocaine cappers, dealers and runners so long as 'rent' was paid up the line to Karam. The gang was also early to recognise the benefit of mobile phones, regularly changing and swapping them to disrupt police surveillance.

It was in 1993, when Karam was said to be out of control and trying to feed a $1000-a-day heroin habit, that he was slated to be the subject of an attack. It was arranged by the husband of a woman with whom he was having an affair and his shooting was designed as a lesson but not a fatal one. It went horribly wrong. On

23 February, the hired gunmen unfortunately went to an incorrect address. Instead of Karam being shot in the legs at No. 50, sixty-year-old Leslie Betcher was shot in the stomach at No. 15 and died that night.

Shortly afterwards Karam was imprisoned for assault and he began to see if not The Light then at least that he needed to control his drug habit and he seems to have made efforts to do so. At the Wood Royal Commission he came out of the woodwork to talk about Kings Cross and his relationship with Bill Bayeh. If he had indeed seen The Light, it soon dimmed to candle-force. On his release he continued to lead a ten-strong gang, which in 1998 killed three innocent people in a drive-by shooting and to have carried out another twenty shootings over Sydney in a twelve-month period. The last had been a drive-by at the EP1 nightclub in Kings Cross when over fifty shots were fired.

DK's Boys included Michael Kanaan, Rabeeh Mawas, Wassim El-Assaad, Charlie Gea Gea and a number of others who were later given pseudonyms for their own protection. One of these, code-named Rossini, was close to Kanaan and the two of them were among those seriously dissatisfied with the boss.

On the evening of 13 December 1998, when Karam left his Randwick home in his Toyota RAV4 to go to a meeting in Surry Hills, four men were waiting for him. He was shot through the open window and at least five bullets hit him in the chest and body. As the gunmen escaped, another man ran over to the dying Karam and stole his wallet and mobile phone. In his hurry he missed the 12-gauge pump-action shotgun on the back seat.

As these things do, it took a little while to sort out just who had killed Karam and why. The answers, when they came, were that it was Michael Kanaan and other members of the gang, tired of doing the work while Karam took the profits. In 2002 Kanaan received life imprisonment for the three murders. Mawas a non-parole period of nineteen years and El-Assaad a year less. By then the killers of the unfortunate Leslie Betcher had also been dealt with. On 18 December 1998, after three trials, John Leslie Baartman, the lookout, was sentenced to fifteen years' imprisonment. The actual gunman, Paul Thomas Crofts, had already pleaded guilty and received the same sentence. The hit had been worth $1000.

Kanaan was in a wheelchair by the time he came to trial for Karam's murder. On 23 December 1998 he had been hit in the back and leg after shooting at police as he tried to escape. He got trapped in Rushcutters Bay while looking for another of the more colourful Sydney identities, John Ibrahim. One officer was shot in the wrist and Kanaan was hit seven times by another.

* * *

It is, perhaps, the Vietnamese who have had the highest profile in the rise of ethnic minority crime in Australia. The Vietnam War had an enormous impact on the demand for, and supply of, drugs. Vietnamese refugees began arriving in the early 1980s and were initially placed in a camp at Villawood from where it was a short walk to Cabramatta, once the home of Italians, Irish and Yugoslavs but soon to be colonised by the new arrivals. Most were hardworking people seeking a better life for their children, but of course some were criminals and ambitious gang wannabes.

Lebanese gangs such as DK's Boys may have roamed Sydney but they took care to avoid Cabramatta, whose youth gangs included the 5T—the most recognised and vicious. The name 5T can stand just about any interpretation, with the most popular suggestion being that it comes from five Vietnamese words beginning with 't' meaning 'love, money, prison, death and conviction', or alternatively 'Young people who lack love and care', the very image the gang members would wish to promote. Whatever the derivation, the gang employed the age-old rackets of any burgeoning community. Restaurant owners holding a wedding party would be told, 'Give me $500 or there will be trouble on the wedding night.' The 5T and other gangs opened or controlled illegal gaming clubs and forced shopkeepers to install their poker machines. The money was recycled into the importation of prostitutes and drugs.

By the end of the twentieth century Sydney was recognised as the national gateway for the majority of illegal imports, and Cabramatta had been targeted as the centre for distribution, sale and purchase of drugs. There, 68 per cent of the population had been born in a non-English speaking country and 69 per cent spoke a language other than English at home.

The 5T enforced a prohibition on senior gang members injecting heroin but not on smoking it. They and other gangs provided what some sociologists saw as a family for youths, often from single-parent families. They clothed members, fed them, found girls and drugs for them and in return demanded loyalty and obedience. In 1992 two youths were killed because they had upset the 5T. One was beaten to death and a second, Duong Van Chu, was shot, a killing said to be witnessed by 200 people. No charges were brought.

By the mid-1990s there was a police crackdown, prompted by a huge increase in heroin overdoses and the 6 September 1994 murder of John Newman, the ALP state MP for Cabramatta. Elected in 1986, Newman was a strong anti-crime campaigner who regarded the Mekong Club in his constituency—run by Phuong Ngo, who had once stood as an independent candidate—as a money-laundering operation. Before his death Newman's car had been firebombed and he had received a series of threatening letters. On the evening he was killed he attended a local branch meeting and was putting a cover on his car when he was shot in his yard. Ngo and three others were arrested after a coronial inquest at which they all gave evidence but had little worthwhile to say.

In June 2001 Phuong Ngo, who had undertaken not to run against Newman while he was a sitting member, was convicted of organising the hit. The sentencing judge said it had been a crime of 'naked political ambition and impatience'. The alleged driver and gunman were acquitted. Phuong Ngo continued to protest his innocence. A report on ABC's *Four Corners* and a submission by a Canberra academic raised questions over analysis of telephone recordings, the evidence given by two indemnified witnesses and evidence not originally disclosed by the police. In 2008 a review of his conviction was conducted by the retired judge David Patten. Over thirty-six days, twenty-three witnesses gave evidence and on 17 April the next year Patten concluded there was no doubt Phuong Ngo had masterminded the murder.

In August 1989 5T members Van Ro Le (known as 'Madonna'), Dung Hing Le and Tri Minh Tran were charged with killing Phu Tuan Nguyen, who was stabbed to death in Cabramatta. Madonna and Dung Hing Le were convicted. Tran was acquitted and became the undisputed head of the 5T. Tran came from a relatively wealthy family and by the age of eleven he had spent six months in a children's institution after being found with a sawn-off rifle. It was said he turned down the $10 000 contract on Newman.

After Madonna was released from prison, a power struggle developed among the 5T, then estimated to have a membership of around forty with 100 wannabes. Tran was unwilling to hand over the reins and Madonna received a bad beating. Then, on 9 August 1995, the twenty-year-old Tran was shot and killed when he opened his front door in McBurney Road, Cabramatta. Bullets went through his hands into his nose and face. A second member of the 5T, Than Hao Nguyen, who was also in the flat, was shot twice in the face and head and twice in the stomach.

After Tran's death the gang splintered. Reprisals came on 30 September when the 5T shot at least seven breakaway members outside the Jadran Hadjuk, a Croatian club at Bonnyrigg, which was holding a Vietnamese fashion show. No one was killed. Some 280 patrons claimed they were in the club's four lavatories when the shooting took place. The *Sydney Morning Herald* noted that if this was really the case the club should seriously consider changing its caterers.

At this stage, it seems the prohibition against gang members injecting broke down, resulting in increased drug addiction and anarchy as the smaller gangs struggled for money and markets. New groups—including The Four Aces, the Black and Red Dragon gangs and Van Ro Le's Madonna Boys, or Mob (Members of the Brotherhood)—came into existence. Where there was one, now there were many. On 5 February 1999 Madonna was killed in a drive-by shooting outside the Cumberland Hotel in Bankstown.

One theory of crime control is that it should begin at the bottom. The anti-drugs strategy included shutting down the drug houses, stopping the illegal trafficking of firearms and clearing the streets of dealers and users as well as decreasing the number of guns floating around the community. A 'Clean-Up Cabramatta' campaign began on 1 July 2001 and by the next year *Cabramatta: A Report of Progress* detailed seventy-five drug houses eliminated, 532 charges of illegal firearm trafficking in New South Wales, and 209 people facing a total of 288 supply charges, an increase of 50 per cent from 2000. Nevertheless gangs such as the Red and Black Dragons still operated, if more quietly. As the authorities seized more and more imports, the reduction in the availability of heroin had a knock-on effect. Car thefts were down. Until then, addicts had been stealing cars to get themselves to Cabramatta.

By the end of the 1990s it was the second generation of Lebanese–Australians who staked out their territories. At least six young Lebanese gangs had been engaged for some eighteen months in tit-for-tat bloodlettings, with more than 115 drive-by shootings, kneecappings and killings—the worst for some four decades.

Indeed one-third of all Australian firearm homicides in the period 1999–2000 took place in New South Wales. By now it was far easier and cheaper to buy a semi-automatic weapon than a sawn-off shotgun in the city.

Over the first years of the twenty-first century the violence escalated. The first victim was a presumed drug dealer, Michael Collins, who was shot dead and wrapped in a blanket at his home in Darlinghurst Road, Roselands, in May 2001. His death was followed a month later by that of another relatively small-time dealer, Bassam Mansour, who was stabbed and then dropped off at the Long Jetty Medical Clinic, where he died. Then, on 13 December 2002, Dimitri Debaz, a senior member of a gang known as the Bronx Boys, was shot by Raymon Youmaran in the car park of the Playhouse Hotel, Sefton, in what the police claimed was a drug-related killing. A fight had broken out at Dimitri's brother Aleck's birthday party, at which Youmaran and his friends arrived armed with a Glock pistol and another gun. Dimitri left the hotel and was shot when Youmaran and (so the prosecution allege) Raphael Joseph sprayed bullets. Debaz was hit three times at close range while he was on the ground sheltering behind a car. There had, it appears, been bad blood between Joseph and his offsider Sandro Mirad and the Debaz family. Aleck was shot in the leg. Sandro Mirad was charged with the murder and warrants were issued for the arrest of two other men. Three days before Christmas, Aleck was alleged to have shot at Hendrick Chekazine, pulling up at an intersection in the outer western suburb of West Hoxton after each had left separate memorial services.

In 2004 Mirad received a thirty-month sentence with an eighteen-month minimum after pleading guilty to being an accessory. Joseph, however, led the authorities on a merry dance, fleeing to the United States, where he fought an ultimately unsuccessful battle to avoid extradition on the grounds that he would be killed by the Bronx Boys on his return to Sydney.

Remaining in Australia, Youmaran stayed out of police hands until he was dobbed in at the end of May 2006. During a period of nearly two years on remand in custody, where he exercised in a two-by-three-metre yard and was kept in handcuffs when he went to use the telephone or see his lawyer, Youmaran took up a Bible class. In July 2008 he received a seventeen-year sentence with a thirteen-year minimum.

The Bronx Boys originated at a housing estate in Villawood, known as the Bronx. They first emerged in the late 1990s, graduating from petty crime and vandalism to more serious crimes. By 1998 they were said to be dealing in $40 000 of cocaine weekly, as well as in cannabis, stockpiling weapons and acting as armourers for other gangs. At one time they had occupied the home of a terminally ill woman and were dealing cocaine from her front yard, divvying up the proceeds in her bedroom. Applications by police for surveillance equipment and outside assistance were rejected. The estate was knocked down that year but by then it was too late to stop the gang's expansion.

It might have been a financially rewarding life but it was a dangerous one. The Bronx Boys were having troubles with the Assyrian Kings—or Spenser Street Boys, also known as Dlasthr (The Last Hour)—a rival gang from West Sydney whose members have a fist tattooed on their backs with the letters 'AK'. In the period between May 2001 and October 2003 there were nine murders, four drive-by shootings, ninety-nine arrests and eighteen weapons seized. Another senior Bronx Boy, Ali Elrich, was doused in petrol in Mandarin Street, Villawood, in February 2003. He died almost two weeks later.

On 12 October 2003, Amar Slwea was shot four times, bound, gagged and, after being doused with petrol, was set on fire and put in the boot of a car. Amazingly, he survived. He had been charged with being an accessory after the fact in the Debaz murder. The same day another man was stabbed. Dimitri Debaz's father

Pierre and brother William were charged over the incidents with conspiracy to murder. Both were acquitted. In the case of William Debaz, who had been in custody for sixteen months, the trial judge ruled that given his alibi, 'fundamentally flawed' identification and the unreliability of a key witness for the prosecution, he should not have been prosecuted.

In October 2003 *Task Force Gain* was established with a specific brief to deal with Middle Eastern gangs. Predictably the move did not appeal to everyone, with more radical elements of the press even going so far as to suggest it was an 'Anti-Arab' squad. On 6 November half the strength of *Task Force Gain* swooped on houses in south-western Sydney, trying to bring an end to the wars between gangs in Fairfield and Liverpool. But the task force was hampered by a lack of Arabic-speaking officers and by the sheer weight of evidence the squad was accumulating. In the meantime, the gangs used Victoria as a dumping ground for stolen white goods, prestige car parts and cigarettes.

A quite separate five-year war over cannabis distribution began around Liverpool, between second-generation families of Lebanese descent. Adnan 'Eddie' Darwiche and his close offsider Khaled 'Crazy' Taleb were distributing cannabis in south-western Sydney in competition with Bilal Razzak and his cousins Gehad and Ziad Razzak. Hostilities commenced when, in February 2001, Taleb and Darwiche quarrelled with nineteen-year-old Bilal and gave him a beating in Nemra's Café in Bankstown. On 25 February shots were fired at Darwiche's car in Punchbowl, and in reprisal Adnan and Abdul Qadir Darwiche, along with Taleb, shot at the Razzak home in Bankstown. Three days later an effort to establish a truce failed when Adnan Darwiche demanded that Bilal be handed over to him or that he leave the country. Discretion always being the better part of valour, Bilal left, but unfortunately returned in May.

Then, on 17 June, Bilal Razzak was in his unit in Sir Joseph Banks Street when he was shot three times in the stomach and legs, which effectively kneecapped him. He lost a kidney. Adnan Darwiche was charged with shooting with intent to murder and acquitted on the curious basis that had he really wished to kill Razzak he could have, but did not. There was another peace offering when Gehad Razzak, recently released from prison, met with Adnan Darwiche, who agreed to pay a sum, suggested to be between $10 000 and $15 000, as compensation.

It seems for a time peace was actually restored and that Adnan Darwiche gave up drug dealing and took a greater interest in religion, attending the Hajj in both 2002 and 2003. But, while Darwiche was abroad, in July 2003 Taleb was shot and badly injured in the legs when he was in a halal butcher's shop. Although the gunmen were masked, Taleb believed they were Gehad and Ziad Razzak. While in hospital he spoke with Darwiche, who regarded this as a breach of the peace agreement and returned to Australia.

On 27 August 2003, the home of Farouk 'Frank' Razzak in Yanderra Street, Condell Park, was sprayed with more than sixty bullets by two men with semi-automatic assault rifles. Two days later Ali Abdul Razzak was shot ten times in the head and chest by masked men as he sat in his car outside the Lakemba mosque. On 1 September gunmen opened fire on a home in Boundary Road, Liverpool, and four hours afterwards another house, in nearby Lurnea, was also shot up. On 22 September a house in Greenfield Park was targeted.

Ziad Razzak was shot through the back of the head at a friend's home in Lawford Street, Greenacre, on 14 October when the house was sprayed with up to a hundred bullets. His friend's sleeping wife, 22-year-old Mervat Nemra, died after she was hit by a stray shot.

The fallout from these gang wars continued unabated. On 30 October, Ahmed Fahda was killed. The prosecution alleged Ramzi 'Fidel' Aouad, a Razzak associate, had been married to Donna Fahda, a Darwiche family member, and when the marriage broke down in August 2003 that year Aouad became afraid the Fahda brothers might kill him. It was a matter of getting a blow in first: Fahda was ambushed as he was filling his car with petrol at a service station in Punchbowl. In all, twenty-nine rounds were fired, a high percentage of which hit Fahda. In 2006 Aouad and Nasaem 'Erdt' El-Zeyat were convicted of his murder. In April 2011 their convictions were quashed and a retrial ordered.

On 7 December 2003 Sayeh Frangeih was killed at his home in Merryland. The police thought it was a case of mistaken identity and that the intended victim had been one of his sons, released earlier in the year after convictions for drug dealing. The same night there was a shoot-out near the Kings Head Tavern in South Hurstville. Two gunmen opened fire on El-Zeyat, Aouad and a friend. The friend was hit and El-Zeyat and Aouad returned fire. When the police arrived and arrested the pair, they found a 9-millimetre Glock in a skip. It had been stolen along with thirty-three other weapons, including thirty-one Glocks, from Obliging Security about three months earlier. It was thought the guns could fetch up to $1800 each on the black market. Another shoot-out followed four days later, this time in the evening at Wattle Grove.

Arrests followed, including that of Adnan Darwiche on 28 November 2003. But things did not stop there. At about 5.20 p.m. on 8 May 2004 Michael Darwiche (who had been hit by a bullet but was not seriously injured), Mohamed Douar, Rami Homsi and Bassim Said were standing at the front of Darwiche's house in Condell Park when they were shot at by three men in a passing vehicle. In March 2007 Mohamed Razzak was sentenced to thirteen years, with a non-parole period of nine over the attack. Later the Court of Appeal quashed some of the jury's findings but his sentence remained the same. Samear Razzak and Rabia Abdul-Razzak were found not guilty.

Prior to that, on 9 August 2006, Adnan Darwiche was convicted of the Lawford Street murders, the shooting of Bilal

Razzak (which effectively began the war) and the Yanderra Street shooting. His former mate Khaled Taleb had dobbed him in, giving evidence under indemnity. Nasaem El-Zeyat and Ramzi Aouad were also found guilty of the Lawford Street murders. All three were sentenced to life imprisonment with no non-parole period set. Abass Osman, the driver in the Lawford Street shooting, was sentenced to twenty-seven years with a non-parole period of twenty-two years. They did appear to have been chastened by the sentences, or at least put on a brave face—talking and joking and calling 'God is great' as they went down. Outside the court Abdul Darwiche, acquitted of the attempted murder of Frank Razzak and now the effective head of the family, told reporters, 'My brother didn't kill anyone. The person that killed the people, he's out there fishing ... This is a political witch hunt.' Bilal Razzak received a fifteen-month sentence for refusing to testify. It sat alongside his four-year sentence for an assault unconnected to the family war.

In 2007 Abdul Darwiche was refused a tow-truck licence, a decision upheld on appeal. Then, on 14 March 2009, he was shot and killed when his four-wheel drive was sprayed with bullets after an argument at a service station in Bass Hill. His children were with him and as he died Darwiche called out, 'What are you going to do? Kill me in front of my fucking family?' Initially the police said they did not believe it was a continuation of the war. Darwiche's family claimed he had turned his back on crime but the press and police remained unconvinced. On 1 April two men were charged and the police appealed to Mohammed Fahda to give himself up, suggesting this had been a killing to revenge his brother Ahmed. He was eventually extradited from Tonga in October. All three men have denied the charge.

There are two postscripts to add. The first came five days after Abdul Darwiche's killing. At 9 p.m. on 19 March 2009, forty-year-old Michael Darwiche, director of a construction company, and Michael

Darwick were arrested by officers from *Strike Force Lieutenant* in Salvia Avenue, Bankstown. A search of their car allegedly found a Glock and a printout from the White Pages directory website listing names and addresses for members of the Fahda family. Initially, Darwiche said he did not know the Glock was in the car but later he changed his story, saying that he had it for his protection—if he waved it about when attacked, it might buy him some escape time. He had hidden it when he was visiting Rookwood cemetery as 'a sign of respect to the people buried at the grave'. On 24 February 2010 he was found not guilty of possessing the gun with intent to fire it 'in a manner likely to injure' people or property. He had already pleaded guilty to four counts relating to the possession of the Glock. On 23 April he was sentenced to fourteen months' imprisonment, a reduction from what would have been the three-year tariff because of 'mitigating circumstances'.

The second postscript is perhaps more surprising. In an attempt to reduce his life sentence, Adnan Darwiche told the authorities he had been dealing in rocket launchers, which had apparently gone missing from the Australian Army. Ammunitions Technical Officer Shane Malcolm Della-Vedova had been ordered to destroy ten rocket launchers containing rockets, which he claimed he put in his car and then forgot about. Later, too embarrassed to fess up, he claimed he had given one to his brother-in-law, who in turn disposed of it to Darwiche. It was in working order but was eventually discarded, possibly because no one had been quite sure how to use it properly in the Lawford Street attack. There was, however, a suggestion that Della-Vedova had hoped to receive up to $20 000 for each of the rockets. By the time of his trial three and a half years later, the nine other rockets had still not turned up. It was not a promising mitigation and Della-Vedova was jailed for ten years, with a minimum of seven pre-parole. With the rockets still not accounted for, his appeal against sentence was dismissed.

On the subject of weaponry on the loose, one of the most dangerous rorts in recent years was that of the Brisbane gun dealer Francis 'Frank' Curr, who from 1998 to 2000 falsified gun buyback scheme certificates, purporting that he had made the weapons harmless. The Queensland police failed to check the guns and accepted the certificates in good faith. The serial numbers were then removed from the guns and they went back into circulation. It is thought Curr may have sold up to 2000 guns, at between $1500 and $3000 apiece, to illegal gun dealers in New South Wales. On 21 February 2007 Curr, who had declined to answer police questions, received a record fourteen years. Sentencing him, Judge Brian Boulton said Curr's legacy was that his illegal handguns— only forty-eight of which had ever been located by the police— would have a long operating life of their own. The guns could be used on the street any time in the next thirty years.

In 2002 Curr's offsider Zivko Stefanovski (better known as the ALP branch stacker Jim Stefan, who had a share in a Pitt Street brothel and was a partner in a security business with Sydney identity Tim Bristow) had received six years for his part in the scam. A short way into his sentence Stefan received a Citizen of the Year award for services to the community from Fairfield City Council. Unable to be present to accept it and, game to the last, Stefan sent a message that he was firefighting in Canberra. The award was later withdrawn.

One unsung Sydney crime family was the Hannoufs. Back in January 1985, Mustapha Hannouf, bailed after pleading guilty to supplying heroin, skipped the country and fled to Lebanon. Meanwhile, his sons Haissam, Rabbi, Ahmad and Wahib, along with cousin Bilal, set about building an empire based, said the police, on manufacturing and supplying amphetamines, armed robbery, demanding property with menaces, possessing illegal firearms and ammunition, and kidnapping as well as car rebirthing, gun dealing and using forged driving licences, credit and Medibank cards.

For years the Hannoufs had remained one step, if not more, ahead of the police, thwarting investigations into their alleged activities. It all went sour for them when, on 7 November 2003, Haissam and Wahib kidnapped their one-time offsider Fadi El Jamal, whom they had known for ten years, beat him and put a pistol in his mouth, telling him, 'You're a dog. We're going to pop you.' When a marked police car passed, sirens screaming, the Hannouf brothers panicked and fled in El Jamal's car, leaving him to walk home and go into hiding.

The next day the two brothers allegedly turned up at the El Jamal family garage, Ojay Smash Repairs at Condell Park, and kidnapped El Jamal's brother, Houssam, holding him hostage for three days until four cars were signed over to them. But by then the El Jamal family had gone to *Task Force Gain*. From then on the Hannouf brothers were under covert surveillance, their phones tapped by police who entered their safe house and installed hidden microphones and a video camera.

The surveillance culminated on 16 January 2004 with a sting operation at the Star City Hotel, when Ahmad and Rabbi allegedly sold 1.36 kilograms of amphetamines to undercover police for $172 800. This led to raids on thirteen Hannouf family homes and businesses. The brothers were remanded in custody. Cousin Bilal was given bail and, when father Mustapha turned up at court to support his sons, he was promptly arrested. Eventually all charges were dropped.

Meanwhile, Mark Nicholls, a man with no criminal convictions, was shot dead on 1 February 2004 at the garage run by Fadi El Jamal in Condell Park. At first it was thought Nicholls had been the mistaken victim of a contract killing but soon the police changed their tune, alleging that he had met El Jamal in December 2001 and for two years the pair had worked happily together, raiding ATMs and dealing in drugs. They believed that Nicholls, far from being a cleanskin, had demanded his share of the profits, which included the proceeds of a $470 000 raid on the National Bank of Australia in Paddington just before the new year. They alleged El Jamal had lured Nicholls to the garage and shot him five times; he was charged with the murder. El Jamal's case stuttered on for five years: one trial was stopped; at a second the jury disagreed; and in 2009, with suggestions that Nicholls had been killed by the Hannoufs (who were, when it came to it, not called to give evidence), El Jamal was found not guilty. In fact the only victim was El Jamal's almost cleanskin brother Rami, who received a short suspended sentence for interfering with a witness.

All this could make other Lebanese gang crime seem juvenile, but it was not—at least not as far as the victims were concerned. Early in 2006 Sydney experienced yet another outbreak of shootings. On 25 March Marcus and Adam Saliba were shot and wounded at the Roxy nightclub in Parramatta, and four days later Bassam Chami and Ibrahim Assad were shot and killed in Blaxcell Street, South Granville. Chami, who was carrying a gun, was shot in the back of the head at point-blank range. He was said to be an enforcer in the drug trade and had served five years for the manslaughter of Larry Cox outside an Auburn hotel in 1998. At the time of his death he was being targeted by the Robbery and Serious Crime Squad. In August 2009 Farhad Qaumi, on trial for the Chami and Assad murders, told the jury he had acted in self-defence and he was acquitted on 3 September 2009.

On the first Sunday in April 2006, Ashoor Audisho, a disc jockey at the Assyrian Australian Association Nineveh Sports and Community Club at Edensor Park, left the club after taking some calls on his mobile phone. At about 7 p.m. the unarmed man with no police record was shot dead in Hamilton Road, Fairfield West, when he was apparently confronted and killed. Three men have been charged with his murder and a fourth with conspiracy to pervert the course of justice. Linard Shamouil later pleaded guilty to Audisho's murder and received a pre-parole sentence of fourteen and a half years. Shamouil was already on bail for an attempted murder, of which he was later found guilty and sentenced to a pre-parole period of nine years. He was also sentenced to a five-year non-parole period for dealing in methamphetamines. The killing of Audisho followed a row over insults allegedly made to Shamouil's female cousin.

In recent years these new gangs have been considerably more violent than the old-time criminals. 'They'll tell you they're going to fuck your mother. Normal crooks will have a bit more respect,' said one detective. 'There was one fellow shot as he came out of the mosque. The killer had waited, "So [the victim] would be clean. I had bits of him all over me. I couldn't eat my dinner." And the man had been a friend in a drug deal gone wrong.'

That is not to say that good, old-fashioned blue-collar players stopped operating. In 2004–2005 the Australian Crime Commission managed to dismantle twenty criminal syndicates and seize drugs with an estimated street value of $66.6 million, up from $19.9 million in 2003–2004 seizures. In 2005 Michael Nicholas Hurley, variously described as a criminal 'head honcho' of a new East Coast Milieu, or the Coogee Mob, was arrested following a five-month investigation known as *Operation Mocha* involving the alleged co-operation of baggage handlers in smuggling drugs through Sydney airport. An October 2004 haul from Chile caught him out. It was the last thing loaded onto an Aerolineas Argentinas flight so that it would be unloaded first and could then be removed before it reached the baggage hall in Sydney and put in a designated bin for subsequent collection. Hurley died before his trial could take place.

In 2008 Sydney identity John David Anderson and his son Michael were convicted of the attempted importation of 27 kilograms of cocaine worth about $11 million. The drugs were in watertight containers strapped to the hull of the *Tampa* and another vessel. The haul was discovered by New Zealand officers and substituted. The *Tampa* was then tracked and Michael Anderson was seen trying to dive to retrieve the drugs. John Anderson received eighteen years and his son, who was said to have acted out of misguided loyalty, to ten. Anderson, also known as 'Neville Tween', is alleged to have been a close friend of disgraced Crime Commission officer Mark Standen and is apparently suffering from both hepatitis C and dementia. Anderson has been a key person of interest in the murder of teenager Trudie Adams, who disappeared on 25 June 1978 after leaving a dance at the Newport Life Saving Club.

At the 2011 inquest into Trudie's death, the coroner was told that in July 1975 Anderson and Garry James Batt abducted a young man near the northern beaches, handcuffed and sexually assaulted him, photographing him in women's clothing. Anderson claimed it had been punishment for the man ripping him off in a drug deal. They had each received six months. After serving his sentence Batt went interstate, fearing that Tween would kill him. When Anderson was produced at the inquest he refused to answer questions and was sent to the cells to consider his position. Later, agreeing he had been 'no angel', if not accepting he was a career criminal, he gave evidence denying that he had ever met Trudie or been involved in any attacks on fourteen women in the northern beaches area. When the inquest reopened in March there were suggestions of new suspects—members of a group known as the Roseland Lads. One witness claimed she had been told Trudie was pack raped and then died when she hit her head leaping from a Kombi van in an attempt to escape. Her body was said to have been buried somewhere between Palm Beach and Avalon.

Anderson has also been mentioned in connection with the disappearance of the drug dealer 29-year-old Antony 'Tony' Yelavich, who vanished after he left his parents' house in September 1985. Yelavich was cycling to meet Anderson at the Manly Pacific Hotel. The bike was later returned to his parents' home.

In May 2010 Standen's co-accused, Bakhos Jalalty, pleaded guilty to conspiring to import a substance which could be used to manufacture a commercial quantity of drugs. The trial of Standen, who has pleaded not guilty, opened in March 2011.

Kings of the Cross

13

"'I didn't shoot my way to the top, I charmed my way there," John [Ibrahim] told the Herald—and the legal history would tend to support him.'

Kate McClymont and Dylan Welch, 'Spotlight turns on band of brothers', *Sydney Morning Herald*, 13 June 2009.

At Abe Saffron's September 2006 funeral service in Woollahra, the rabbi spoke of the club owner—one of the last of the so-called East Coast Milieu—as 'acknowledged as a man of goodwill' and 'a true Australian icon'. Not everyone would agree. In addition to his clubs, Saffron's interests included brothel keeping and arson. He was suspected of being behind the Luna Park fire on 9 June 1979, in which seven people were killed after fire broke out on the Ghost Train. An NCA inquiry found that the fire had been lit 'as a trigger to evict the incumbent tenants', who held their premises on a weekly basis. The New South Wales coroner recommended that Saffron and another man be charged with conspiracy to commit arson and fraud, but no charges were ever brought. Within the next two years seven more fires broke out at Saffron-owned premises. There was also bribery, blackmail, extortion and heavy involvement in illegal baccarat games. Saffron always denied any participation in drugs but his employees' comments seem to give the lie to this. In 1974 he was dubbed 'Mr Sin' at the Moffitt Royal Commission. To his great annoyance, the name stuck.

In the early 1980s Saffron had free access to high-ranking police and, in particular, to the office of Bill Allen, the Assistant Commissioner—something that contributed to that officer's speedy dismissal. Saffron was also named by Senator Don Chipp in federal parliament as 'one of the most notorious, despicable human beings—if one can use that term loosely—living in this country'. In 1988, Saffron fell out with James Anderson, his former nightclub partner, who gave evidence against him about their bookkeeping. Capone-like, Saffron went to prison for three years for tax fraud and served seventeen months. It cannot have been that hard a sentence because he organised the cabaret from his Les Girls club to give a performance for his fellow prisoners. Another prisoner had food brought in for the concert from a Chinese restaurant he owned.

In his book *Mr Sin*, author Tony Reeves claims that Sydney photographer, prostitute and blackmailer Shirley Begh was shot and killed by her husband after she had stolen photographs from Saffron and refused to return them. The matter was hushed up by the allegedly corrupt detective Herb Talarico, who had her body spirited away.

Saffron married Doreen Kratz in November 1947 but much of his life was spent with his mistress, one-time Tivoli showgirl Biruta Hagenfelds, with whom he had a daughter, Melissa. He remained spiky to the end, suing the *Gold Coast Bulletin* over a crossword clue 'Mr Sin (3,7)' and, rather less successfully, John Silvester and Andrew Rule over his entry in their *Tough: 101 Australian Gangsters*. He settled the action on part payment of his lawyers' costs. The sales of the book increased enormously.

Saffron died on 15 September 2006. Karl Bonnette, another East Coast Milieu survivor, said, 'He was always a gentleman and I don't believe any of the things that were written about him being a criminal.' One of his former employees thought differently, saying, 'He made sure his girls had enough heroin to work and make him a dollar. He always took 60/40. He was a hoon.'

In Saffron's early days one of the flies in his ointment was the cauliflower-eared policeman, Newtown Blueboys' international forward Frank 'Bumper' Farrell, who was at one time the scourge of villainy in Kings Cross. Farrell was chief of the vice squad that led the raid on Saffron when he was charged with indecent behaviour.

One of the many stories about Farrell is that when he saw crims in an alley he would drive the police car straight at them, with the doors thrown open so there was no escape. A prodigious drinker in his days on the force, he would go for a swim at dawn in Bondi to sober up. In July 1945 he was alleged to have bitten off part of the ear of St George player Bill McRitchie. After a long inquiry, in which he maintained he had left his dentures in the dressing room, he was cleared. Apparently he continued to deny any misconduct until he died in 1985. Whoever was the culprit, McRitchie spent twenty-two weeks in hospital. In an interview in 1976 Farrell told *Daily Mirror* reporter Jack Darmody, 'The old crims were manly sort of blokes. They took it and they gave it. Today they are slimy types with hearts as big as the buttons on their shirts. There's not too many men of action around now.' Sadly, by the end of his working life he was acting as Abe Saffron's bagman.

For some years Mr Sin's lieutenant was James McCartney 'Big Jim' Anderson, sometimes known as 'The Overlord' and no relation to Paddles. Anderson, born in Glasgow in 1930, joined the Marines at the age of sixteen and later became a coach driver before becoming a traffic policeman in New Zealand. He could clearly turn his hand to most things because in the late 1950s he came to Sydney as manager of the Hi-Fives, a Maori showband that played at Andre's nightclub. It was then he met Saffron. Superficially, Anderson was a friendly, gregarious man, but those who knew and feared him thought he had a very nasty temper.

In the late 1960s, in partnership with Saffron, Anderson owned a number of clubs, strip joints and bars, including the Venus Room in Orwell Street and the transvestite cabaret Carousel, otherwise known as Les Girls, which he managed. When asked whether the girls were renting rooms above the Venus Room for the purposes of prostitution, he replied, 'I don't think they were playing Scrabble.'

In 1970 he encountered the fearsome standover man Donny 'The Glove' Smith in the Venus Room. Smith hit Anderson, breaking his jaw, and in turn Anderson shot Smith three times in the chest and back as Smith was running away. He claimed self-defence on the basis that Smith was running away to get a gun. His initial charge of murder was reduced to manslaughter and the case was then 'no-billed', a decision which the Parliamentary Joint Committee found 'difficult to understand' except that it was made under the corrupt Askin government where certain criminals held at least partial control over both the police and the administration.

The disappearance of the beautiful and socially conscious Juanita Nielsen remains one of the great unsolved mysteries of Australian crime. Heiress to the Mark Foy department store fortune, she led a somewhat chequered life. Born in 1937, she married a Danish seaman and lived with him in Europe until, on the breakdown of her marriage in 1973, she returned to Australia. She started *Now*, a local newspaper in Kings Cross, taking a strong social line and opposing in particular a project at Victoria Street, Potts Point, where builder Frank Theeman was planning to redevelop much of the street into a 400-unit block of flats. Nielsen's campaign cost Theeman something in the region of $3 million. Operating a green ban for two years, the Builders Labourers' Federation refused to tear down the existing buildings and when, following government pressure, that ban was relaxed, Nielsen persuaded the Water Board Union to refuse to work on the site. Theeman was losing $3000 a day.

On the morning of 4 July 1975, Nielsen visited the Carousel, in theory to discuss the inserting of an advertisement into *Now*. She was never seen again. At the thirteen-week inquest, her friend John Glebe told the jury that in 1976 he had received a call telling him to back off and that Nielsen's death, which had been a mistake, happened shortly after her abduction. The jury ruled that she was dead but was unable to say when, where or at whose hands she had died. It was at this inquest that Lennie McPherson denied telling a federal officer that the corrupt police officer Fred Krahe had admitted responsibility. Another name in the frame was the standover man Tim Bristow, who also denied involvement, putting the blame on Krahe.

Over the years bits and pieces of the story have leaked out, but another opportunity to solve the riddle died with Anderson on 15 July 2003. In fact it is surprising that he had lived long enough to die of cancer. In the 1980s Anderson had been badly burnt in a petrol bomb attack. He had also been a police informer, an occupation which carries an inordinate number of risks, and had been shot in the hallway of a supposed police safe house in early January 1988. That year he saved six sailors during a typhoon and received a bravery award. In 1995 Anderson suffered a heart attack and moved to the Blue Mountains, from where he regularly visited Las Vegas and the Philippines, where he was a welcome visitor. Later he contracted avian pneumonia from feeding rosellas and was taken to hospital, where his cancer was diagnosed.

Anderson, who always denied any involvement in Nielsen's disappearance, was yet another to name Krahe as the actual killer. Certainly Krahe had connections. It was he who organised the gangs that terrorised the Victoria Street redevelopment protesters.

The theory that Anderson had been involved in Nielsen's death was based principally on circumstantial evidence and association. His club had been the place where she was last seen; he knew the three men later convicted of conspiracy to kill her; and he was a close friend of the developer Theeman and his son Tim. Over the years there were rumours that Anderson was blackmailing Theeman and that he had been 'lent' hundreds of thousands of dollars which had, of course, never been repaid.

After Anderson's death two transvestites who were in the club on the morning of Nielsen's visit spoke to reporter Emma Alberici. Then twenty-seven years old, Loretta Crawford was acting as the receptionist. She maintained that Anderson was not in the club that morning but that Nielsen's meeting was with the barman Shane Martin Simmonds and the night manager Eddie Trigg. Monet King (once Marilyn, a cocktail waitress in the club) was the live-in lover of Trigg and she maintained that after the visit there was blood on Trigg's shirt and that his hand was badly bruised and swollen. Trigg had told King that, if she was asked by the police, she was to confirm that Trigg had hit her. Crawford claimed that she saw Nielsen lying on the stairs going down to the storeroom and a third person, not Trigg or Simmonds, was there with a gun. 'The bullet wound was only very, very tiny. It was, like, probably like a cigarette butt, the size of a cigarette butt, but there was, like, maybe a trickle of blood that I saw.'

Theeman did not live long after the killing of Nielsen, dying in 1979. In 1983 Trigg received three years and Simmonds two for their involvement in her disappearance. Trigg told the police that the advertising story was just a ruse and she was going to be kidnapped but that when she came to the club she was not alone and the plot was aborted. In fact another anti-development campaigner, Arthur King, had also been kidnapped, snatched from his car, and taken first to Victoria Street and then outside Sydney. He was released after three days once he undertook to stop his anti-development campaign.

* * *

Bill and Louis Bayeh may never have been kings of the Cross but they were certainly courtiers. By the 1980s the brothers had become major Kings Cross standover men and drug dealers, and much of the drug trade in the area revolved around Bill Bayeh's video and games parlours, and 'shooting galleries' where, for $6, addicts could rent a room for ten minutes in order to shoot up.

In June 1990 Louis Bayeh was arrested outside a Kings Cross club and agreed to become a police informant. Later he alleged that evidence had been fabricated and the charge against him was dismissed. He offered to give evidence to the ICAC but the terms and conditions for his co-operation were set too high. In April 1993 he complained that a senior officer had taken out a contract on his life. Certainly on 12 July that year Louis Bayeh's home in Ermington, North West Sydney, was sprayed with bullets. He believed that it was done on the orders of Robert Daher, who at one time ran the Budget Hotel in the Cross. Two men were charged but were later 'no-billed'. A police officer arranged to have a meal with Daher and Bayeh's other brother Joe at a restaurant, the Water's Edge. For the moment peace was restored.

It is a Bayeh protégé, the charismatic identity John Ibrahim, who has become the current and undoubted king of the Cross. Ibrahim, of Lebanese descent, may have been born in Australia or in Tripoli and in 2010 may have been thirty-nine or eight years older. His father Wahib, whom he describes as a 'well-known businessman', travelled between Sydney and Lebanon and one day simply disappeared. Ibrahim was always interested in martial arts and, as a teenager, was good enough to represent New South Wales at tae kwon do. He began hanging around the Cross after his older brother Sam became a bouncer there at the age of sixteen. For a short time after he left school John worked as a bricklayer but then in the 1980s he became a driver and odd job man for the Bayehs. Shortly before his sixteenth birthday he had gone to the rescue of Bill Bayeh, who was being attacked, and he ended up in hospital with multiple stab wounds. His survival established him as a force to be reckoned with. Now, as with many identities, he would want for nothing; tributes in the form of free coffee, entry to clubs and more would be offered. Three years later he bought into The Tunnel Cabaret in Earl Place, paying $70 000.

In 1985 the Bayeh brothers told the Wood Royal Commission that Ibrahim and his brother Sam were taking over the Cross. John Agius QC then asked John Ibrahim, 'You are the new life blood of the drugs trade in Kings Cross, aren't you?' 'So it would seem, but no, I'm not,' he deflected neatly and modestly. Sam Ibrahim, who had gone down the biker route and was president of the Parramatta chapter of the Nomads, accepted that it was possible the Nomads had been protecting drug dealers in Kings Cross, acting as doormen at Porky's nightclub.

On 21 April 1994, when drug dealer Talal Assaad was knocked to the ground near the Kings Cross fountain by Russell Peter 'The White Rhino' Townsend, John Ibrahim's scuba-diving friend Wendy Hatfield was the first police officer on the scene to help him. She massaged Assaad's chest while Ibrahim gave him the kiss of life. Townsend was committed on a murder charge by magistrate Pat O'Shane. She had heard evidence from a convicted drug dealer that Townsend was himself a dealer and wanted Assaad off the streets. However, at the trial the jury heard that Townsend was a fitness fanatic who never dealt in drugs and had been offended when Assaad approached him, saying, 'Do you want to score?' Cleared by the jury of murder but convicted of assault, Townsend was placed on a bond by Justice Abadee, who told him, 'You are a big man; keep your hands to yourself and exercise self-control and restraint at all times.' Townsend left the Cross and went on to have a short and partially successful career in the ring, knocking out his first six opponents in short order. But, when it came to it, he accepted he was no match for men who approached top class, and retired.

By the late 1990s John Ibrahim and his clan were well on their way to dominating the nightclub scene and in March 2001 he took over The Embassy from the later disgraced businessman Rene Rivkin and his then partner Joe Elcham. For most of his life, after a teenage skirmish that earned him some criminal stripes, Ibrahim has retained a relatively clean bill of legal health.

In 2003 a rival family to the Ibrahims, the Maloufs, suffered extensive damage. Roy Malouf claimed that during an altercation with Michael Ibrahim and three Nomad bikers, his leg was broken in two places. While he was in hospital he took a call from his mother, who said that she was on her way there because Roy's younger brother, Richard, and his father, Pierre, had been shot. Michael Ibrahim faced charges arising from their shooting outside their Guildford home. A secret police recording resulted in John Ibrahim being arrested and charged with perverting the course of justice, but the tape was ruled inadmissible and the charges against him were dropped in December that year. The case against Michael Ibrahim and his co-accused, on charges of assault, malicious wounding and shooting with intent to murder, was dismissed in 2005. After the case John Ibrahim told reporters that he had been unfairly branded a criminal.

At an earlier remand hearing of the case, police made submissions opposing bail which described John Ibrahim as a 'major organised crime figure' who had been the subject of no less than '546 police intelligence reports in relation to his involvement in drugs, organised crime and association with outlaw motorcycle gangs'. He was said to have a 'team of henchmen' at his beck and call. Bail was granted and the case faded away.

In 2008 Michael Ibrahim was not so fortunate. He was sentenced to nine years, with six pre-parole, for the manslaughter of Robin Nassour, brother of the comedian and *Fat Pizza* star George. On 2 January 2006 Nassour was stabbed to death in a basement car park in The Promenade, Chiswick. A meeting had been arranged there between Michael Ibrahim, who had been working for brother John as a spotter, and the Nassour brothers, who had been involved in a minor fracas when Robin Nassour was thought to have made an obscene gesture towards John Ibrahim outside the former DCM nightclub (now the UN nightclub) in Kings Cross. When the Nassours went to the car park, they were attacked by four men. George was stabbed in the leg but managed to escape. His brother was knocked to the ground and given a kicking before being stabbed. It was believed that Faouzi Abou-Jibal, who was with Ibrahim, was the one who stabbed Robin Nassour. Abou-Jibal was wanted by the police for the murder when he was found shot dead around midnight on 14 May 2006 in a park in Punchbowl. He seems to have been lured there by soi-disant friends. His parents had been the victims of a home invasion the previous month.

In October 2009 John Ibrahim told reporter Brendan Hills, 'I don't need it,' and if he meant all the aggravation then he was right. In April that year, Semi Ngata—the mullet-wearing 'Tongan Sam' who was Ibrahim's bodyguard for over a decade—was arrested on drug and weapons charges. Ibraham's sister, Maha Sayour, was arrested and charged over $3 million allegedly found concealed in her ceiling. Committed for trial in April 2011, she denies any wrongdoing. Meanwhile, Sam Ibrahim was back in the courts, this time charged over an alleged kidnapping. Disgraced detective Roger Rogerson told reporter Marcus Casey that he was providing a generally supportive shoulder on which John Ibrahim could lean in these difficult times.

But there was more trouble to come for the family when on 5 June 2009 John's brother Fadi Ibrahim was shot while sitting with his girlfriend, the model Shayda Bastani Rad (once engaged to the late Faouzi Abou-Jibal), in his Lamborghini in the driveway outside his Castle Cove home. He survived thanks to Ms Bastani Rad, who, despite being shot in the thigh herself, rang triple-0 and followed instructions on how to staunch the blood. It is then alleged that Fadi Ibrahim conspired with his friends Rodney 'Goldy' Atkinson, Amerigo Gerace and Sid Habkouk to murder convicted drug dealer

John Macris, who he thought had carried out the shooting. This led to more trouble, particularly for Michael. It was suggested he had used a mobile phone smuggled into his cell at the minimum security Broken Hill prison to give instructions about the killing of Macris. All the men deny any involvement in a conspiracy, saying they have been set up. All this, followed by the shooting of brother Sam, may turn out to be just too much for John Ibrahim. There have been suggestions he may move his operations to the up-and-coming nightlife of Parramatta.

* * *

One of the relatively unacknowledged families of the Cross, the Vincents, is led by patriarch Tony, whose three sons Jamieson ('Jamie'), Thomas Anthony ('Tony') and Seamus have, to a greater or lesser extent, followed in their father's footsteps. At one time Vincent senior had not only a security company but also an interest in the 777 Café in Goulburn Street with Ned Bikic (or Pikic) as his partner. It was frequented by Sydney identities such as Roger Rogerson and Tom Domican. More recently Vincent has opened a strip club in Market Street, the Lady Jane, sometimes known as Little Jenny's. Con Kostas, Lennie McPherson's one-time offsider, is said to have had a consultancy at the club.

In 1993 the bouncer Europa Sio was shot dead in the lavatory of another Kings Cross café, JJ, in a killing for which Bikic was found not guilty and another man fled the country amid allegations of a police cover-up. Bikic had something of a talent for not being the shooter when things went down. In January 1999 a number of people, including Bikic and the medical student turned biker Russell Oldham, assembled at the 777, where it was decided that two men would be taught a lesson. A punitive expedition, minus Bikic, set off to Bankstown. The men were, however, expecting a visit and had arranged for some help to be with them. In the ensuing melee, two people were killed. It took place in the dark and it was never clear who fired the fatal shots. Bikic argued that since the expedition had only been intended to be punitive, not fatal, and he had stayed behind, he could not be guilty of murder. It was not an argument that appealed to either the judge, the Court of Appeal or the High Court. Bikic received a sentence of life imprisonment, with the possibility of parole from 2011. The other men, including Oldham and Benny Puta, were convicted of manslaughter and received nine years.

One of the more bizarre cases to which the Vincent family was linked was the death of Mark Gibson, a heroin addict and one-time member of the Bandidos, who was seen running away minus part of his buttock from a burning mansion in Tara Street, Woollahra, in February 1997. He was closely followed by Tony Vincent junior, who was wearing only one shoe. The owner was a week away from selling the property to the controversial developer Jim Byrnes when it was torched. The police alleged Gibson, whose blood and wallet were found at the scene of the fire, had been the bomber, along with Tony junior. Two years later Gibson was appointed director of a number of companies owned by Byrnes.

It was on the second day of his trial that Gibson disappeared and on 26 March 2001 his decomposed body was found in a drain in Gardners Street, Marrickville. He had died from a heroin overdose. At first it was thought it was self-administered but when it was discovered the left-handed Gibson had been injected in the left arm, that his mobile phone was missing and his body had been moved after his death, it was suggested that 'Big Peter' Milardovic, once a bodyguard for Lennie McPherson, and Ned Bikic might have been responsible, something both men strenuously denied. Milardovic had been dobbed in by Michael 'No Thumbs' Pestano, a one-time friend of Tim Bristow. Sadly, Pestano was not available to give evidence at the inquest because he himself had been shot and killed while standing over Timothy John Nam in an effort to get his family out of a property at Arthurville near Orange. After Gibson's death Tony Vincent junior was acquitted of arson.

At the subsequent inquest the magistrate Jacqueline Milledge found that Gibson was administered a 'hot shot' by a person or persons unknown with the intention of taking his life. She said there was a 'motive for his demise' and those who had 'sufficient reason' to want him dead were Tony Vincent and Tony junior as well as developer Jim Byrnes. She also severely criticised the police for what she called an alarming lack of commitment in investigating Gibson's death.

In January 2004 Tony Vincent senior allegedly arranged to sell a kilogram of cocaine to a police informant and that year Tony junior, who had not learned from his father's experience, was befriended by two more undercover officers who, he said, intimidated him so much that he became both depressed and a drug addict. This time he pleaded guilty to selling a .357 Magnum handgun to the officers and to supplying drugs. In January 2005 Seamus Vincent received five years, later reduced on appeal, and Tony junior eight years. In February 2007 Tony senior received ten years along with another three for his part in a superannuation bust.

In 2010 Jamie Vincent was sentenced to twenty months in prison for the attempted theft of $150 million in a sting: phone lines at the Telstra phone exchange were hotwired and a fax was sent authorising the transfer of funds to overseas bank accounts. It all came undone when 'Ltd' was added by mistake to a personal account and a receiving bank became suspicious.

At the end of George Orwell's *Animal Farm*, the animals that were left saw their masters, the pigs, and the humans, their former hated enemies, strolling arm in arm. It had become difficult for them to tell the difference. The general community may still be yet to embrace multiculturalism wholeheartedly but crime has often been a step ahead. The once disparate elements in the underworld have merged, proving that, when necessary, crime can show the way. All-white OMCGs scramble to recruit Muslims and Pacific Islanders. Bikers patch over to other clubs, something they would not have considered, let alone dared, a decade earlier. Italian drug dealers recruit white hitmen. Corrupt police officers and ex-police officers hire themselves out. The young fighting gang MBM (Muslim Brotherhood Movement), said to have around 600 members, and the smaller Asesinoz street gangs now have links to Notorious.

The New South Wales prison system has also witnessed a kind of fusion. Biker networks are mingling with organised crime networks; members of Dlasthr (The Last Hour), Pacific Islanders, Aboriginal gang members and the surfing Bra Boys are joining in networks of conflict and alliance. To mix metaphors, the old motto 'Leave your colours at the gate' has gone out of the window. Outside, these figures and others align themselves with foreign importers and local amphetamine cooks. Sydney's gangland has become one big amorphous bubbling pot.

Notes

Abbreviations used in Notes

A Crim R	Australian Criminal Reports
HCA	High Court of Australia
IRTA	Immigration Review Tribunal of Australia
NSWADT	New South Wales Administrative Decisions Tribunal
NSWCA	New South Wales Court of Appeal
NSWCCA	New South Wales Court of Criminal Appeal
NSWIRComm	New South Wales Industrial Relations Commission
NSWSC	Supreme Court of New South Wales
QSC	Supreme Court of Queensland
VSCA	Victorian Supreme Court of Appeal
WASCA	Western Australian Supreme Court of Appeal

Foreward

Page viii, 'You are a flag': Reeves, *Mr Big.* **Page ix, In March 1958 he survived:** Hickie, The Prince and the Premier, pp. 383–7. **Page x, A suitably penitent piece:** Somewhere in archival papers the names may yet be unearthed. Conversation with Richard Neville, 25 March 2011.

1. Founding Fathers

Page 2, An immediate reward of 100 pounds was posted: *Sydney Gazette,* 17 September, 10 November 1828. **Page 3, The Appeal Court for the first time:** *Sydney Gazette,* 14 June 1831. **Page 3, He received only seven years' transportation:** *Sydney Herald,* 23 July 1832, 25 February 1833. **Page 3, Back in Sydney he continued to commit:** Other versions of Blackstone's death have him found in a swamp at Woolloomooloo in 1842. Baxter, *Breaking the Bank.* **Page 4, The Bank of Australia never recovered:** Sharpe, *Crimes That Shocked Australia,* Ch. 3. **Page 4, Watches were sent abroad:** Anon, A pupil of the Late Professor John Woolley DCL, *Vice and Its Victims in Sydney,* pp. 67–9. **Page 5, Foley later conceded the match:** Foley went on to become the official demolition contractor for New South Wales. Later he owned a public house in York Street and a gymnasium off George Street. He died on 12 July 1917. Lancashire-born William Miller, once a stationmaster for the Melbourne and Hobson's Bay Railway Co, was among other things a champion walker and weightlifter. He also drew an eight-hour bout with the Scottish wrestler Donald Dinnie despite suffering a broken leg. A champion broad swordsman, he emigrated to America where he became athletic instructor to the New York Police. He died in Baltimore on 11 March 1939. Roberts, *Captain of the Push: Chronicle of Australian Pugilism*, p. 351; *Australian Dictionary of Biography*, vol. 4, p. 193; *The Bulletin*, 10 June 1882. **Page 6, The seventeen-year-old Joe Martin:** Despite his blunder on this occasion, Robert 'Nosey Bob' Howard, the official New South Wales hangman from 1873 to 1903, took his job seriously and appeared on the scaffold sober and dressed in a frock coat and white necktie. He acquired his nickname after he was kicked in the face by a horse. **Page 6, There was an outcry when the men:** *Maitland Mercury*, 13 March 1884. **Page 6, The reprieved boys in the Mount Rennie:** Clune, *Scandals of Sydney Town*, pp. 1–50; Karstens and Rogowsky (eds.), *Histories of Green Square*, pp. 65–6. **Page 6, Nine men were put on trial:** *The Sydney Morning Herald*, 26 June 1893. **Page 7, It was this incident that led:** *Daily Telegraph*, 16 February, 1 June 1894; *Australian Star*, 3 February, 4 April 1894; *Truth*, 8 April 1894; *Justice and Police Museum Handbook*. **Page 7, The Railway Mob specialised:** Hickie, *Chow Hayes: Gunman*, p. 17. **Page 9, Two months later, in separate trials:** *The Sydney Morning Herald*, 1 March, 25 September, 21–22 November 1905. **Page 10, 'We commend to the Government's notice':** *The Sydney Morning Herald*, 11 June 1914. **Page 11, They found 300 pounds:** *The Mercury* (Hobart), 11 September 1914. **Page 11, He had tried, and failed:** *Brisbane Courier*, 11 September 1914; '"Shino" Ryan Australia's Master Criminal', *The Advertiser* (Adelaide), 18 September 1914. **Page 12, She received five years:** *The Sydney Morning Herald*, 30 March 1915. **Page 13, And although, along with his offsider:** *The Advertiser* (Adelaide), 6 August 1917, 23 November 1921; *The Argus*, 23 August 1920; *The Mercury* (Hobart), 31 October 1927.

2. The Rip Roaring Twenties

Page 14, The marriage ended when: Habitual criminal Barry had convictions going back to 1916. The pinnacle of his career came in February 1929 when he and prostitute Vera Carr robbed the one-legged William Snell of his gold watch and chain. Barry received six months' hard labour and was once again declared a habitual criminal. Carr received twelve months' hard labour. New South Wales Police Gazette, 1929, p. 300; Writer, *Razor*, p. 11. **Page 16, She was promptly, if a bit ambitiously:** *The Sydney Morning Herald*, 11 July 1931. **Page 16, Clearly there was a great deal of money:** *Canberra Times*, 25 September 1931; *The Sydney Morning Herald*, 10 October 1931. **Page 16, Then he worked as a bootboy:** In 1941 Trautwen served twelve months for tax frauds. His daughter, Kathleen, married the legendary jockey Darby Munro. **Page 16, He also worked as a strongarm man:** For an account of Kingsley's career see Morton and Lobez, *Kings of Stings*. **Page 18, Her allegation seems to have come:** Morton and Lobez, *Gangland Australia*; *The Sydney Morning Herald*, 9–10 May 1928; *Truth* (Sydney), 11, 18 March, 1 April, 13 May 1928. **Page 18, 'I've been considering committing all your witnesses':** *The Argus*, 28 November 1929. **Page 18, In February 1938 he was fined:** *The Sydney Morning Herald*, 23 April 1938. **Page 18, Regarded as one of the hardest razor men:** *Daily Mirror* (Sydney),

20 December 1972. **Page 18, The fourth, if rather less permanent:** NAA. A.471.21795. **Page 19, In an interview after his death:** 'Five Bullets—and Death—for Razor Slasher Bruhn', *Truth* (Melbourne), 2 July 1927. **Page 20, Asked what she saw in the disagreeable man:** Writer, *Razor*, p. 60. **Page 20, Waldhoer, who boxed as the lightweight:** Hickie, *Chow Hayes: Gunman*, p. 53. **Page 20, Charged with his murder, on 15 December:** *The Sydney Morning Herald*, 16 December 1927. **Page 22, 'Pentridge is half full of men':** Wright, *Razor*; 'Whose Was the Hand That Held the Gun?', *Truth* (Sydney), 16 July 1927, 5 May 1956. **Page 23, The pair met at Richmond Racecourse:** Buggy, 'How "Squizzy" Taylor Died by the Gun', *The Argus*, 3 December 1949. **Page 23, Taylor then staggered out:** *The Age*, 28, 29, 31 October 1927. **Page 24, Good was charged with manslaughter:** *The Sydney Morning Herald*, 17 October 1930. Curiously, in December the next year Saidler's father William dropped dead after grappling with his son-in-law in an argument over politics. No charges were brought. *The Sydney Morning Herald*, 29 December 1931. **Page 25 The first king:** *Morning Bulletin (Rockhampton), 11 March 1925.* **Page 25, A number of women had been found:** *The Argus,* 30 May 1923. **Page 25, Tom Kelly, now described:** *The Sydney Morning Herald*, 29 November 1929, 1, 8 March 1930. **Page 25, She told them she had got them:** *The Sydney Morning Herald*, 18, 28 September 1928. **Page 26, The article claimed underworld czars:** *Truth* (Sydney), 23 December 1928. **Page 26, Now she was required to find:** *The Sydney Morning Herald*, 27 July 1929. **Page 28, Castles also suggests:** Castles, *The Shark Arm Murders*; *The Sydney Morning Herald*, 26 April, 13, 18 May, 15 June, 11 September, 11 October, 13, 14 December 1935. **Page 28, Unsurprisingly, Twible was unhappy:** *The Argus*, 27 October 1920. **Page 29, They were increased to four:** *Courier-Mail*, 10 March 1934. In Vince Kelly's *The Shadow*, Williams is named Roy Manders. **Page 29, Now the police found a newspaper:** *The Sydney Morning Herald*, 17 August 1931. **Page 29, The trio immediately left:** *The Courier*, 9 September 1932; *The Sydney Morning Herald*, 22 November 1932. **Page 30, No gun could be found:** *The Sydney Morning Herald*, 14 January 1929. **Page 30, Naturally, by the beginning of September:** *The Sydney Morning Herald*, 8 May, 19, 23 July, 6 September 1929. Sorlie was another identity sometimes described as a taxi driver who appeared regularly in the Sydney courts charged with a variety of offences of dishonesty. In 1925 he was convicted of indecently assaulting a fourteen-year-old girl.

3. The Game, gambling and cocaine

Page 31, The charge of biting Lewis: *The Sydney Morning Herald*, 16, 25 July 1929. **Page 33, Green went into smoke:** *Western Argus*, 10 December 1929. **Page 33, In March 1930 McDonald:** *The Sydney Morning Herald*, 21 March 1930. **Page 33, Later she would say:** *The Sydney Morning Herald*, 9 April 1930. **Page 33, And if, in a fit of temper:** *The Sydney Morning Herald*, 16 April 1930. **Page 34, He merely told the police:** *The Sydney Morning Herald*, 23 April 1930. In his day a very reasonable fighter and crowd pleaser who occasionally topped the bill, Walker took a fearful amount of punishment throughout his contests and became punchy. In late 1945 he was involved in a row with some servicemen who threw him off the ferry from Luna Park. They then threw a life belt after him but the punch-drunk Walker swam away from it and drowned. He came from a family of standover men, all of whom used the alias 'Walker'. His older brother Joseph began his career as a thief in 1921 working with Valerie Lowe. The next year she received eighteen months for breaking and entering and in July 1928 she alleged he had abducted her at knifepoint. He was acquitted but it did him little good because in August the next year he was sentenced to five years for assault and robbery. In 1930 Joseph Messenger was described in the New South Wales Criminal Register as a man who 'violently resists arrest ... frequents wine saloons, billiard halls and racecourses ... consorts with prostitutes.' *Truth* (Sydney), 2 December 1945. **Page 34, There was also the suggestion that:** Later that year Bourke went to Queensland, probably to avoid consorting charges under the new legislation and also to conduct a little piece or two of business there. On 30 December he was charged with shooting a police officer at Breakfast Creek and on 12 March 1931 the Chief Justice, Sir James Blair, sentenced him to five years' hard labour. *The Sydney Morning Herald*, 19 April 1930; *Canberra Times*, 21 April 1930. **Page 35, For good measure, Devine:** *The Sydney Morning Herald*, 10, 17 January 1931. **Page 35, Devine, now described as a fruiterer:** *The Sydney Morning Herald*, 10 September 1931. **Page 36, This time he received:** *The Sydney Morning Herald*, 12 September 1931; *Canberra Times*, 1 September, 8 October 1932, 10 March 1933. **Page 36, In the meantime, on 3 January:** In October 1946, described as 'one of the last survivors of the old razor gang', Brame received two years for standing over two men in Glebe pretending he had a gun and persuading them to hand over 250 pounds. *Adelaide Advertiser*, 6 August 1929; *The Sydney Morning Herald*, 26–7, 31 October 1931; *Canberra Times*, 28 October 1931, 16 March 1932, 1 October 1946. **Page 37, He received an encomium:** *The Sydney Morning Herald*, 23 June 1932. **Page 37, Happily, he was acquitted:** *The Sydney Morning Herald*, 11, 12 May 1931. **Page 37, *Truth* now claimed, 'she had held:** *Truth* (Sydney), 1 February 1931. **Page 38, There being no other evidence:** *The Sydney Morning Herald*, 12, 23 December 1931. **Page 38, He was given a 250-pound fine:** In August 1926, after a fifteen-day trial, the jury had failed to agree over a case in which Dangar, Joseph Kearns, Norman Riley, Sylvester Fennell and Richard Williams were charged with conspiracy to cheat and defraud the railway commissioners over stolen consignments of goods. In the October retrial Riley was acquitted, and Dangar and the others were convicted with, as was usual at the time, a recommendation to mercy. Dangar received two years. *Brisbane Courier*, 25 August 1926; *The Sydney Morning Herald*, 22 October 1926, 14 February 1931. **Page 38, 'No, I won't,' replied the judge:** *Truth* (Sydney), 26 March, 3 June 1933; *The Sydney Morning Herald*, 2 August 1933. **Page 39, The police generously described him:** *Truth* (Sydney), 16 April 1933, 20 April 1941. **Page 39, In 1936 *Truth* named Alam:** *Truth* (Sydney), 27 September, 4, 11 October, 5 November 1936. **Page 40, When the club was raided in March:** *Truth* (Sydney), 3 April 1938. **Page 40, As sociologist Alfred McCoy:** NSW Parliament, Debates, 4 August 1937, pp. 22–6; McCoy, *Drug Traffic*, pp. 150–1. **Page 41, His shooting**

Notes

may have been over gambling: *The Sydney Morning Herald*, 9 October 1937; Buggy, 'When Sydney Gun Gangs Waged War', *The Argus*, 15 July 1950. 'The Robert Walker Story', *The Argus*, 20–21 September 1953. **Page 41, In May 1924 Thomas:** Roy Governor, who claimed he was the younger brother of the notorious James, had received twelve years in October 1923 for a variety of offences, including shooting police officer Sergeant Young, who had been tracking him. Governor was himself shot in the lung. **Page 42, With Finnie blaming:** *The Sydney Morning Herald*, 7 December 1937, 17 February 1938. **Page 42, Myles Henry McKeon, known as 'Face':** *The Sydney Morning Herald*, 1 April, 11 June 1938. Two years later he and Florrie Riley were among fifteen charged with distributing forged five-pound notes. *R v. Riley, The Sydney Morning Herald*, 20 April 1940. **Page 42, 'Big Bill' George Plaisted and Pulley were charged:** *The Sydney Morning Herald*, 4, 9 September 1936. **Page 43, It wasn't the women who shot Pulley:** Hickie, *Chow Hayes: Gunman*, p. 72. **Page 43, Back in Sydney in February 1944:** *The Sydney Morning Herald*, 23 February 1944. **Page 44, Naturally Reeves was acquitted:** Hickie, *Chow Hayes: Gunman*, pp. 161–2; Morton and Lobez, *Dangerous to Know; Truth* (Sydney), 21 January 1951. **Page 44, He had convictions for assault:** *Canberra Times*, 6 August 1932. **Page 44, Nor did they get any change:** *The Sydney Morning Herald*, 15 September, 5 November 1938. **Page 45, Labourer Thomas Craig was charged:** McDonald was normally staunch. When in late 1927 he was shot by Alphonse Clune, he refused to identify his attacker. This was, however, merely professional courtesy. When he had shot Clune a few weeks earlier, Clune would not identify him. *Truth* (Sydney), 3 June 1928; *Canberra Times*, 28 November 1933. **Page 45, No charges were ever brought:** *The Argus*, 30 September 1933; *The Sydney Morning Herald*, 2 October 1933. **Page 45, He was acquitted after telling the jury:** *The Sydney Morning Herald*, 18 September, 9 December 1936. **Page 45, Finnie continued his high-profile:** *The Sydney Morning Herald*, 21 November 1936, 11 December 1937. **Page 45, After Maisie Wilson accused Siddy Kelly:** *Truth* (Sydney), 2 February 1930. **Page 46, Sinclair and Kelly were acquitted:** *The Sydney Morning Herald*, 25 September 1930. In February 1936 Penfold was fined five pounds for attacking his step-daughter, Lavinia Richards, with a plate after she had thrown a bowl of stew over him. He denied using a broken bottle on her and she later claimed she could not remember him doing so. *The Argus*, 26 February 1936. **Page 46, The superior court agreed with him:** *R v. Barr* [1928] CCA; *The Sydney Morning Herald*, 2 June 1928. On 26 February 1934 Barr pleaded guilty to possession of and uttering counterfeit coins and was sentenced to two years. John Gillan, a bookmaker's clerk who was passing them at the races, received twelve months. *The Sydney Morning Herald*, 27, 28 February 1934. **Page 46, In turn Siddy Kelly shot at:** '"Revenge Is Sweet", Declared Diamond Dolly', *Truth* (Sydney), 29 June 1928. **Page 46, He also worked as a debt collector:** *The Sydney Morning Herald*, 6 February 1930. For an account of Kingsley's long career, see Morton and Lobez, *Kings of Stings*. **Page 47, As it was carried out:** *The Sydney Morning Herald*, 9 August 1939. For a highly entertaining account of the Calletti–Green feud over Cameron and the period generally, see Hickie, *Chow Hayes: Gunman*. **Page 48, He was acquitted on the direction of** the judge: *The Sydney Morning Herald*, 26 September, 13 October, 28 November 1939, 13 March 1940. **Page 48, On 2 June he was found not guilty:** *The Sydney Morning Herald*, 3 June 1939; *Truth* (Sydney), 4 June 1939. **Page 48, And that, more or less:** *The Sydney Morning Herald*, 1 May 1939.

4. Some Grey and other fleeting Shadows

Page 49, Soon there was an influx of Shadows: *The Sydney Morning Herald*, 12 March 1931. **Page 49, But no one believed:** *The Sydney Morning Herald*, 1 November 1929. **Page 49, The charge of attempting to obtain money:** *The Sydney Morning Herald*, 27 September 1929. **Page 50, If it was indeed the Shadow:** *The Sydney Morning Herald*, 26 August 1929. **Page 50, Whether he was the real Grey Shadow:** *The Advertiser* (Adelaide), 7 February 1930. **Page 50, Another man whose name had come up:** *The Sydney Morning Herald*, 19 October 1929. **Page 53, Morris also knew Alexander:** For an account of the shooting of Snowy Jenkins, see Morton and Lobez, *Gangland Melbourne*. **Page 53, On 2 December 1935:** Tedeschi, 'History of the New South Wales Crown Prosecutors 1901–1986', *The Forbes Flyer*, Autumn 2006, issue 11. **Page 54, 'Always impeccably dressed':** Quoted in Doyle, *Crooks Like Us*, p. 246. **Page 55, The public never really forgave it:** Blaikie, *Remember Smith's Weekly* p. 192 *et seq.*; Kelly, *The Charge Is Murder*; Evans, *William John Mackay and the New South Wales Police Force 1910–1948: A Study in Police Power*. **Page 56, As a result of the escape:** *The Argus*, 30 November 1940; *Canberra Times*, 26 August, 1 September 1942; *The Sydney Morning Herald*, 21 March 1939, 7 January 1942, 11 April, 20 August 1946. **Page 57, His career continued into the 1950s:** Kelly, *The Shadow*; *The Sydney Morning Herald*, 2 November, 12 December 1928; 'Criminal Who Posed as a Woman', *Sun-Herald*, 11 October 1953. **Page 59, One of the conditions imposed on her:** *R v. Killick* [2002] NSWCCA 1; *R v. Dudko* [2002] NSWCCA 336; Tame, *Deadlier Than the Male; Sunday Mail* (Brisbane), 28 March 1999; *Daily Telegraph*, 22 December 2000. **Page 61, One victim had been buried:** *The Sydney Morning Herald*, 30 December 1969. It has been suggested McPherson was actually allowed into Long Bay to hold mock trials there. **Page 61, Levy, who consistently denied:** *R v. Levy* [2000] NSWSC 355. **Page 62, When one of the guards opened:** *The Sydney Morning Herald*, 5–6 March 1970. **Page 62, According to underworld legend:** Read, *Chopper: Hits and Memories*, pp. 90–2. **Page 62, It was many years before he returned:** *The Sydney Morning Herald*, 1 July, 14 August 1971. For an account of Woon's career, see Morton and Robinson, *Shotgun and Standover*, pp. 108–10. **Page 63, It was only after she had done so:** Read, *Chopper: Hits and Memories*, p. 89. **Page 63, It appears, though, that he was completely:** *Applicant: Pauline O'Driscoll Principal: Linus Patrick O'Driscoll* [1994] IRTA 3532. **Page 63, In turn, the Melbourne hardman:** Reeves, Getting Away with Murder, Part 3. **Page 63, The men had all met at Grafton jail:** In 1972 Harbecke tried to escape from Long Bay with Earl Heatley after beating a warder with a Braille printing machine. On his release in 1981 Harbecke was deported to Germany but returned to Australia and, in 1983, was convicted of a robbery in Queensland. He served thirteen years and was again deported. This time he remained in Germany where he was sentenced to fifteen years for a series of bank robberies. Morton and Lobez, *Dangerous to Know*, p. 212. **Page 64, In December 1977 he was charged:** *The Age*, 17 December 1977. **Page 65, 'He left the indelible impression':** Ramachandran, 'How bikie Peter Zervas survived hail of bullets', *The Sydney Morning Herald*, 31 March 2009. **Page 65, It was thought the killing:** Morton and Lobez, *Dangerous to Know*, pp. 267–8; *The Sydney Morning Herald*, 5 July 2003; *Sunday Telegraph*, 12 December 2004. **Page 66, The constable pulled his own revolver:** Silvester, *Leadbelly*; Silvester and Rule, *101 Australian Gangsters; The Sydney Morning Herald*, 13 February, 13 June, 7–8, 20 December 1992, 26 July 1994, 30 May 1998; *Sun-Herald*, 20 December 1992. **Page 66, He had lost the sauce-bottle top:** *The Sydney Morning Herald*, 19 July 1947. **Page 67, It was the first robbery in New South Wales:** *The Sydney Morning Herald*, 14 April 1945. **Page 67, Because the brothers looked almost identical:** *New Straits Times*, 22 October 1980. In August 2006 a bag of diamonds worth $1.6 million, due to be displayed at the Australian Jewellery Fair at the Sydney Convention and Exhibition Centre, Darling Harbour, vanished. It had been sent from Melbourne and either disappeared en route or from a vault in Sydney before being put on display. *The Times*, 24 August 2006. **Page 67, He had been suffering from cancer:** *Daily Telegraph*, 20 June 2001; McClymont, 'Slipping the Net', *The Sydney Morning Herald*, 24 January 2007.5.

5. The War Years: 1940–1945

Page 68, There was the opportunity to work variations: *Truth* (Sydney), 30 January, 6 February 1944. **Page 69, In September 1940 a magistrate:** *Truth* (Sydney), 29 September 1940. **Page 69, Two years later, in October 1942:** Later in the war Jeffs was persuaded out of retirement by the 1944 Sydney baccarat boom, and organised clubs with Siddy Kelly and the young, up-and-coming Perce Galea. When Jeffs died in October that year it was suggested that the cause was the lingering effects of bullet wounds from the 1929 Cocaine War. **Page 71, By the early 1950s he owned:** New South Wales Parliament, *Royal Commission on Liquor Laws*, pp. 70, 168–72, 176, 219. **Page 71, Appearances are deceptive, though:** *Truth* (Sydney), 7 December 1940. **Page 71, Harry Barker (also known as Harry James):** *Canberra Times*, 24 January 1935. **Page 72, Smiley behaved like a proper gentleman:** *The Sydney Morning Herald*, 17 October, 7 December 1935. **Page 72, On 7 September the police prosecutor:** In May 1952 McIvor received four years and was declared a habitual criminal after being found with gelignite and detonators at the back of the Waterloo Post Office. Earlier, in 1933, he had been given five years for breaking and entering, with, as a repeat offender, an additional two years under the little used section 443 of the Crimes Act. In 1937 he had been shot in the leg from a passing car in the Domain. *The Sydney Morning Herald*, 7 February 1933, 10 May 1952; *Truth* (Sydney), 20 July, 24 August 1940; *Canberra Times*, 7 September 1940; *West Australian*, 22 July 1937. **Page 72, In 1943 the licensee:** *Truth* (Sydney), 12 December 1943. **Page 73, At the retrial they were again:** Allen, *Sex and Secrets*, p. 185; *The Sydney Morning*

Herald, 12 May 1944; *Truth* (Sydney), 8 August, 24 October 1943. **Page 73, In November 1943 the president:** *Truth* (Sydney), 14 November 1943. **Page 73, When the prime minister, John Curtin:** Ross, *John Curtin,* p. 268. **Page 74, Police officer Lilian Armfield:** Kelly, *Rugged Angel: The Amazing Career of Policewoman Lilian Armfield,* p. 68. **Page 74, The military police were employed:** *Truth* (Sydney), 10 December 1944. **Page 74, Many of the women preferred the black servicemen:** Hickie, *The Prince and the Premier,* p. 203. **Page 74, Armfield commented:** Kelly, *Rugged Angel,* p. 68. **Page 75, This was her heyday:** Wright, *Razor,* p. 228; *Truth* (Sydney), 10 December 1944. **Page 78, The trade broke down when a newspaper:** *The Argus,* 31 May 1946. **Page 78, Cooks took the drug:** Joseph Riedle, 'The Smuggling Traffic in Time of War', *The Sydney Morning Herald,* 31 January 1945. **Page 79, In the wash-up he was never charged:** *The Sydney Morning Herald,* 13 May 1944; *Canberra Times,* 20 May 1944. **Page 80, In due course Humby and Jordan:** *The Sydney Morning Herald,* 30 March, 4 April, 9 November 1944. **Page 80, There were 6225 arrests:** *The Sydney Morning Herald,* 5 January 1945. **Page 81, A .38 or a Beretta:** *Truth* (Sydney), 1 December 1945, 2 August 1947. **Page 81, Others were used as muscle:** *The Age,* 30 August 1929; *Canberra Times,* 8 November 1943. **Page 81, It was not a tactic that appealed:** Kelly, *The Shadow;* Boy 'Basher' Gangs, *The Sydney Morning Herald,* 5 April 1944. **Page 82, His costs were paid for him:** For Hayes's account of the quarrel, killing and subsequent trial, see Hickie, *Chow Hayes: Gunman,* pp. 174–93. **Page 82, The case against Renee was dropped:** *The Sydney Morning Herald,* 30 January 1931. **Page 84, One version of Bailey's killing:** Webster, *Beyond Courage; The Sydney Morning Herald,* 10, 13 January, 8 February 1945. **Page 84, Prendergast prudently absented himself:** *The Sydney Morning Herald,* 3 February 1945. **Page 84, The papers described her:** *The Sydney Morning Herald,* 19, 23 February 1945; *The Argus,* 31 March 1945; *People,* 6 May 1953.

6. After the War Was Over

Page 86, Apart from the jury no one had any real doubt: *The Sydney Morning Herald,* 7, 11 May 1946; *Truth* (Sydney), 1 April 1956. **Page 86, He does not say why Bollard:** *The Sydney Morning Herald,* 29, 30 March, 10 May, 26 June 1946. **Page 87, Amazingly, Hollebone was acquitted:** *The Sydney Morning Herald,* 30, 31 August 1946. **Page 87, To his surprise, Dowden:** *Truth* (Sydney), 26 February 1956. **Page 88, Later his wife and executrix:** *The Sydney Morning Herald,* 22 November 1948, 3 December 1949. **Page 89, Marcovics also ran a scam:** Bottom, *Connections 2;* Morton and Lobez, *Kings of Stings.* **Page 90, The article glowingly described him:** Blaikie, *Remember Smith's Weekly,* pp. 192–3. **Page 90, She had underestimated hers:** *Canberra Times,* 6 October 1950. **Page 91, It is said that when a toast to her memory:** For a full account of the lives of both Kate Leigh and Tilly Devine, see Writer, *Razor;* Hickie, *Chow Hayes: Gunman; People,* 6 May 1953. **Page 91, Hayes received five years:** *The Sydney Morning Herald,* 21 August 1948; *Canberra Times,* 6 November 1948. **Page 91, Hayes's defence was probably paid for:** For Hayes's version of the incident, see Hickie, *Chow Hayes:*

Gunman, pp. 213–15. **Page 93, There was enough confusion for the jury:** *The Sydney Morning Herald,* 27–29 November 1951. **Page 94, This time there were no more court appearances:** In August 1956 Hayes's son Patrick received five years for robbery. He had, so the court was told, taken up with a 'widgie-type' girl who had the 'unstable combination of an adult body and an immature mind'. She also received five years and so did another young man. *Truth* (Sydney), 26 August 1956. **Page 94, The charges were later dropped:** Dower, *Deadline; The Sydney Morning Herald,* 11 September 1962, 23 September 1964. **Page 95, In October that year, after telling the jury:** Kelly, *The Shadow,* p. 166; *Truth,* (Sydney) 29 April, 7 October 1956. **Page 95, Money was paid in cash at a pub:** 'Sydney's Casinos: A Fact of Life Becomes a Scandal', *The National Times,* 25–30 June 1973. **Page 96, Warren transformed his centre of operations:** *The Sydney Morning Herald,* 7 May 1968. **Page 97, Within an hour the *Sydney Morning Herald*:** *The Sydney Morning Herald,* 26–28 June 1967. **Page 97, Shortly before his death, Brouggy:** Kidman, 'Confessions of a Hit Man Who Fooled Them All', *The Sydney Morning Herald,* 15 June 2008. **Page 98, Commissioner Norman Allan liaised:** Reeves, *Getting Away with Murder.*

7. The 1970s

Page 100, Before his death he is reputed: Whitton, *Can of Worms.* **Page 101, By the 1960s he was a man to be feared:** Brown, 'A Cut above a Common Criminal', *The Sydney Morning Herald,* 19 November 1994. **Page 102, It cannot have been a case of robbery:** *The Age,* 1 August 1960. **Page 102, What made the killing a first:** This Robert Walker should not be confused with the much superior (in the gangland pantheon) standover man who operated principally in Melbourne and who killed himself in Pentridge after taking a number of men hostage. See Morton and Lobez, *Gangland Melbourne.* **Page 102, The girlfriend then told Smith:** Smith, *Catch and Kill Your Own,* pp. 3–5. **Page 102, The gunman most favoured for Walker's killing:** *Daily Telegraph,* 11 July, 5 December 1963, 20–21 February 1964; *Sunday Mirror* (Sydney), 5 May 1964; *The Sydney Morning Herald,* 1 August, 5 December 1963. **Page 103, In turn Bourke remained staunch:** *The Sydney Morning Herald,* 6 May 1939. For an account of Bourke's career, see Hickie, *Chow Hayes: Gunman,* pp. 162–8. **Page 103, The man holding the machine gun:** Hickie, *The Prince and the Premier,* p. 128; *The Sydney Morning Herald,* 10–11 February 1964. **Page 104, When questioned by the police Steele:** *The Sydney Morning Herald,* 29 November 1965. **Page 105, A woman sitting at a nearby table:** *The Sydney Morning Herald,* 27, 29–30 November 1965. **Page 106, Her body was never found:** Hickie, *The Prince and the Premier; Sunday Mirror,* 4 June, 19 October 1967; *The Sydney Morning Herald,* 20 October 1967. **Page 106, In short order he too disappeared:** *The Sydney Morning Herald,* 17, 18 January 1967. **Page 107, The *Sydney Morning Herald* took a slightly different view:** Freeman, *George Freeman: An Autobiography; The Sydney Morning Herald,* 18 September 1994. **Page 107, McPherson and a solicitor:** *The Sydney Morning Herald,* 26 August 1951. **Page 108, Unsurprisingly there were suggestions:** *Truth* (Sydney), 28 October 1956. **Page 109, In 1980 Moylan died:**

McCoy, *Drug Traffic*, pp 273–81. **Page 109, He took over a string of brothels:** See Chapter 9. **Page 111, One story that circulated was that Freeman:** Small and Gilling, *Smack Express*; Bottom, *In the Firing Line*, pp??. **Page 113, What was even worse was the other line:** On 18 October 1983 Humphreys was re-tried on the charges and fined $4000. Within a month of his conviction he was employed as a publicity manager for the Illawara Turf Club. There is a full and most enjoyable account of the Street inquiry in Whitton, *Can of Worms*. **Page 113, At the end he made a plaintive:** Freeman had no love whatsoever for Bottom, who was, for the period from April to September 1978, a special investigator into crime attached to the Attorney General's department. Freeman blamed Bottom for many of his misfortunes and in his autobiography he mounts an attack on him. This may be one of the reasons why the book was privately published. **Page 114, Dr Nick Paltos, who was unavoidably:** Freeman's sons, David George and Adam Sonny, close friends of the Kings Cross identity John Ibrahim, run the Lady Lux club in Darlinghurst Road. Whitton, 'Freeman: He Was Big Crime's Artful Dodger' and McClymont, 'Dash to Hospital Too Late', *The Sydney Morning Herald*, 21 March 1990. **Page 117, A small-time identity with a liking:** Harvey, 'A Violent End for a Small Time Hoodlum', *The Sydney Morning Herald*, 1 June 1991. **Page 118, He was also a witness:** Stewart, *Recollections of an Unreasonable Man*, p. 33; *The Sydney Morning Herald*, 15 February 2003; *Daily Telegraph*, 19 February 2003. **Page 118, He had been run over:** Small, *Smack Express*. **Page 118, Bonnette is now the last:** Brown, 'The Good of Stan The Man Is Not Interred with the Bones', *The Sydney Morning Herald*, 22 January 2010; Duffy, 'Alive and Kicking, a Quiet Achiever of the Underworld', *The Sydney Morning Herald*, 16 April 2010.

8. War in the 1980s

Page 120, Its tolerance for that corruption: McCoy, *Drug Traffic*, p. 34. **Page 122, She had been shot in the chest:** Mr Justice DG Stewart, Royal Commission of Inquiry into Drug Trafficking, *Report* [1983]. **Page 123, However Justice Stewart:** Stewart, *Recollections of an Unreasonable Man,* p. 149. **Page 123, The fifth and most dangerous:** *Sun-Herald*, 7 April 1985. **Page 126, Smith received life imprisonment:** *R v. Smith*, Matter No 007/93 [1994] NSWSC 2. Salvietti's niece, the prostitute Virginia Perger, was involved in the so-called Love Boat scandal, a failed attempt to discredit a politician with faked photographs. **Page 127, Suspects have included Michael Sayers:** Small and Gilling, *Smack Express*, pp. 80–4. **Page 128, Present at his home were Neddy Smith:** On 23 March 1986 James William 'Bill' Duff was dismissed from the force over allegations of offering a bribe in relation to a drug deal. In 1997 he was jailed for eighteen months for heroin trafficking. He had been found with some $40 000 worth of the drug and $17 380 in cash. See Silvester and Rule, *Tough*; Whitton, *Can of Worms*, pp. 31–9. **Page 128, The killer was said to be Flannery:** *The Sydney Morning Herald*, 17 February, 24 April 1985. **Page 129, What is absolutely clear:** Khazar, 'Chopper's Whoppers', *Australian Penthouse*, December 1994. For a full review of the Flannery theories see McGeough, 'Flannery Fictions', *The*

Sydney Morning Herald, 11 May 1996. **Page 129, After all, as Jackie:** Smith, *Catch and Kill Your Own,* pp. 176–7. **Page 130, When Savvas was on trial for fraud:** Small and Gilling, *Smack Express,* p. 98. **Page 130, In 1998, after an unsuccessful:** Smith, *Catch and Kill Your Own; The Sydney Morning Herald,* 3 January 1988, 18 February 1990. **Page 131, Nye was acquitted the following year:** *Nye v. State of New South Wales and ors* [2003] NSWSC 1212. **Page 131, Throughout the trial, Kidd:** *Kidd v. Chief Executive, Department of Corrective Services* [2000] QSC 405; Morton and Lobez, *Dangerous to Know,* pp. 267–8; *The Sydney Morning Herald,* 5 July 2003; *Sunday Telegraph,* 12 December 2004.

9. Sex and the Sydney Citizen

Page 138, Then, as now, many of the city's: Anon. A pupil of the Late Professor John Woolley DCL, *Vice and Its Victims in Sydney,* pp. 42–6. **Page 139, Throughout the 1920s and 1930s:** McCoy, *Drug Traffic,* pp. 101–2. **Page 139, What the girls had to say:** Blaikie, *Remember Smith's Weekly,* p. 192. Not all Italian crime in Sydney in the early twentieth century was prostitution or blackmailing Black Handers. There were some highly talented safebreakers, including the trio of Giovanni Lucci, Alberto Borri and Geioli Martini, arrested in July 1926 by the New South Wales undercover detective Frank Fahey, known as 'The Shadow'. They served three years for attempted bank robbery before two of them were deported. Another gang of housebreakers of the era was led by Giomi Menotti, who received fourteen years, halved on appeal, for shooting at Constable Joass. His offsider, the Spanish Joseph Bisla, later received two years for a breaking. *Truth* (Brisbane), 3 May 1925. **Page 140, A girl with the looks:** Blaikie, *Wild Women of Sydney,* pp. 183–99. **Page 140, The reason given for the early release:** *The Sydney Morning Herald,* 16 June 1931; *Canberra Times,* 2 December 1931. **Page 141, After all, hairdressers often need:** *The Sydney Morning Herald,* 8 January, 17 March 1938. **Page 141, Rather ungallantly, Williams:** *Canberra Times,* 12 July 1945. **Page 142, But by the time the case:** In May 1950 Hamilton and Twist received nine months each for assaulting the catering manager of the Alfred Hospital. Hamilton's sentence was later reduced to three months. *Barrier Miner,* 3 August 1950; *The Advertiser* (Adelaide), 24 April 1952; *Canberra Times,* 11 June 1952. **Page 143, The next year she received a two-month sentence:** *Canberra Times,* 12 March 1932. **Page 143, Green stole a car:** *Brisbane Courier,* 15 April 1934. **Page 144, He was said to have framed:** *Calletti v. Truth and Sportsman Ltd and anr.* 20 November 1934; *Truth* (Sydney), 10 June 1934. **Page 144, Quite what that was all about:** *Canberra Times,* 16, 30 July 1937. **Page 145, It was certainly not a life sentence:** *The Mercury,* 18 February 1929; *The Sydney Morning Herald,* 18, 27 February 1929, 30 May 1931. **Page 145, Not a bad epitaph:** Blaikie, *Wild Women of Sydney;* Hickie, *Chow Hayes: Gunman;* Wright, *Razor; Sun-Herald,* 15 November 1953; *The Sydney Morning Herald,* 3 December 1953, 26 January 1954. **Page 146, In fact the only reason he did not commit him:** *Truth,* 9 February, 2 March 1947; *The Argus,* 31 May 1952. **Page 148, At the time of his death in 1968:** Perkins, *Sex Work and Sex Workers in Australia,* p. 57. **Page 148, Despite the convictions:** Morton and Lobez, *Gangland Australia,*

p. 234. **Page 149–50, According to a report on the out-of-control industry:** *The Sydney Morning Herald,* 30–31 August 1999. **Page 150, The first jury conviction:** *R v. Wei Tang* [2009] VSCA 182. **Page 150, Appeals against both convictions:** *Sieders, Johan v. R; Somsri, Yotchomchin v. R* [2008] NSWCCA 187. **Page 150, Perhaps generously, the trial judge:** *R v. Netthip* [2010] NSWDC 159; Wells, 'Sydney Mother Forced Thai Women into Prostitution', *ABC News,* 30 July 2010. **Page 151, In 2007 the brothel black market:** Mitchell, 'Illegal Brothels Function across Sydney', *The Sydney Morning Herald,* 10 December 2006; Welch, 'Brothel Black Market Worth $500m: Report', *The Sydney Morning Herald,* 14 February 2007. **Page 151, In August 2005 Attallah's life:** *R v. Attallah* [2005] NSWCCA 277. **Page 151, It was after this that the manager:** *R v. Eleter* [2002] NSWCCA 1224; *R v. Attallah* [2005] NSWCCA 277. **Page 152, There Kim Hollingsworth:** Silvester, *Underbelly: The Golden Mile,* Chapter 5. **Page 152, An effort to sell the premises:** Reines as told by Powell, *Touch of Class: Life in Australia's Best Known Bordello;* McClymont and Tadros, 'Curtains for Little House of Ill Repute—Secret Sydney', *The Sydney Morning Herald,* 15 September 2007; Marks, 'Sydney Brothel-Goers Lose a Touch of Class', *The Independent* (UK), 9 October 2008. **Page 152, In 2009 it was thought:** Chris Seage, 'Found: Sydney's Biggest Illegal Brothel', *Crikey,* 1 May 2009. **Page 152, A statewide survey:** *Daily Telegraph,* 12 November 2010.

10. The Best That Money Can Buy

Page 153, 'In the end, by the late 1980s': Conversation with JM, 6 November 1996. For an analysis of what constitutes corruption in a police force, see McCoy, *Drug Traffic,* pp. 32–3. **Page 154, He was removed from office:** *Sydney Herald,* 18 June 1841. **Page 154, He died three years later:** Phillips, *William Augustus Miles: Crime, Policing and Moral Entrepreneurship in England and Australia.* **Page 154, The third, Captain Joseph Innes:** Morton and Lobez, *Kings of Stings; The Sydney Morning Herald,* 24 August 1849. **Page 154, By 1850 the New South Wales:** Grabosky, *Sydney in Ferment,* pp. 75–6. **Page 154, Unsurprisingly the police denied this:** *Papers Relating to Statements Made by Dr Ralph Worrall before the Select Committee on Prevention of Venereal Diseases in Connection with Certain Improper Practices Alleged to be Prevalent in the Police Service in Connection with Prostitution.* New South Wales Parliamentary Papers, 1915, p. 899. **Page 155, The eighteen-year-old Joseph Swan:** *The Argus,* 29 August 1930. **Page 157, He died, aged sixty-one:** For an account of the careers of Kelly, Krahe and Fergusson, see Hickie, *The Prince and the Premier,* pp. 280–300. **Page 159, Despite leaning towards a verdict:** Maguire, 'The Case of the Missing Victim', *The Bulletin,* 19 January 1982; Keenan, 'Purge of Corruption Seems Doomed to Fail', *The Sydney Morning Herald,* 28 February 1988; Curtin, 'Death of Former Policeman Remains a Mystery', *The Sydney Morning Herald,* 31 August 1990; Gosman, 'Heroin in the Ice Cream', *The Sydney Morning Herald,* 10 November 1991. **Page 159, His most disastrous act:** Hickie, *The Prince and the Premier;* Whitton, *Can of Worms.* **Page 160, The coroner dispensed with an inquest:** Hickie, *The Prince and the Premier,* pp. 273–9. **Page 161, Less than six**

months into a five-year sentence: *The Age*, 5 April 1993. **Page 162, Doyle lasted only three months:** Brown, 'Nemesis of Crims and Corruption', *The Sydney Morning Herald*, 9 August 2002. **Page 165, An internal inquiry headed by Superintendent:** Ralph, along with drug dealer Morres George, was convicted of conspiracy to receive money on the evidence of a superdobber. They each received fourteen years but the convictions were quashed by the Court of Appeal, which held that the evidence of the grass was wholly unreliable. 'Career Check for Supergrass', *The Sydney Morning Herald*, 7 July 1988. **Page 166, After a five-week trial:** Dale, *Huckstepp: A Dangerous Life*. **Page 167, In February 1998:** Dempster, *Honest Cops*, Ch. 11. **Page 168, In 2010 he could be found giving solace:** *R v. Rogerson* [1992] HCA 25; [1992] 174 CLR 268; [1992] 60 A Crim R 429; Whitton, *Can of Worms*, pp. 328–9; Silvester and Rule, *Tough*. **Page 170, In 2006 he was ordered to pay over:** *R v. Eade* [2002] NSWCCA 257; *State of NSW v. Eade* [2006] NSWSC 84; *O'Sullivan v. The Queen* [2002] NSWCCA 98. **Page 172, She later dropped out:** Silvester, *Underbelly: The Golden Mile*, Ch. 5. **Page 173, Patison and Jasper received:** *R v. Patison* [2005] NSWSCCA 257; *R v. Jasper* [2003] NSWSC 287; *R v. Caccamo* [2005] NSWCCA 257. **Page 173, It was reissued in 2009:** *Operation Florida*, Vol. 1 and 2; *The Sydney Morning Herald*, 29 June 2004. **Page 173, An appeal to the Court of Appeal was rejected:** *Hatfield v. TCN Channel Nine Pty Ltd* [2010] NSWCA 69; Sexton and Clune, 'John Ibrahim and Underbelly 3', *Daily Telegraph*, 7 June 2009. **Page 174, She failed in her action:** *Jessica Parfrey v. Commissioner of Police* [2010] NSWIRComm 19.

11. Bikers

Page 175, That autumn the gang: Welch, 'Religious Divide Drives Bikie War', *The Sydney Morning Herald*, 16 February 2009. **Page 175, In 2003 Professor Arthur Veno:** Veno with Gannon, *The Brotherhoods: Inside the Outlaw Motorcycle Clubs*. **Page 176, In the early months of 2009:** In May 2009 Richard 'Rebel Rick' Roberts, a Maori and former president of the Rebels Motorcycle Club, and his offsider Gregory Carrigan were shot dead in Chisholm, south Canberra. 'Polynesians on the Rise in Sydney Gang Crime', *Dominion Post*, 6 April 2009. **Page 177, In 2009 former Bandido Caesar:** 'Caesar Campbell Comes Clean', *Daily Telegraph*, 15 April 2009. **Page 177, As a result of the massacre:** *R v. Garry George Annakin and Ors* [1987] NSWCA; Caine, *The Fat Mexican: The Bloody Rise of the Bandidos Motorcycle Club*; Stephenson, *Milperra: The Road to Justice*. **Page 178, Their appeals against conviction:** *R v. Georgiou and Harrison* [2000] NSWSC 287; *R v. Georgiou, R v. Harrison* [2005] NSWCCA 189. **Page 179, He was only found by police in 2006:** O'Brien, 'Murder of Bikie Gregory Haystacks McDonald Leads to Trail of Killings', *The Australian*, 21 January 2009; Kidman, 'The Body in the Seven Bags Still Hides Its Secrets', *Sun-Herald*, 2 March 2003; Heary, 'Kidnapping Charge', *St George and Sutherland Shire Leader*, 21 April 2010; 'Witness Tells of Abduction of Terry Falconer', *St George and Sutherland Shire Leader*, 11 June 2010. **Page 180, In New South Wales seventy-two labs:** Lozusic, New South Wales Briefing Paper, 2002. **Page 181, He and Melinda Love:** *R v. Walsh and Little* [2005] NSW SC 28; *R v. Zdravkovic* [2002] NSW SC. **Page 182, A**

woman in the queue: Gibbs, 'Now the Streets Go to Hell', *The Sydney Morning Herald*, 21 April 2006. **Page 182, The police claimed that the victim:** Walsh, Kennedy and Gibson, 'Bandidos Deadly Fall Out', *The Sydney Morning Herald*, 21 April 2006. **Page 182, Although reports said the shooter:** Gibbs, 'Now the Streets Go to Hell', *The Sydney Morning Herald*, 21 April 2006. **Page 183, Bandido Rodney Monk was killed:** Walsh, Kennedy and Gibson, 'Bandidos Deadly Fall Out', *The Sydney Morning Herald*, 21 April 2006. **Page 183, Oldham joined the Bandidos:** *R v. Puta, R v. Nitrovic, R v. Curry, R v. Mackic, R v. Oldham, R v. Nanai* [2001] NSWSC 225. **Page 183, The buyers, who had ripped off Sande:** *The Sydney Morning Herald*, 24 November 2005. **Page 183, He also suspected Oldham of being involved:** *The Sydney Morning Herald*, 13 May 2005; *Border Mail*, 13 May 2006. **Page 184, His former employer Player:** *The Sydney Morning Herald*, 16 May 2006; *Daily Telegraph*, 16 May 2006. **Page 184, He was convicted but in June 2002:** Tony Olivieri and Ray Johnson were in on a plan to recover $5.4 million in gold bullion that had been stolen from magnate Kerry Packer. *R v. Johnson* [2001] NSWCCA 465; *R v. Johnson and Olivieri* [2002] NSWCCA 348. **Page 184, Norman was also convicted:** *R v. Norman; R v. Olivieri* [2007] NSWSC 142; *Olivieri v. NSW Police Force* [2010] NSWADT 299. Brown, '$3m Fraud of Man Who Hired a Killer', *The Sydney Morning Herald*, 29 June 2007. **Page 185, Because of the exceptional help:** Davies, 'Cut-price Jail Term for Crim on a Roll', *Daily Telegraph*, 29 May 2010. **Page 185, After he was made bankrupt:** Carson, McClymont and Jacobsen, 'McGurk's Sledgehammer Justice Went Awry', *The Sydney Morning Herald*, 28 September 2009. **Page 185, If not there then Lyle:** Carson, 'McGurk Confidant Accused of Fraud', *The Sydney Morning Herald*, 8 September 2010. **Page 186, No money was taken:** *The Sydney Morning Herald*, 16 March 2007. **Page 187, This was generally regarded as surprising:** Kennedy and Hawkins, 'Three Bikies Shot at New Clubhouse', *The Sydney Morning Herald*, 1 March 2009. **Page 187, A police source has alleged:** In October 2010, 28-year-old Charles Moa, alleged to be a Comanchero, was charged with conspiracy to murder Zervas and with membership of an illegal organisation. **Page 188, Two more Comancheros pleaded guilty:** In 2008 Hawi was acquitted of the glassing of an English tourist in the Sapphire Rooms. It turned into a double triumph when he won a High Court action to retrieve a pair of sand shoes seized as evidence. *McQueen v. Hawi and anr* [2008] NSWSC 136. **Page 188, Unsurprisingly it brought a wave of support:** Jacobsen and Kontominas, 'Hells Angels High Court Challenge Delays Police Bid to Outlaw Club', *The Sydney Morning Herald*, 23 July 2010. **Page 188, One reason is that in July:** Davies, 'Notorious Gang Member Breaks Ranks', *Daily Telegraph*, 17 February 2010. **Page 189, In December he was given bail:** Vereker, *The Fast Life and Sudden Death of Michael McGurk*; McClymont and Kontominas, 'Accused Unite Against Medich', *The Sydney Morning Herald*, 18 November 2010. **Page 190, Others are understood to have been warned:** Kennedy, Carson and Duff, 'Exposed: the Gruesome Underbelly of A Turf War', *The Sydney Morning Herald*, 5 December 2010; 'Golden Mile Gang Busters', *The Sydney Morning Herald*, 5 December 2010. **Page 190, The financial blow to Notorious:** The Real Underbelly, 16 September 2010, therealunderbelly. com **Page 190, At the end of November shots:** Kennedy, 'Bikies Fight for Lucrative Drug Trade', *The Sydney Morning Herald*, 5 December 2010.

12. The Drug Trade

Page 192, After 1970 there was the emergence: New South Wales detective, conversation with JM, 9 February 2006. **Page 193, They were involved in all sorts of crime:** *Australian Story*, 10 October 2005. **Page 193, Australia was a short sail away:** Lintner, *Blood Brothers*, p. 323. **Page 194, Two years later he was described:** *R v. Bayeh* [1999] NSWCCA 82; Sutton, 'Fences and Gates Don't Stop Bullets', *Sun-Herald*, 9 July 2000. **Page 194, On 27 July Bayeh limped:** *The Sydney Morning Herald*, 31 January, 28 July 2001. **Page 194, On 26 February 2002:** *Daily Telegraph*, 27 February 2002. **Page 195, In May 1999 brother Bill:** *R v. Bayeh* [2000] NSWCCA 473. **Page 197, The hit had been worth $1000:** *Kanaan and ors v. The Queen* [2006] NSWCCA 109. *The Sydney Morning Herald*, 24 February 1993, 18 December 1998, 16 April, 30 August 2002. **Page 197, The name 5T can stand just about:** Lintner, quoting his interview with a Vietnamese diplomat, in *Blood Brothers*, p. 309. **Page 199, Over thirty-six days:** *R v. Phuong Canh Ngo* [2001] NSWSC 1021; [2003] NSWCCA 82; Jacobsen, 'Murder of MP: Report Vindicates Jury Verdict', *The Sydney Morning Herald*, 18 April 2009. **Page 199, A second member of the 5T:** *The Sydney Morning Herald*, 9–10, 12 August 1995. **Page 200, The Sydney Morning Herald noted:** *The Sydney Morning Herald*, 2, 4 October 1995. **Page 200, Until then, addicts:** *The Sydney Morning Herald*, 8 March 2003. **Page 202, In July 2008 he received:** *R v. Mirad* [2004] NSWSC 701; *R v. Youmaran* [2008] NSWSC 762. **Page 203, In the case of William Debaz:** 'Judge Criticises Prosecution of Murder Victim's Brother', *AAP General News Wire*, 19 September 2005. **Page 204, There was another peace offering:** *R v. Bilal Razzak* [2006] NSWSC 1366. **Page 204, His friend's sleeping wife:** 'Gangster Style Murders Hit Suburban Sydney', *The Sydney Morning Herald*, 17 October 2003. **Page 205, In all, twenty-nine rounds:** *R v. Darwiche and ors* [2006] NSWSC 929. **Page 205, Another shoot-out followed:** Davey, 'Robbers Steal 34 Guns from Obliging Security', *The Sydney Morning Herald*, 4 September 2003. **Page 205, Later the Court of Appeal quashed:** *Mohamed Razzak v. The Queen* [2008] NSWCCA 304. **Page 206, His former mate:** The indemnity was not to be prosecuted. See *Darwiche v R* [2011] NSWCCA 6. Appeals in this and linked cases were dismissed on 8 April 2011. **Page 206, They did appear to have been chastened:** *R v. Abdul Darwiche and ors* [2006] NSWSC 878; *R v. Abdul Darwiche and ors* [2006] NSWSC 1167. **Page 206, Bilal Razzak received a fifteen-month sentence:** Allan, 'No Joking—Life in Jail', *Daily Telegraph*, 10 November 2006. **Page 206, In 2007 Abdul Darwiche:** *Darwiche v. Two Truck Authority of New South Wales* [2007] NSWADT 20; Mercer, 'Loving Families, but Crime Is a Way of Life', *Sunday Telegraph*, 16 September 2007. **Page 206, All three men have denied:** Kent, 'Abdul Darwiche—a Loving Family Man', *Daily Telegraph*, 17 March 2009. **Page 207, On 23 April he was sentenced:** Andrew Drummond, 'Bail Refused for Murder Victim's Brother', *Nine News*, 20 March 2010; Margaret Schelkowski, 'Gun Hidden at Cemetery out of "Respect"', *Adelaide Now*, 23 February 2010. **Page 207, With the rockets still not accounted for:** *Shane Della-Vedova v. The Queen* [2009] NSWCCA 107. **Page 208, The guns could be used on the street:** Kennedy, 'The Big Sting', *The Sydney Morning*

Herald, 10 February 2007. **Page 208, The award was later withdrawn:** Mitchell, 'Fraudster Forced to Hand Back Award', *Sun-Herald*, 9 February 2003. **Page 210, In fact the only victim was El Jamal's:** *R v. Rami El Jamal* [2009] NSWSC 686; Jones, *Firearms Restrictions: Recent Developments*, Briefing Paper No. 3/04; Hon Peter Breen, Law Enforcement (Controlled Operations) Amendment Bill, 5 April 2006; Cornford, 'Crime Gang Too Clever to Catch', *The Sydney Morning Herald*, 20 January 2004, and 'Secretive Brotherhood of Crime', *The Sydney Morning Herald*, 24 January 2004; Kennedy, 'Criminal Dispute Led to Shooting Death in Car Yard, Police Allege', *The Sydney Morning Herald*, 9 September 2005. **Page 210, In August 2009 Farhad:** *Qaumi v. Director of Public Prosecutions* [2008] NSWSC 675; *The Sydney Morning Herald*, 4 September 2009. **Page 211, The killing of Audisho:** *R v. Shanouil and David* [2009] NSWSC 24. **Page 211, Hurley died before his trial:** Small and Gilling, *Smack Express*, p. 184 *et passim*. **Page 213, When the inquest reopened in March:** *The Sydney Morning Herald*, 1–3 February 2011. **Page 213, Her body was said to have been buried:** *The Sydney Morning Herald*, 22–23 March 2011. **Page 213, The bike was later returned:** *Sun-Herald*, 3 August, 30 November 2008; *The Sydney Morning Herald*, 28 November 2009. **Page 213, The trial of Standen:** *The Sydney Morning Herald*, 18 May 2010; 1 February 2010.

13. Kings of the Cross

Page 214, Within the next two years seven more fires: McClymont, 'Niece Links Abe Saffron to Luna Park Deaths', *The Sydney Morning Herald*, 26 May 2003. **Page 215, The matter was hushed up:** During his career Herb Talarico had spats with bank robber and multiple escapee Darcy Dugan and on 1 October 1971 he shot and killed Noel Ronald Gaffney in a gun battle in Bruce Street, Petersham. Talarico died at Tuggerah Lakes on 1 October 2003. Reeves, *Mr Sin: The Abe Saffron Dossier*. **Page 215, 'He was a hoon':** Reeves, *Mr Sin: The Abe Saffron Dossier*; Silvester and Rule, *Tough: 101 Australian Gangsters*; McClymont, 'Mr Sin of Sydney Dead at 86', *The Sydney Morning Herald*, 16 September 2006. **Page 216, Sadly, by the end of his working:** Reeves, *Mr Sin*; Williams, *Out of the Blue*; Wright, *Bumper: The Life and Legend of Frank 'Bumper' Farrell*. **Page 218, Another name in the frame was the standover man:** For a very full analysis of the case, see Cornford, 'Juanita's Lament', *The Sydney Morning Herald*, 1 July 1995; Bacon, 'Juanita, the Story behind the Story', *National Times*, 14–20 October 1983. **Page 218, Later he contracted avian pneumonia:** Saffron, *Gentle Satan*; Mercer, *The Sydney Morning Herald*, 3 January 1988, 18 February 1990, 22 July 2003. **Page 220, His father Wahib:** John Ibrahim, 'The Tunnel' in *People of the Cross*; Welch, 'How the King of the Cross Won his Crown', *The Sydney Morning Herald*, 17 January 2009. **Page 221, 'So it would seem, but no':** *The Sydney Morning Herald*, 19 October 1985. **Page 221, But, when it came to it, he accepted:** Sexton, 'Ibrahim's Bid to Save Dealer's Life', *Daily Telegraph*, 5 July 2009. **Page 222, The case against Michael Ibrahim:** Sexton, 'Secret Recordings Reveal Ibrahim World,' *Sunday Telegraph*, 21 June 2009. **Page 222, Bail was granted and the case:** *The Sydney Morning Herald*, 22 October 2004. **Page 223,**

Notes

He seems to have been lured there: *R v. Ibrahim* [2008] NSWSC 268; *Sunday Telegraph*, 2 April 2006. **Page 223, Disgraced detective Roger Rogerson:** Hills, 'John Ibrahim "I Don't Need It"', *Daily Telegraph*, 17 October 2009; Casey, '"Depressed" King John Ibrahim Seeks Wisdom from Artful Roger Rogerson', *Daily Telegraph*, 16 July 2010. **Page 223, But there was more trouble to come:** Lawes, 'Woman's Ex-fiance Was Shot, Too', *The Sydney Morning Herald*, 8 June 2009. **Page 224, In 1993 the bouncer Europa:** Lavatories in the Cross could generally be dangerous places. A frequenter of the Sweethearts coffee lounge in Kings Cross, Ali Ghazzwi was shot dead in June 1989. Arben 'Benny' Puta, allegedly part of the Albanian drug connection and owner of gambling clubs in Parramatta and Bondi, was charged and acquitted. He told the jury he had been washing his hands in the ladies lavatory when Ghazzwi had approached him, saying, 'This one's for Johnny.' Puta added, 'I pick up brick from floor and I hit him two times, took the gun off him and shot him.' Meanwhile the owner of Sweethearts, Regina Ashley-Riddle, known as the 'Princess', counted the takings, unperturbed. **Page 225, The other men, including Oldham:** *Bikic v. The Queen*, S245/2002 [2003] HCATrans 675. *R v. Puta; R v. Nitrovic; R v. Nanai* [2002] NSWCCA 495. **Page 225, Sadly, Pestano was not available:** In August 2006 Nam was given a minimum two-year pre-parole sentence, which meant he was immediately available for parole. Pestano's family complained bitterly, saying No Thumbs had merely been trying to mediate. For the judge's view on how the mediation was conducted, see *R v. Nam* [2006] NSWSC 802. **Page 226, After Gibson's death:** *Vincent v. The Queen* [2006] NSWCCA 78. **Page 226, She also severely criticised the police:** McClymont, 'Criminals Linked to Arson Suspect's Murder', *The Sydney Morning Herald*, 3 June 2008. **Page 226, In January 2005 Seamus:** *Vincent v. The Queen* [2006] NSWCCA 78. **Page 226, It all came undone when:** McClymont, 'Vincent Tribe Salutes Own in Going Away Party', *The Sydney Morning Herald*, 20 November 2010. **Page 227, Outside, these figures and others:** Masters, 'Hell on Wheels—the Cycle of Sinners', *Daily Telegraph*, 7 April 2010.

Selected Bibliography

Books

Allen, JA, *Sex and Secrets: Crimes Involving Australian Women since 1880*, Oxford University Press, Melbourne, 1990.

Anderson, H, *The Rise and Fall of Squizzy Taylor, Larrikin Crook*, Pan Books, Sydney, 1981.

Anon. *A pupil of the Late Professor John Woolley DCLJ, Vice and Its Victims in Sydney*, privately published, Sydney, 1873.

Australian Dictionary of Biography, ed. D Pike, vol. 4, Melbourne University Press, Melbourne, 1972.

Blaikie, G, *Remember Smith's Weekly*, Rigby, Sydney, 1966.

——*Wild Women of Sydney*, Rigby, Sydney, 1980.

Bottom, B, *Connections*, Sun Books, Melbourne, 1985.

——*Connections 2*, Sun Books, Melbourne, 1987.

Boyle, D, *Call me Jimmy: The Life and Death of Jockey Smith*, Floradale Productions, Melbourne, 2003.

Caine, A, *The Fat Mexican: The Bloody Rise of the Bandidos Motorcycle Club*, Allen & Unwin, Sydney, 2010.

Campbell, C with D Campbell, *Enforcer: The Real Story of One of Australia's Most Feared Outlaw Bikers*, Pan Macmillan, Sydney, 2010.

Castles, A, *The Shark Arm Murders: The Thrilling Story of a Tiger Shark and a Tattooed Arm*, Wakefield Press, Kent Town, South Australia, 1995.

Clune, F, *Scandals of Sydney Town*, Angus & Robertson, Sydney, 1957.

Dale, J, *Huckstepp: A Dangerous Life*, Allen & Unwin, Sydney, 2000.

Dempster, Q, *Honest Cops*, ABC Enterprises, Sydney, 1992.

Dettre, A, G Keith and P Walker, *Infamous Australians*, Bay Books, Sydney, 1985.

Dower, A, *Deadline*, Hutchinson, Melbourne, 1979.

Freeman, GD, *George Freeman: An Autobiography*, George Freeman, Sydney, 1988.

Goodsir, D, *Line of Fire: The Inside Story of the Controversial Shooting of Undercover Policeman Michael Drury*, Allen & Unwin, Sydney, 1995.

Grabosky, PN, *Sydney in Ferment: Crime, Dissent and Official Reaction, 1788–1973*, Australian National University Press, Canberra, 1977.

Haken, T and S Padraic, *Sympathy for the Devil*, ABC Books, Sydney, 2005.

Hay, R, *Catch Me if You Can: The Life and Times of Darcy Dugan*, Pan Macmillan, Sydney, 1992.

Hickie, D, *The Prince and the Premier*, Angus & Robertson, Sydney, 1985.

——*Chow Hayes: Gunman*, Angus & Robertson, Sydney, 1990.

Jenkings, B, *As Crime Goes by: The Life and Times of 'Bondi' Bill Jenkings*, Ironbark Press, Sydney, 1992.

Karskens, G and M Rogowsky (eds), *Histories of Green Square*, University of New South Wales, Sydney, 2004.

Kelly, V, *Rugged Angel: The Amazing Career of Policewoman Lilian Armfield*, Angus & Robertson, Sydney, 1961.

——*The Charge Is Murder*, Rigby, Adelaide, 1965.

——*The Shadow*, Mayflower-Dell, London, 1967.

Lintner, B, *Blood Brothers*, Allen & Unwin, Sydney, 2002.

McCoy, AW, *Drug Traffic*, Harper & Row, Sydney, 1980.

Moffitt, A, *A Quarter to Midnight*, Angus & Robertson, Sydney, 1985.

Morton J and S Lobez, *Gangland Australia*, Melbourne University Press, Melbourne, 2008.

——*Dangerous to Know*, Victory Books, Melbourne, 2009.

——*Kings of Stings*, Victory Books, Melbourne, 2011.

Morton, J and R Robinson, *Shotgun and Standover*, Pan Macmillan, Sydney, 2010.

Newcombe, L, *Inside Out: The True Story of the Simmonds–Newcombe Gaol Escape*, Angus & Robertson, Sydney, 1979.

Perkins, R et. al. (eds), *Sex Work, Sex Workers in Australia*, University of New South Wales Press, Sydney, 1994.

Phillips, D, *William Augustus Miles (1796–1851): Crime, Policing and Moral Entrepreneurship in England and Australia*, University of Melbourne Press, Melbourne, 2001.

Read, MB, *Chopper 2: Hits and Memories*, Floradale Productions, Kilmore, Victoria, 1992.

Reeves, T, *Mr Big: The True Story of Lennie McPherson and His Life of Crime*, Allen & Unwin, Sydney, 2005.

——*Mr Sin: [The Abe Saffron Dossier]*, Allen & Unwin, Sydney, 2007.

——*Getting away with Murder*, Reeves Lourensz Group, Brisbane, 2009.

Reines, R, *Memories of a Touch of Class*, Penguin, Melbourne, 1987.

Roberts, K, *Captain of the Push: Chronicle of Australian Pugilism*, Angus & Robertson, London, 1963.

Saffron, A, *Gentle Satan: My Life with Abe Saffron*, Michael Joseph, Melbourne, 2008.

Shand, A, *King of Thieves*, Allen & Unwin, Sydney, 2010.

Sharpe, A, *Crimes That Shocked Australia*, Atrand, Sydney, 1987.

Silvester, J and A Rule, *Tough: 101 Australian Gangsters*, Floradale Productions and Sly Ink, Melbourne, 2002.

——*Leadbelly: Inside Australia's Underworld Wars*, Floradale Productions and Sly Ink, Melbourne, 2004.

——*Underbelly: The Golden Mile*, Sly Ink, Melbourne, 2010.

Small, C and Gilling, T, *Smack Express: How Organised Crime Got Hooked on Drugs*, Allen & Unwin, Sydney, 2009.

Smith, N with T Noble, *Catch and Kill Your Own*, Ironbark, Sydney, 1995.

Stephenson, R, *Milperra: The Road to Justice*, New Holland Publishers, Sydney, 2004.

Stewart, DG, *Recollections of an Unreasonable Man: From the Beat to the Bench*, ABC Books, Sydney, 2007.

Tame, A, *Deadlier than the Male: Australia's Most Notorious Female Criminals*, Pan Macmillan, Sydney, 2009.

Thompson, J, *Snitch: Crooked Cops and Kings Cross Crims by the Man Who Saw It All*, Allen & Unwin, Sydney, 2010.

Veno, A with E Gannon, *The Brotherhoods: Inside the Outlaw Motorcycle Clubs*, Allen & Unwin, Sydney, 2002.

Vereker, R with M Abernethy, *The Fast Life and Sudden Death of Michael McGurk*, Allen & Unwin, Sydney, 2010.

Webster, D, *Beyond Courage: The Circumstances of New South Wales Police Officers Who Have Lost Their Lives*, Police Association of New South Wales, Sydney, 2004.

Whitton, E, *Can of Worms*, The Fairfax Library, Sydney, 1986.

Williams, T, *Out of the Blue: The History of Newtown RLFC*, Newtown RLFC, Tempe, New South Wales, 1993.

Writer, L, *Razor: A True Story of Slashers, Gangsters, Prostitutes and Sly Grog*, Pan Macmillan, Sydney, 2001.

Articles, Pamphlets, Reports, Unpublished Manuscripts etc.

Allan, L, 'No Joking—Life in Jail', *Daily Telegraph*, 10 November 2006.

Arnold, J and M Shiels, 'Outlaw Motor Cycle Gangs', *Policing Issues and Practice Journal*, vol. 8, no. 1, January 2000.

Bacon, W, 'Juanita, the Story behind the Story', *National Times*, 14–20 October 1983.

'Boy "Basher" Gangs', *The Sydney Morning Herald*, 5 April 1944.

Brown, M, 'Nemesis of Crims and Corruption', *The Sydney Morning Herald*, 9 August 2002.

——'$3m Fraud of Man Who Hired a Killer', *The Sydney Morning Herald*, 29 June 2007.

——'When Crooks Were Almost Celebrities', *The Sydney Morning Herald*, 18 January 2010.

——'The Good of Stan The Man Is Not Interred with the Bones', *The Sydney Morning Herald*, 22 January 2010.

Buggy, H, 'How "Squizzy" Taylor Died by the Gun', *The Argus*, 3 December 1949.

——'Razor Gang', *The Argus*, 25 February 1950.

——'When Sydney Gun Gangs Waged War', *The Argus*, 15 July 1950.

——'The Muscle Man of Fitzroy', *The Argus*, 3 November 1950.

——'The Robert Walker Story', *The Argus*, 20, 21 September 1953.

Cabot, C, 'Jest and Earnest', *Brisbane Courier*, 24 March 1928.

'Career Check for Supergrass', *The Sydney Morning Herald*, 7 July 1988.

Carson, V, 'McGurk Confidant Accused of Fraud', *The Sydney Morning Herald*, 8 September 2010.

Carson, V, K McClymont and G Jacobsen, 'McGurk's Sledgehammer Justice Went Awry', *The Sydney Morning Herald*, 28 September 2009.

'Comanchero MC Attack Takes $25 Million+ from Notorious MC', *The Real Underbelly.com* (viewed 16 September 2010).

'Conman and Gunman', *Truth* (Sydney), 21 September 1924.

Cornford, P, 'Juanita's Lament', *The Sydney Morning Herald*, 1 July 1995.
—— 'Crime Gang Too Clever to Catch', *The Sydney Morning Herald*,
   20 January 2004.
—— 'Secretive Brotherhood of Crime', *The Sydney Morning Herald*,
   24 January 2004.
'Criminal Who Posed as a Woman', *Sun-Herald*, 11 October 1953.
Curtin, J, 'Death of Former Policeman Remains a Mystery', *The Sydney
   Morning Herald*, 31 August 1990.
Davies, L, 'Cut-price Jail Term for Crim on a Roll', *Daily Telegraph*,
   31 August 1990.
Drummond, A, 'Bail Refused for Murder Victim's Brother', *Nine News*,
   20 March 2010.
Duffy, M, 'Alive and Kicking, a Quiet Achiever of the Underworld',
   The Sydney Morning Herald, 16 April 2010.
Evans, RW, William John Mackay and the New South Wales Police
   Force 1910–1948: A Study in Police Power, thesis, Monash
   University, Melbourne, 2005.
Fife-Yeomans, J, 'John Ibrahim, the Teflon Man of Kings Cross, Looks
   After His Own', *Daily Telegraph*, 13 June 2009.
'Five Bullets and Death for Razor Slasher Bruhn', *Truth* (Melbourne),
   2 July 1927.
'Gangster Style Murders Hit Suburban Sydney', *The Sydney Morning
   Herald*, 17 October 2003.
Gibbs, S, 'Now the Streets Go to Hell', *The Sydney Morning Herald*,
   21 April 2006.
Gladstone, C, 'A Golden Mile in Crooked Shoes', *The Sydney Morning
   Herald*, 13 May 2010.
Gosman, K, 'Heroin in the Ice Cream', *The Sydney Morning Herald*,
   10 November 1991.
Harvey, S, 'A Violent End for a Small Time Hoodlum', *The Sydney
   Morning Herald*, 1 June 1991.
Heary, M, 'Kidnapping Charge', *St George and Sutherland Shire
   Leader*, 21 April 2010.
—— 'Witness Tells of Abduction of Terry Falconer', *St George and
   Sutherland Shire Leader*, 11 June 2010.
Jacobsen, G, 'Murder of MP: Report Vindicates Jury Verdict', *The
   Sydney Morning Herald*, 18 April 2009.

Jacobsen, G and B Kontominas, 'Hells Angels High Court Challenge Delays Police Bid to Outlaw Club', *The Sydney Morning Herald*, 23 July, 2010.

Johns, R, *Firearms Restrictions: Recent Developments*, Briefing Paper no. 3/04, Parliament of New South Wales, Sydney.

'Judge Criticises Prosecution of Murder Victim's Brother', *AAP General News Wire*, 19 September 2005.

Keenan, A, 'Purge of Corruption Seems Doomed to Fail', *The Sydney Morning Herald*, 28 February 1988.

Kennedy, L, 'Criminal Dispute Led to Shooting Death in Car Yard, Police Allege', *The Sydney Morning Herald*, 9 September 2005.

——'The Big Sting', *The Sydney Morning Herald*, 10 February 2007.

——'Bikies Fight for Lucrative Drug Trade,' *The Sydney Morning Herald*, 5 December 2010.

——'Golden Mile Gang Busters', *The Sydney Morning Herald*, 5 December 5, 2010.

Kennedy, L, V Carson and E Duff, 'Exposed: the Gruesome Underbelly of a Turf War', *The Sydney Morning Herald*, 5 December 2010.

Kennedy, L and P Hawkins, 'Three Bikies Shot at New Clubhouse', *The Sydney Morning Herald*, 1 March 2009.

Kent, P, 'Abdul Darwiche—a Loving Family Man', *Daily Telegraph*, 17 March 2009.

Khazar, M, 'Chopper's Whoppers', *Australian Penthouse*, December 1994.

Kidman, J, 'The Body in the Seven Bags Still Hides Its Secrets', *Sun-Herald*, 2 March 2003.

——'Confessions of a Hit Man Who Fooled Them All', *The Sydney Morning Herald*, 15 June 2008

Lozusic, R, *Gangs in New South Wales*, Briefing Paper no. 16, Parliament of New South Wales, Sydney, 2002.

Maguire, T, 'The Case of the Missing Victim', *The Bulletin*, 19 January 1982.

Marks, K, 'Sydney Brothel-goers Lose a Touch of Class', *The Independent* (UK), 9 October 2008.

Marr, D, 'Crime Fighters Taxing War on Big Shots', *The Sydney Morning Herald*, 15 May 2009.

Masters, C, 'Hell on Wheels—the Cycle of Sinners', *Daily Telegraph*, 7 April 2010.

——'Why Sydney's Hitmen are Deadlier', *Daily Telegraph*, 8 April 2010.

McClymont, K, 'Dash to Hospital Too Late', *The Sydney Morning Herald*, 21 March 1990.

——'Niece Links Abe Saffron to Luna Park Deaths', *The Sydney Morning Herald*, 26 May 2003.

——'Mr Sin of Sydney Dead at 86', *The Sydney Morning Herald*, 16 September 2006.

——'Slipping the Net', *The Sydney Morning Herald*, 24 January 2007.

——'Criminals Linked to Arson Suspect's Murder', *The Sydney Morning Herald*, 3 June 2008.

——'Vincent Tribe Salutes Own in Going Away Party', *The Sydney Morning Herald*, 20 November 2010.

McClymont, K and B Kontominas, 'Accused Unite against Medich', *The Sydney Morning Herald*, 18 November 2010.

McClymont, K and E Tadros, 'Curtains for Little House of Ill Repute — Secret Sydney', *The Sydney Morning Herald*, 15 September 2007.

McClymont, K and D Welch, 'Spotlight Turns on Band of Brothers', *The Sydney Morning Herald*, 13 June 2010.

McGeough, P, 'Flannery Fictions', *The Sydney Morning Herald*, 11 May 1996.

Mercer, N, 'Loving Families, but Crime Is a Way of Life', *Sunday Telegraph*, 16 September 2007.

Mitchell, A, 'Illegal Brothels Function across Sydney', *The Sydney Morning Herald*, 10 December 2006.

——'Fraudster Forced to Hand Back Award', *Sun-Herald*, 9 February 2003.

New South Wales Government, *Cabramatta: A report on progress*, Sydney, 2002.

O'Brien, N, 'Murder of Bikie Gregory Haystacks McDonald Leads to Trail of Killings', *The Australian*, 21 January 2009.

Oz, October 1965.

Papers Relating to Statements made by Dr Ralph Worrall before the Select Committee on Prevention of Venereal Diseases in Connection Certain Improper Practices Alleged to be Prevalent in the Police Service in Connection with Prostitution, New South Wales Parliamentary Papers, 1915.

'Polynesians on the Rise in Sydney Gang Crime', *Dominion Post*, 6 April 2009.

Ramachandran, A, 'How Bikie Peter Zervas Survived Hail of Bullets', *The Sydney Morning Herald*, 31 March 2009.

Report to Parliament: Operation Florida, Police Integrity Commission, Sydney, 2004.

Riedle, J, 'The Smuggling Traffic in Time of War', *The Sydney Morning Herald*, 31 January 1945.

Schelkowski, M, 'Gun Hidden at Cemetery Out of "Respect"', *Adelaide Now*, 23 February 2010.

Seage, C, 'Found: Sydney's Biggest Illegal Brothel', *Crikey*, 1 May 2009.

Sexton, J, 'Ibrahim's Bid to Save Dealer's Life', *Daily Telegraph*, 5 July 2009.

Sexton, J and R Clune, 'John Ibrahim and Underbelly 3', *Daily Telegraph*, 7 June 2009.

'"Shino" Ryan Australia's Master Criminal', *The Advertiser* (Adelaide), 18 September 1914.

Royal Commission of Inquiry into Drug Trafficking, *Report, 1983,* (DG Stewart, commissioner), Australian Government Publishing Service, Canberra, 1983.

Sutton, C, 'Fences and Gates Don't Stop Bullets', *Sun-Herald*, 9 July 2000.

Tedeschi, M, 'History of the New South Wales Crown Prosecutors 1901–1986', *The Forbes Flyer*, Autumn 2006, issue 11.

Welch, D, 'How the King of the Cross Won His Crown', *The Sydney Morning Herald*, 17 January 2009.

——'Religious Divide Drives Bikie War', *The Sydney Morning Herald*, 16 February 2009.

——'Brothel Black Market Worth $500m: Report', *The Sydney Morning Herald*, 14 February 2007.

Welch, D, L Kennedy and J Gibson, 'Bandidos Deadly Fall Out', *The Sydney Morning Herald*, 21 April 2006.

Wells, J, 'Sydney Mother Forced Thai Women into Prostitution', *ABC News*, 30 July 2010.

Whitton, E, 'Freeman: He Was Big Crime's Artful Dodger', *The Sydney Morning Herald*, 21 March 1990.

'Whose Was the Hand That Held the Gun?', *Truth* (Sydney), 16 July 1927.

Index

Note: page numbers in **bold** type refer
to images.

Index

Index

Shaw, Bernard 79
shoplifting 7, 65
Sieders, Johan 150
Silvester, John 215
Simmonds, Kevin 156
Simmonds, Shane 219
Simmons, Danny 92–3
Sinclair, Joe 'The Pig' 46, 88
Sinclair, William 125
Sio, Europa 224
Skinner, Thomas Herbert 50
Skyrus, Johnny 180
Slater, Henry 13, 71
Sloss, Albert 98
Slwea, Amar 202
Sly, Justice 11
sly-grog shops 14, 37, 39–40; American
    troops and 68–9
Small, Clive 129
Smiley, William 71–2
Smith, 'Botany May' 25
Smith, Donny 'The Glove' 149, 157, 217
Smith, James 122
Smith, James Edward 'The Jockey' 63–6,
    146
Smith, Jim 27–8
Smith, Neddy 102, 111, 123–5, 127–9,
    164–6, 168
Smith, Stan 'The Man' 101–2, 107, 118
Smith, Stephen Allan 126
Smith, Teddy 125
smuggling 27, 77–8; *see also* drugs and
    drug trafficking
Somme, Louis 28–9
Somsri, Yotchomchin 150
Spencer, Anthony 176
sportspeople 32, 75, 82, 89–90, 100, 119,
    124–5, 160, 220–2; boxers 20, 25, 27,
    34, 41, 48, 65, 76, 89, 92, 129, 142, 183,
    189; *see also* horseracing and training
Sproule, Lilian 25
Standen, Mark 212–13
standover/enforcement 23–4, 27, 37, 46,
    73, 91–2, 95–6, 101, 106, 109–10, 157,
    195, 214; abortion and abortionists 75;
    bookmakers and gambling 40–8;
    building industry 117; motorcycle
    gangs and 177; Safe Protection
    gang 12
Stanley, Bill 5
Stanton, Alfred 37
stealing, *see* burglary; robbery; theft
Steele, Jackie 'Iron Man' viii, ix, 104–5,
    129, 148

Steele, Rose 25
Stefan, Jim 208
Stefanovski, Zivko 208
Stein, Danny 112, 116
Stelio, Armani 190
Stewart, Justice 112, 118, 123
Stokes, Edgar Ronald 29
Stokes, Henry 90
Street Inquiry 113
Stuart, John 61
Stuart-Jones, Reginald 39, 76–7, 82–3,
    88–9
suicides 11, 18, 49, 78, 145, 157, 159–60,
    177
Sullivan, Garry 60
Summers, Paul 179
Surridge, Barbara Phyllis 69
Surridge, Stella 89
Surridge, William 69
Swan, Joseph 155
Sweeney, James 156
Sweetman, Charles 5
Sydney suburbs: Cabramatta 197–200;
    Darlinghurst 8, 26, 81, 147

Talarico, Herb 215
Taleb, Khaled 'Crazy' 203–4, 206
Tang, Wei 150
Taplin, Arthur 140–1
Tarlington, Harold 42
Tatham, Arthur 10–11
taxation 88, 90–1, 215
Taylor, Ernest James 30
Taylor, Joe viii, 7, 84, 87, 114–15
Taylor, Squizzy 12–13, 23
Temby, Ian 168
Testa, Joe Dan ix, 107
Theeman, Frank 217–19
theft 51, 61–2, 67, 81, 92–3, 96, 157, 226;
    ginger game 9; of luggage 83–4;
    of rocket launchers 207; of
    vehicles 157–8; *see also* burglary;
    robbery; shoplifting
Theilman, Julie 122
Theobald, Kevin 128
Thomas, Clarrie 41–2
Thompson, Cliffie 76–7, 83
Thompson, Inspector 80
Thompson, John 58
Thompson, Violet 17
Thompson, William Joseph 101–2
Thornton, James Patrick 63
Thurgar, Roy 65, 124, 126, 130–1
Tidmarsh, Lloyd 64